Praying for Peace

A Journey to Serenity

Naima P. Tryman

iUniverse, Inc.
New York   Bloomington

Praying for Peace
A Journey to Serenity

iUniverse books may be ordered through booksellers or by contacting:

iUniverse
1663 Liberty Drive
Bloomington, IN 47403
www.iuniverse.com
1-800-Authors (1-800-288-4677)

Because of the dynamic nature of the Internet, any Web addresses or links contained in this book may have changed since publication and may no longer be valid.

ISBN: 978-1-4401-8661-5 (sc)
ISBN: 978-1-4401-8662-2 (ebk)

Printed in the United States of America

iUniverse rev. date: 4/20/2010

Dedication

To my son, Sha-Quaan Terrell Charles Jackson, without whom I never would have found the inspiration to write this book. You are special, and can do anything you put your mind to. I love you, now and forever.

To my mother, Patrice Mosley Tryman. Through your actions I have learned unconditional love and grace in the face of adversity.

To all of those that died so young, your living was not in vain, and your memory will live on through this book and in the hearts of those that loved you.

Acknowledgements

I spent a great percentage of my life bemoaning life's pitfalls and wondering why God had put me through so much. Having undergone a spiritual rebirth in the writing of this book, I realize that it was all in preparation for a triumphant victory over all of my demons. Everything I have was a gift from God, and I am truly grateful for every second of life that I have been blessed with.

Mom, words simply cannot express ... nothing I could possibly say here would do you justice, so just know that being the mother that you've been has left me speechless with respect to my gratitude. To Jerry Citro, as with my mother, I don't have the words Coach. I never would have become who I am without your love and guidance. I owe my life to you. To Donnie DiGeronimo, you will always have my undying gratitude and respect for the role you played in turning my life around. When I was at the lowest point in my life, you were the best friend I could have asked for. Thanks for all the diner talks.

There are hundreds of people that helped me to become the person I am today, and to attempt to identify you all would be futile. You know who you are, and I know who you are, and I love and appreciate each and every one of you. There were also a number of people that read this book in its elementary stages and gave me great feedback. I want to reaffirm my gratitude here, and let you all know how deeply that was appreciated. I would be totally remiss if I didn't give special thanks to Marisol and Alexis Dennis. Marisol, your feedback on the previous ending was monumental in the final product. Thanks for telling me how bad it was. Alexis, thank you for editing this twice for me, and also for passing along *The Shack*, without which this book may never have found it's ending.

A Letter to My Son

Dear Sha-Quaan,

I love you. I don't know when or even if you will ever read this, and that makes writing this hard. You may no longer remember me, but when you were a child, I was your step-mother. Your mother and I were very close at one time, and I considered you my son. I still do. I was very sick for a long time, and made a number of bad choices. Your mother decided that I was not a good person for you to be around and she took you away from me. I can't say I blame her.

I miss you every day, more than you can imagine. I have your face tattooed on my arm and I think of you constantly. That tattoo will be there forever, and when my children ask me who you are I will tell them that you are their older brother that I lost because I acted badly when I was sick. Not one day goes by that I don't think about you and wish I could have gotten better in time to keep you in my life.

What's done is done, and I cannot change my mistakes. I will spend my life trying to be someone that you would be proud of, and I pray everyday that you will somehow find your way back to me. If you ever need anything, I will be here for you. I don't care if it is college tuition, bail money, or just a hug… I hope that you will not be too shy to come to me, because I will NEVER deny you. Love doesn't seem to be a strong enough word, but it's all I have for now. I love you… I love you… I love you.

Na-Na

Foreword

For years I struggled with the hand I'd been dealt. I wondered what I'd ever done that was so bad to earn the life I'd gotten, until I learned that it was all in preparation for my impending success. The hardships I've experienced have taught me great lessons, and without enduring them, I would not have the knowledge that I now possess. Growth is painful, and for the majority of my life I did any and everything I could to avoid it, but I could not outrun it. My life changed when I decided to use my past troubles as fuel for a spectacular spiritual growth spurt.

I used to wonder why I had to deal with seemingly so much more heartache and pain than those around me. In time, I came to realize that every tear I shed, and every pain I endured, were investments into a prosperous future. The decision to write this book came from the understanding that my suffering has not been in vain, and that by sharing my experiences, I may be able to give hope to those that are as far down spiritually as I once was… This too shall pass.

"I finally came around, I'm back on solid ground, can't let it get me down. Life perfect ain't perfect if you don't know what the struggle's for. Falling down ain't falling down if you don't cry when you hit the floor. It's called the past 'cause I'm getting past and I ain't nothing like I was before, you ought to see me now. Yes, I was burned, but I called it a lesson learned. My soul has returned so I called it a lesson learned. Another lesson learned."

-Alicia Keys, Lesson Learned.

Chapter 1
Childhood

One of the primary reasons I drank so heavily was so that I would completely pass out when I slept. I never dreamt when I passed out, but more importantly I wouldn't be subjected to the horrible nightmares recounting my father terrorizing us all. We didn't live with him anymore, but nevertheless he haunted me for years. Night after night I suffered through images of him charging up the stairs with that belt in his hand. Sometimes I would wake up in a cold sweat before he actually got to me, but more often than not I was beaten for no reason at all and then left to whimper in a corner. The nightmares became too much for me when I started fighting back with chairs and blunt objects, leaving him bloody and lifeless on the floor. Drinking negated those nightmares. I always woke up tired and hung over, but it was better than waking up in a panic.

On this particular night, the alcohol didn't work though. Although I'd been drunk for a week straight, I had a life-changing dream. It wasn't just a dream though, it was a conversation. It began with me lying on my back on the side of a dark, dirt road. I tried with all my might to sit up but I couldn't move. I was dizzy and disoriented, and I spent what felt like hours trying not to choke to death on my tears. Then out of nowhere, in a matter of seconds, the sun rose and I was able to sit up, but I couldn't stop the tears. I cried out to God, begging for help but not really expecting a response.

"Help me. I can't do this anymore. Nobody cares about me, and I clearly care too much about everyone else. No one understands me and every day just seems to bring more pain than the last. I don't want you to save me Lord, I want you to take me. I've been trying so hard to change the course of my life, but it only seems to get worse. I walk through every day with such incredible tension in my neck, ashamed of who I have become and terrified of the consequences of my actions. I don't want this life anymore. Please just take me away."

Then I heard His voice. It was soft and gentle, brimming with empathy for me. "Naima, I'm not finished with you." It sounded like He was sitting right next to me, but as I looked around I could see nothing but forest and a long road to nowhere. "You have nothing to be ashamed of. I know that you have suffered tremendously, but please don't give up. You are my child. I created you with very special intentions, and if you will follow me I will turn every one of your hardships into a gift. I will take the pain away, but you have to trust me."

"Trust You? How can I trust You? I don't even know You. I mean I've always assumed that You exist in some capacity, but what have You ever done for me? My life is a wreck. My childhood was torture, and somehow as an adult things have only gotten worse. I have tried to live right, but what do I have to show for it? My life has been tragedy after tragedy, misery complicated with more misery. Nothing I do seems to work out and my efforts are never good enough for anyone. I'm just so tired."

"Naima, I am working for you as we speak. It may not seem that way to you, but that does not make it untrue. Have you ever really tried? I have given you many tools, but you have chosen not to use them. I want to help you, but you have to fight for me. I can bring you to a life filled with such joy and happiness that you won't even be able to remember what misery feels like, but I need your help. What do you have to lose? You've been trying to live this life on your own terms, and look what that has gotten you. If you continue to walk this path you will get your wish soon enough, but I don't really think that's what you want, and it surely isn't what I want for you. Take a chance. For once in your life, step out on faith. If you take one step towards me, I will take ten towards you. The choice is yours."

Everything went black, and the dream was over. When I awoke I was back to the sad reality my life had become, and a smell that will stay with me forever. It was an awful mix of vomit, urine, feces, cigarette smoke, and dog. It wasn't the first time I'd woken up to it, but today would be the last. It was a Saturday morning in September, and day six of my latest rampage of drinking and vomiting. I didn't remember very much of the past week, but none of what I remembered was good. I'd gone on countless treks to the liquor store, bought food that I was too drunk to eat, lost my cell phone, broken up with Shonte, and called out sick to work.

I had been way too drunk and lazy to let my scrawny excuse for a pit bull out to relieve himself, so he made a huge mess in the kitchen. I was being threatened with eviction and my pay would be docked because I called out sick. I hated my job, I hated my father, I hated my apartment, I'd crashed my car, I had no money, and worst of all I'd lost my son. How could anyone blame me for trying to check out, twice? The rancid, awful stench reeking throughout every inch of my tiny apartment is an unpleasant memory, but it was the beginning of my enlightenment.

How did I get here? Surely this was not my purpose. God didn't create me to suffer through my existence, yet here I was... drunk, dirty, and absolutely miserable. This couldn't have been the plan, but where did I go wrong, and more importantly how was I to fix it? I prayed for strength and guidance, because I was lost and desperate. I was dying, and in jeopardy of wasting my entire existence. I couldn't handle my life anymore and something had to give. I was so ready to do God's Will, but what did that mean? Before I could determine that, I had to find the source of my troubles and deal with them head on. I would have to be startlingly honest and bear the weight of my sins, because the alternative of death was staring me in the face. I had to begin a search of my soul. I had to dig through my history from the very beginning to understand where I'd developed the defense mechanisms that eventually doomed me.

The Basics

All things considered, most would think my childhood was pretty good. I grew up in a large, aging house in Montclair, NJ. In fact it was the same house that my father had grown up in. My father, Jimmy, was a teacher in town, and was something of a hero to many. He grew up as an excellent athlete, starring in football, baseball, and track. He graduated from Montclair High School in 1961 and worked odd jobs for about eight years. In 1967 he had a baby girl named Juno with a woman I never met.

Following a violent fight with this woman he went to Oregon, and then Pasadena, California for junior college. After working construction in California for a while he returned to New Jersey to cut hair in his father's barbershop and complete his education. My mother, Patrice, was born in Bay St. Louis, MS, the baby of four other siblings. She moved to Montclair with her mother and siblings when she was 17. She played Varsity basketball and was the band majorette. She graduated from Montclair High in 1969, at which point she enrolled in county college to study secretarial science.

My brother Jay was born to my parents in December of 1970, and so began a twenty-five year journey. My parents bought the house from his father and that would be the only home any of us knew for years to come. The house was big by general standards. It was definitely too big for a young, upstart family, so they rented out the third floor as a two bedroom apartment and half of the second floor as a small one bedroom, thus making the house both affordable and sensible.

The next ten years brought waves of happiness crippled by my father's furious tyrannical rants. He wanted to be a good man, and by most accounts he was. He was a teacher that honestly enjoyed being with children. He was a third generation barber that was well connected within the community. He constantly volunteered his free time with his Black male students and he was a boyhood baseball hero to those that came behind him. But somewhere deep inside him was a terrible mean streak. This was a man that was drunk with control issues, and whenever he felt his control or authority was being questioned or denied he snapped.

Jimmy Tryman was an individual that was not in any way comfortable with denial. He only had one sibling, a brother Donald five years his junior, on whom he absolutely trampled. He was a known neighborhood bully, never in fear of a fight. My father may have been 5'8", 170 pounds on a generous scale, but he had the heart of a lion. It was that courage that made him such a fierce competitor. However, it was also the eventual source of his foolish pride and resulting alienation.

My father and brother have always had a rocky relationship. Juno was back and forth between parents, but Jay was stuck. For almost ten years, there was no one around to deflect or distract my father's fits of rage from my brother. I've always believed Jimmy's greatest flaw to be pathological inconsistency. Everyone walked on eggshells around him, even in times of joy, because you never knew just what might flip his switch. My mother has always been petite, even through her pregnancies. She is 5' tall, and gets excited when her weight hits 110 pounds. Try as she did, she was not much defense against an enraged bully trained in the arts. My father boxed golden gloves and was a brown belt in karate, and Jay and Jimmy had an adversarial relationship to say the least.

In August of 1980, God sent a little distraction to take some heat off of Jay. My mother gave birth to me on August 8th, and my parents named me Naima Patrice. Jimmy was a huge John Coltrane fan and named me after a song of his that he loved. Although his relationship with Jay had not yet been damaged beyond repair, something in him decided that this would be the child he raised right. He would rear Jay, but this one he would raise.

A Gifted Child

I don't remember much from my pre-school years, but everything I am told illustrates a story of an exceptional child with boundless potential. I was reading at four years old, and at the same age I stood in front of my entire church congregation and recited a Langston Hughes poem from memory. When I was five years old I could solve a Rubik's cube in minutes. I was the apple of my father's eye, and he took me everywhere he went. I looked just like him, and he would spend the next fifteen years trying to mold me into the son that he wanted Jay to be. My parents had two more daughters after me, Khalea and Amina, but I always seemed to be the one that occupied the most of Jimmy's time and attention.

My elementary school years were filled with joy. My father worked as a teacher every day, came home for an hour, and then went to cut hair. My mother would come home from her job in Newark around five, usually just long enough to round us up and whisk us off to some activity. Jimmy would come home around seven and turn on *The Rockford Files, The Fugitive,* or *Sanford and Son.* As a young child I shadowed him. Although Khalea and I were the closest siblings in age (twenty months), the sisterly bond was with her and Amina who was two years younger than her. Jay and I were close, but it wasn't the same because he was a teenager and I was his kid sister, so I clung to my father.

My relationship with Jimmy has always been at the very least a little awkward. I adored him for the good father that he tried to be, but I was terrified of him. I spent my days under his wing, but out of his way. I cherished my mother and her soft nature, but I longed for my father's approval. He took me to the park a lot, and we decided together that I would play baseball instead of softball. I wouldn't just be a player though-- I was going to be a pitcher like him.

Baseball was always the core bond with my dad and me. Jay never really took to the sport, but once I got a taste I was insatiable. He started to teach me about pitching mechanics, and I was obsessed. There was a chimney that ran up the back of our house adjacent to a patio space. Sometimes I would spend hours throwing a tennis ball against the house and fielding the carom. On countless occasions I broke windows with errant throws and paid dearly, but that never put a damper on my enthusiasm for the game. Every day when my father came home from the barbershop, I would harass him to catch for me on the side of the house before it got dark.

It didn't end there though. We spent many summer days in the park. First I would pitch to him, then he would hit me ground balls. Eventually I'd move to the outfield and he'd hit me flies. There was always something comfortable to me about baseball. I could stay outside and play baseball all day every day, but not Jimmy. Our sessions always ended with him hitting balls well out of my reach until I was tired of running. I think that my ability to play baseball fortified his affinity for me, and looking back over the years he never hid his favor for me particularly well.

My siblings and I were always given the choice to participate in activities we enjoyed. Thankfully, our parents allowed us to each find our own respective niche. Jay was an exceptional soccer player, Khalea was at one time a nationally ranked swimmer, and Amina has been to a number of different countries playing with all-star soccer teams. I was not so decisive. I played anything I was good at, which spanned a number of activities. Ultimately I settled on three that I was really passionate about: basketball, baseball, and karate.

I started taking karate classes when I was five years old. The local YWCA was offering classes and I jumped at the chance. I loved karate. Within a few months I enrolled at the school that was sponsoring the classes, NJKA. I practiced every day, and the days I didn't have class I practiced even harder. Martial arts made me into a perfectionist. The best part about it though, was the look on my father's face when we did demonstrations. I'm not sure I can remember another time when his pride was so apparent. More importantly, martial arts created an incredible outlet for me later in life and probably kept me from exploding in high school.

The Way It Was

I'm sure that I'm quite prejudiced, but I consider myself extremely fortunate to have grown up in Montclair. I loved the town for many reasons as a child. It was a suburban township with lots of parks and playgrounds. The school system was excellent and the township offered all types of recreational activities. It was a safe, quiet town and my sisters and I frequently went bike riding and to the park by ourselves. It was also extremely diverse, and in 1997 Interrace magazine rated Montclair as the number one city in the country in which to raise an interracial family.

I have also always taken great pride in the celebrities that my hometown has produced and/or been home to. Astronaut Buzz Aldrin was born and raised here. I went to middle school with actress Christina Ricci. I graduated from high school with national track stars Mikele and Melisa Barber as well as NFL star David Tyree. Actor Frankie Faison lived around the corner from me, and Yankee legend Yogi Berra was on the other side of town. Maybe one day I would add my name to the list.

I received my first five years of formal education at Northeast Elementary School. Those were my glory days. I was so exceptional back then that sometimes when I stop and look at who I became it makes me shudder. I never skipped a grade in school, but in first and second grade I was excused during math and reading class and sent to the next grade level because I was so far advanced. I loved to read. I absolutely loved it, and math was second nature to me.

My father took a lot of trips down south to visit his brother, and I always went with him because I was so close to my cousin, Nyerere. He is a year younger than me, but we were like twins. We were always just so happy to be together that we didn't have time to argue. On those trips my father and I did three things to pass the time. He would quiz me on my multiplication facts, he'd think of difficult words for me to spell, and we would sing along with his homemade doo-wop tapes, which I was crazy about. It was all a big game to me, but in hindsight I realize just how much those trips helped to enrich my educational foundation.

Every year, from first through fifth grades, I was a member of the "One Hundred Book Club." We had an optional reading enrichment program and every year I finished among the top two or three students in my grade. Back then the school administered the IOWA standardized test for grades one through eight, and every year I was ranked in the ninety-sixth percentile or above nationally. My mother takes credit for my intellect. She comments all the time, somewhat jokingly, on how she ate lots of tuna fish when she was pregnant with me. When she realized my reading abilities, she fortified my natural gifts with tons of books and computer programs that further drove my quest for knowledge.

Physically, I'm not quite sure what made me stand out. At that age gender doesn't make much of a difference and at the time, I was one of the faster kids in school. I always came home with blue ribbons on field day, and I received the Presidential Physical Fitness Award almost every year. As much as I loved martial arts, my main claim to fame was playing baseball with the boys, and I was good. I was a decent fielder and hitter, but man could I pitch. Most of the boys were nice to me because they wanted to win, but I was never quite comfortable. I always felt as though I had something to prove, and pitching allowed me to go head to head with the boys and show that I was for real.

At the end of my third grade year, our principal transferred to another school. He was a nice man, but that is not why I remember. I remember because my father detested his replacement. He'd had past altercations with her as a teacher and did not want my sisters and I subjected to her brand of discipline. My parents transferred us to Watchung School for the next school year and that's where we stayed. Tragically, the principal that we left Northeast because of was crushed by a tree one morning during a freakish thunderstorm as she got out of her car to come to work. She was killed instantly.

Turmoil

Fourth grade is when I believe the course of my life changed drastically. The arguments that my father had with my mother and brother began to increase in frequency and intensity. Jay was not around that often, but when he was there was constant turmoil. He had lost most, if not all respect for my father. He was now eighteen, and refused to be constantly subjected to Jimmy's mood swings. In the previous three years he had run away on numerous occasions, and eventually found a deeper sense of family with my grandmother and cousins. He also found a better father figure in a man named Al that my mother had known since moving to New Jersey. To this day I don't know who my father hated more, Al or my grandmother. He saw the control that he once had over his son slipping away as if he were trying to hold water in his hands. The harder he tried to hold on, the more he lost.

I can only imagine the pain and resentment my mother endured watching Jimmy push her firstborn further and further away. To make matters worse, my father forbade us to see my mother's family because they offered Jay refuge from his tyranny. On Saturdays they often gathered for cookouts to laugh and catch up on the week's happenings. On Saturdays my father was at the barber shop from six in the morning until two in the afternoon, so to keep us from the family gatherings he piled an extraordinary list of chores on us, and God forbid they weren't done when he got home. At a bare minimum our measly allowances were withheld, and more often than not we were beaten with the leather belt that he kept solely for that purpose. He would actually call home around eight to see that we were awake. While every other kid in America was sleeping in or up watching cartoons, he saw to it that we were working.

I can't expressly remember the chores that my sisters had, but I still remember mine. At this point in time we no longer had third floor tenants, as we were all old enough to have our own rooms and our parents were making more money. My chores began with emptying the waste cans in every room except the kitchen, which was Khalea's. I was then to take the shop-vac up to the third floor and vacuum the stairs down to the basement. There was a two inch space on the other side of the banister that was not carpeted, so my next chore was to take a rag and a bottle of polish back up to the third floor and polish the banister and that small space of wood all the way down.

Next I went down to the basement which consisted of two rooms, plus a bathroom, and a laundry area. I vacuumed the rug, cleaned the bathroom, cleaned the lint trap on the dryer, and dusted. Jimmy had a barber chair with a large mirror down there, so I was also to make sure that area was straightened up, and clean the mirror. Then I emptied the shop-vac, washed it out, and cleaned the filter. When Khalea finished her chores we would fold all of the week's laundry. Now to some this may not seem like a lot, but keep in mind that I was nine and Khalea was seven. My father paid us according to grade, so for all of this I got four dollars a week and Khalea got two.

In the event that we finished our chores before Jimmy got home, my mother would whisk us down to my grandmother's house for some family time. At two o'clock, however, the control freak would come to get us. I had so much fun running around with my cousins, and my heart would always sink as I saw him pull up. He would barely even speak to my mother's family. He'd step out of our van and stand at the edge of the yard.

"Let's go girls! What are you going to do Patrice? I don't care if you stay here or come along, but the girls are going with me."

Although I know it hurt her, I think that my mother reserved her objections for arguments that spoke to our direct well-being. A great many of the arguments between my parents stemmed from her trying to defend Jay. Jimmy's temper was so volatile that it didn't make any sense to argue about him taking us from my grandmother's house, because it would only result in him making a scene.

There is no doubt that my issues at home greatly contributed to my ensuing depression, but I dealt with two major issues at the age of nine that I would struggle with for the next fifteen years of my life. I was a star when I was at Northeast. Everyone there had known me since pre-kindergarten. I was accepted as an athlete and a generally good friend. When I switched to Watchung, I was the new kid on the block. I never liked being a girl. I was always a tomboy and at Northeast that was okay. Back then I thought God had made a mistake. I felt like I was supposed to be a boy. Playing sports and wearing jeans was how I was most comfortable, and I didn't like being a girl at all.

I was born with a full head of black, curly hair. My mother spent hours between my sisters and myself washing, blow-drying, and braiding our hair. I always wanted short hair though, and the summer before arriving at Watchung I got my wish. My father has never been a fan of girls having short hair, but I guess I nagged him so much that he couldn't take it anymore. There was a catch though. If he couldn't have his way, I wasn't going to have mine either. He cut my hair like a little boy, tail and all. Now I realize that I wanted to be a little boy, but I was nine... what did I know?

When I came to school that September I was teased mercilessly. I was mistaken for a boy, and often times called names like "She-man" and "The Bush" because of my haircut. My classmates would constantly refer to me as "him," and I began to dread going to school. It didn't help that I refused to wear dresses either. I had some friends, but I was ridiculed far more than I was accepted. My gender identity was a huge issue with me from that point on, although it took a long time for me to realize why I felt so different.

The second issue that haunted me for years was that of my ethnicity. My sisters and I are all fair in skin tone, but they look Spanish or mixed. I, on the other hand, have always been very pale. I'm not light skinned, I look White. Montclair is a town that prides itself on its diversity, and the pressure I felt to "be" Black did not come from my friends or any other outside influence. I felt it all the same though, and it was crippling. That pressure came from my father. He wanted us to consider ourselves only black, and ignore the multiple ethnicities encompassed in our heritage. His belief is that if you have one drop of black blood you're black, period. He taught a black history class in school, and had volumes of video tapes at home of *Eyes on the Prize* and Ku Klux Klan documentaries.

To make matters worse, he hated White people. Now he didn't walk around making racist remarks or try to block our friendships with White kids, but it was obvious. We were forbidden to watch *The Brady Bunch*. He hated the Yankees because he felt they were a "White franchise," and he hated the Celtics and the University of Notre Dame because they had Irish mascots. Being considered "a brother" was more important to Jimmy than anything. He pledged Omega Psi Phi in college and I spent my entire childhood wearing hats, jackets, and t-shirts that said, "My dad is a Q." There was to be no mistake about it. We were Black, and to be thought of as anything else was unacceptable.

As an informed adult I have come to consider myself Black, but I am also aware and proud of my entire heritage. As I mentioned at the outset, my mother was from a town on the Gulf of Mexico, where immigrants from so many different countries arrived and assimilated. I am Black, Spanish, Italian, Irish, German, Native American, British, French, and even a little Chinese, but I was taught to respond "Black" when asked what I was.

If you look at a picture of me, the only indication that I am not totally Caucasian is the texture of my hair, and even that might lead you to believe I am Spanish or Jewish, not Black. Now I was not intrinsically concerned with my ethnic make-up, but something in me shrunk every time someone asked my ethnicity and then snickered or laughed at my response. It constantly diminished me as an individual, and filled me with self-doubt and apprehension. Between my gender and ethnic identity issues I had no idea who I was, and became very reclusive and fearful of rejection. I lost myself that year, and would not find myself again for almost twenty years.

Friendship Deferred

Throughout the next two years of turmoil and confusion, I had three friends that accepted me for who I was, and never once judged me. One was a girl named Monique that went to Watchung with me, and lived right around the corner. I went to her house every day, and when I played with her and her siblings I could forget my problems at home for a while. Al had a daughter named Tiffany, and we'd been friends since pre-school. Our mothers had become close friends and we spent many weekends at their house, laughing and running around with our siblings without a care in the world. Through Tiffany I met a girl named Meikel and we became fast friends. Meikel and I would sit at her computer for hours printing signs and banners for our mothers.

As the arguments in my household became worse and worse, I began to crumble. My desire to perform academically dissolved rapidly, and my grades plummeted severely. I guess it never occurred to Jimmy that my struggles were emotional. His response to my poor academic performance was the same as his response to everything else he didn't like when it came to his kids… punishment. He took sports, television, and karate away from me. When that didn't work, he blamed it on my friends. He decided that Monique and Tiffany were bad influences, and forbade me to be friends with them. Meikel was okay, though I'm not sure what criteria he was using, because Tiffany was getting better grades than I was.

As I now realize is his way, he deflected any culpability he may have owned in my deterioration, punished me, and blamed others. What he didn't realize was that those three friends were like crutches to me. Their friendship was the only thing supporting my self-esteem, because they were the only people in my life, outside of my family, that never wanted anything from me, and never asked me to change one thing about myself. He didn't have to remove Meikel; she moved to California in middle school and we lost touch. Looking back, his taking my friends away marked the death of all the potential I was born with.

Me and Jimmy

Sometimes I wonder if I've been too hard on Jimmy. After all, he did a lot of good things for us over the years. I realize that in the grand scheme of things my life could have been worse. I could have been molested, punched and kicked, or orphaned. I could have been poor, homeless, or totally neglected. But we all live in our own personal realities, which are separate from what perceived reality is. What everyone around you sees or thinks about you has nothing to do with how you experience life, and the true reality lies somewhere in between. For my self-evaluation to be complete, I must look at things in total honesty, and try to refrain from unfairly vilifying anyone.

I had a childhood that ranged from terrifying to thrilling. For all of my father's negative tendencies, he also gave us a lot of benefits. My strongest memories are of the negatives though, and even though he is widely popular in town, the thought of him made my blood boil for a long time. My relationship with him has always been confusing and complicated. In my opinion he single-handedly bred depression in all five of his children, but to most of his students and customers he was a charismatic, caring, funny father and husband. One major hump I had to overcome with respect to my feelings was a severe case of resentment. It wasn't just that he was a jerk; he was getting away with it!

It was very difficult for me to sort through my feelings for him. I hated him for the poor decisions he made when it came to our family, but I also loved him for the things he did right, and pitied him because I believed that in his dementia he really believed he was doing right by us. I don't know. His brand of discipline was always yelling and hitting, and I have two fundamental problems with that. The first is that he rarely showed that much energy when we deserved praise. We were punished and chastised severely when we did something wrong, yet our successes in school and athletics were met with a smug smile and some comment about how we should always perform like that-- no hugs, no allowance bonuses, not even ice cream.

The second issue I have is that when he beat or punished us, that was it for the day. He never supplemented the punishment with the understanding that he loved us and he never seemed to care how his treatment of us affected our self-images. How do you love yourself when you don't think your father likes you? When I got older I made a decision to always follow up on discipline with an explanation, a hug, and a heartfelt, "I love you."

The Good Old Days

I was probably the most confused growing up. Aside from my gender and ethnic identity issues, I had no clue where I stood in my father's life, or even how I felt about him. I kind of knew that I was his favorite. I look just like him, except I have my mother's eyes. I walk just like him, and I starred in baseball just like him. Our trips down south bonded us forever in a love for "golden oldies," and I got the most opportunities as a child.

We all went to summer day camp when we were old enough, but somehow he convinced the camp to let me come when I was a year younger than everyone else. We all went to sleep-away camp in middle school, but

I went to a "college camp" at Wellesley College while my sisters were at a YMCA camp in the mountains. Not for nothing, Frost Valley is a great camp and I went there as well, but my camp was on a whole different tier.

We would all go up to Boston Fourth of July weekend and spend the night in a hotel. The next day I checked in at Wellesley and was assigned a roommate and a counselor with whom I would check-in at certain points in the day. The counselors were students from the best colleges and universities in the country. I took two classes that I pre-selected from the camp brochures. If I remember correctly, one summer I had logic and psychology of law, and the other summer I had mock trial and public speaking. The days were filled with various activities, as well as lots of leisure time. Weekends offered a wide variety of field trips, including amusement parks, concerts, and trips to Harvard Square. It was an extraordinary experience, and it was only for exceptional students. I wasn't even a teenager yet and was already living college life, even if it was only for three weeks.

In the seventh grade I was a member of a program for gifted and talented students called ROGATE. We met primarily after school and to be perfectly honest, I don't really remember what we did. The only thing from the program I still remember is that we got to go to Space Camp. I don't remember much about Space Camp either, but I do remember thinking it was the coolest place in the world. The sleeping quarters looked like space stations and we got to simulate missions, just like they did in the movie.

Another summer my father and I went on a rafting trip down the Colorado River. The two of us flew to Las Vegas and met up with a friend of his and his two sons. We spent the night at Circus Circus Hotel, and the next day we were flown in a thirty-passenger plane to a ranch in Arizona. We spent a day of horseback riding, skeet shooting, and stories around a campfire. The next day we were flown by helicopter into the Grand Canyon, where there were two eighteen passenger motorized rafts awaiting our group. We spent four days on the river, and I had the time of my life. We camped out on the river banks each afternoon, and participated in the preparation of extravagant dinners. We hiked and explored, swam and fished.

Another summer I got to go on a twenty-day trip out west. My parents drove me up to Frost Valley, where I met up with nine boys and two counselors. We loaded up in a van and drove up to Albany, where we all boarded a train set for Montana. A few days later we arrived and again hopped into a van. We spent the next two weeks traveling throughout Montana, Wyoming, and Colorado. We stayed in a different campsite every night or two, and visited numerous National Parks. We hiked many trails and scaled snow-capped mountains, in July. I even got to see Old Faithful, and taking the train out there with a layover in Chicago was an experience in itself.

Aside from the personal trips I got to take, we took nice vacations every summer. We took three separate cruises to Bermuda, a trip to Cancun, and two trips to Disneyworld. In addition to that, we spent a week at the Jersey Shore every summer. My father also had a lot of free time in the summer being that he was a teacher, so when we weren't off in camp he took us on numerous day trips. We went to every children's attraction New Jersey had to offer, as well as the American Museum of Natural History and the Bronx Zoo in New York. He tried to take us camping once a year as well.

My father also did a lot for us around the house. My parents had a playground company come and dig up a fifteen foot by twenty foot area behind the garage and fill it with sand, and then erect a swing set complete with a jungle gym and slide. He also built us a two-story playhouse all by himself. It had plastic windows that opened, and a front door that locked. Every once in a while we even got to sleep out there. When we got older the large above ground pool and the billiards table in the basement made us the fun house on the block.

Terror

So what was so bad about this guy? It sounds like you're reading the story of a spoiled ingrate looking for a soapbox, right? Well I wish that was the case, I really do, but it just isn't. It took me a long time to sort through my feelings for him. It was hard to appreciate the good things he did when my heart was so tainted by anger, and possibly hatred, for the mistakes he made. It's like an Alaskan trying to remember the sunlight after four months of darkness. It's very hard.

I will never forget the beatings. There is a huge difference between a spanking and a beating. A spanking is one or two hits with an open hand to the rear end, or maybe the legs, intended to instill discipline or make an immediate point. I believe any and every thing physical beyond that is abuse--period. When we got in trouble we were beaten.

My father had a leather belt that was perfect for exacting pain. It was so limp that it felt like a whip. I can't recall one time in my life that I actually saw him wear that belt. All we had to do was see the belt in his hand and we fell down crying, praying that our tears would somehow touch a soft spot in him, never to any avail. Once that switch flipped in him there was no turning back, and the terror didn't stop until his sadism was satisfied.

My father has always been a control freak. He is the embodiment of an absolute spoiled brat. He is happy and agreeable as long as he gets his way, and he throws a fit if he doesn't. He ran his house with an iron fist. For instance, he woke us up at five forty-five for as far back as I can remember, so that he knew we were ready for school when he left at seven, and not to help my mother or because he had a long commute to work. It took five minutes for him to drive to school. School started at eight, but he wanted to get in at seven so that he could get "his" parking space next to the door and read the paper. In order to accomplish this, he woke his five, seven, and nine year-old daughters up before the crack of dawn every morning.

Our house was huge and our rooms were on the third floor, so he bought and installed an intercom system. It made communication within the house a great deal easier. It would eventually prove to be a curse for Amina, though. Every morning when breakfast was ready Jimmy would come through on the intercom telling us to wake up and come down to the kitchen. One by one we would stagger groggily out of our bedrooms and down the stairs. Khalea and I were pretty good at getting up, but Amina never has been.

One day we were sitting at the table for three or four minutes and Amina hadn't come down yet. Jimmy didn't say a word. He grabbed his belt and went up the stairs. Khalea and I looked at each other in misery because we knew what was going to happen, and we knew we couldn't stop it. Thirty seconds later we heard Amina screaming and crying as she stumbled her way down the stairs. She was woken from her sleep with the sting of his belt because she drifted back to sleep. It happened at least five times a month. Khalea and I would try and wake her, but sometimes we couldn't and knew better than to stick around trying. Jimmy's temper always seemed to be exceptionally short when it came to Amina, and it's no coincidence that she had the worst childhood. I could go on recounting more of his sadistic antics back then, but they are unfortunately a primary theme throughout, so I will not belabor the point.

Chapter 2
Middle School

In the sixth grade I began attending Glenfield Middle School, where my father was a social studies teacher. Most of my classmates from Watchung went to the other middle school in town, Mt. Hebron, but since my father taught at Glenfield I wasn't given a choice. I always felt accepted at Northeast, but the teasing I endured when I transferred to Watchung made me extremely apprehensive when it came to meeting new people. My sisters and I were bused to Northeast, but Watchung was too close for us to be eligible so we walked. When I started middle school, I was faced with a dilemma. I could take the bus and risk additional teasing, or I could come to school an hour early everyday with my father. Ultimately, my social anxiety overwhelmed me and I decided to go with Jimmy.

For the second time in three years I was thrust into an environment of people that I did not know and thus terrified me. On the first day of school as I walked to my homeroom, I watched longingly as everyone around me greeted each other with hugs and smiles, while I just tried not to be noticed. I wanted to make friends, but what if they didn't like me? What if I was teased and ridiculed as I had been at Watchung? I decided to stay to myself and hope that someone equally as scared and reserved would gravitate to me.

Sneaking By

In elementary school, we took gym class in the clothes we wore to school, but in middle school we had to change in the locker room. I was never comfortable with my body, or how it might be perceived by others. I don't exactly know where that came from. I do know that the sideways looks I often received when entering public restrooms always created extreme anxiety within me, to the point where I almost urinated on myself on numerous occasions to avoid the encounter. I was constantly stared at as if I belonged in the boys' room.

There were always one or two cruel girls that made passing comments about me being in the wrong locker room. Just entering the locker room was a daily challenge in itself, let alone removing my clothes to change for gym. I had a special routine for changing, and I executed it as quickly as possible. I would put one shirt on top of the other, slip my arms out and then pull the bottom shirt up through the neck-hole of the top shirt so I never had to reveal my stomach or sports bra. My gym shirt always came about midway down my thighs so that my underwear was not visible when I removed my bottoms. I would then throw my sneakers on and rush out the locker room as fast as I could, with my shoes untied. Being in the locker room felt like being in the lion's den.

Playing sports provided the only environment in which I felt any type of acceptance. Gym class was the only time in middle school that I had any fun. Whether it was basketball, football, or soccer, I was wanted. I was always chosen in the top three, often times over many of the boys, and I could play any position I wanted no matter the sport. For thirty-five minutes a day I was comfortable, but that feeling was short-lived. Far too soon the whistle would blow and it was back to reality. Back to the lion's den I went, and then into my world of alienation and fear.

Academic Trouble

My grades began slipping for a number of reasons. The primary and most obvious was my home life. It now occurs to me that the more my father abused and alienated my mother, the deeper his misery and anger became. He was grumpy much of the time and short-tempered as usual. Their arguments were getting worse and occurring more often, and I had no idea how to deal with it so I shut down. I went to karate class an hour early every day and hung around an hour late, just to be out of the house. That obviously didn't leave a lot of time for homework, but I had no interest in doing busy work anyway.

My successes were never enough for Jimmy, so I believe that the second reason my grades slipped was attention. It is basic psychology that if a child's need for attention is not fulfilled through positive means, they will seek attention through negative actions and/or poor behavior, for negative attention is better than none at all. My will to succeed was greatly diminished in those years, because I felt like I was being held to unrealistic standards.

A C was commendable for my siblings, but not for me. If I got a B, it should have been an A. If I scored a ninety-two, it should have been one hundred. If I scored one hundred but missed the extra credit, I had once again come up short, and when I got a perfect score I was told that was how I was expected to perform. The gift of natural intelligence was ultimately my childhood curse.

The summer before sixth grade, Jimmy came to me with a proposal of incentive. He said he would give me fifty dollars for every A I received on my report card. Armed with this knowledge I tried to turn over a new leaf. For as much as I loved to read as a child, I'd grown to completely resent the practice of reading an assigned passage and regurgitating the knowledge I had gained through worksheets and essays, so I didn't. I was always quiet and attentive in class and I always performed well on tests, but something deep within prevented me from ever committing myself to homework and reports for English and Social Studies.

My first quarter in school I got A's in everything else, and C's for those two subjects, but I only received one-hundred dollars. Jimmy said that he wasn't paying for A's in aesthetics, only the basics. I got the exact same grades for the second quarter, but this time I received nothing. He decided that I would not be rewarded for C's at all, regardless of my other grades.

That was all it took for me to throw my hands up in despair and confusion and resign from the attitude of scholarship altogether. I wonder what would have happened if he would've looked into trying to figure out why I had so much difficulty when it came to the redundant busy-work that my classes entailed. Could it have been that I was not being challenged? Jimmy refused to consider that I may have been crying out for help, or that my circumstances at home were affecting my ability to concentrate and desire to achieve, so nothing changed.

A Bit of Guidance

In my sixth grade year I found two women that proved to be staunch allies in my time of need. One was my social studies teacher, Mrs. Springfield. Often times I would sit with her while my father was in a meeting or grading papers, and she would listen to me as I vented about my problems at home. She knew I was much more intelligent than my performance in her class indicated, and she genuinely wanted to help me.

Her willingness to listen along with her soft voice and motherly nature were such an incredible comfort to me. I could talk to her about anything. She was disappointed when I didn't hand in my work and she never favored me or gave me grades I hadn't earned, but the mentorship that she offered me after and sometimes before school proved exponentially more beneficial than anything I could have learned in class.

The other woman was the school secretary, Ms. Lance. She was a young, sweet, vibrant woman. Sometimes the faculty meetings ran well over an hour, so I would sit in the office and talk with her. She was always so cheerful and nice. My father would usually give me three dollars after school so that I could go to the store around the corner and get a bean pie and a soda. Sometimes for no reason in particular he would say no, without explanation. It was always such a huge disappointment when he turned me down, especially when I felt I hadn't done anything wrong. Sometimes I would be hurt to the point of tears. If Ms. Lance was around when he denied my request, she would ever so quietly go into her purse and retrieve three singles. She would hand them to me without a word, just a wink and a smile.

Ms. Lance

Two days after my sixth birthday my twenty year-old cousin Terri was gunned down in front of her house by her boss, an older man with a crush that was extremely jealous and wanted complete control over her. He was upset that she had gone to a party so he came there, and they left arguing. He lost his temper, pulled out a gun, and shot her numerous times. To this point I made no mention of this because I was so young I have very limited memories of her or that period of time in general. I remember the crying, I remember the pain I saw, and I remember the sorrow, but I remember it as a witness because I was too young to truly grasp what was happening. I refer to it now because it was my first experience with traumatic death, and it seemed to be a precursor for things to come.

The first bell rang at seven-fifty every morning, signaling that it was okay for students to enter the building. Any student that entered before that had to have a pass from a teacher. My father's classroom was at the end of the hallway on the second floor, and he took this rule very seriously. His desk was positioned in such a way that he could see the doors leading to the stairwell, and it was a rare occasion when a student was able to sneak by before the bell.

One morning in May, three or four students came through the door a few minutes early. As my father went to send them back downstairs they exclaimed that the principal had sent them up without explanation. As he headed down to investigate he was overrun by a sea of students rushing up the stairs. There was a great deal of confusion and anxiety, and I had no idea what was going on. When my father returned to the classroom there was a look on his face that I had never seen before. It seemed to be a mixture of sorrow, confusion, discomfort, anguish, and fear. It was a look that I would eventually get to know very well, regardless of whose face it was on. By this time his room was full of students, so he walked up and put his hand on my back. "Naima, come in the coat room with me."

I didn't know what was coming next, but I knew it wasn't good.

"There's been a shooting in the parking deck. Someone grabbed Ms. Lance and shot her in the head. They're taking her to the hospital."

I began to weep, and he wrapped me in his arms and held me. It was without a doubt the most tender moment I ever remember sharing with my father. She was taken by ambulance to a nearby field, where she was then put in a helicopter and flown to the trauma center at University Hospital in Newark.

There were obviously no classes that day. We spent the day in our classrooms and our teachers did their best to comfort us. Many students were picked up by their parents, and counselors were brought in to deal with students that were having an especially hard time. I never spoke to a counselor, but I probably should have. We learned later on in the day that Ms. Lance's ex-boyfriend had been waiting for her in the parking deck. He shot her, and then himself. We didn't hear any more about her status for the rest of the day. When it was time to go home, my horror was intensified exponentially. She had not just been shot in the parking deck-- she was shot right next to our van. When we came out the door to leave, I saw a huge, dark stain where a pool of blood had soaked into the concrete.

I learned by way of the five o'clock news that Ms. Lance had been pronounced dead at four o'clock. I was crushed. Apparently, two nights prior to the incident her ex-boyfriend was threatening to jump off the top of her three-story apartment building because they had broken up. She was called and asked to talk him down, which she was able to do successfully. He was taken to Mountainside hospital for observation. Now, all understanding I have about psychiatric observation leads me to believe that it is supposed to last for at least forty-eight hours following a suicide attempt. He was not found to be committable and released at three-thirty the next morning. I don't know if the standard was different back in 1992, but I can't understand how someone suicidal could be cleared for release by a licensed mental health physician after such a short period of time. It was an egregious mistake, and Angela Lance paid for it with her life.

I had been to a few funerals before, but they were nothing like this one. Every funeral I'd ever been to was for an older family member that had succumbed to an illness or natural causes (I was not allowed to go to Terri's). The mood at them was one of sorrow, but it was tempered as in most cases their death was somewhat expected after a period of illness or a very long life; but this was a tragedy. Ms. Lance was twenty-five years old and widely loved and appreciated. Her wake and funeral were held at St. Paul's Baptist Church, which is one of the larger churches in town. The night of the wake and in the hour preceding the funeral, the line to her casket stretched up along the side of the sanctuary, through the foyer, out of the church to the sidewalk, and up the sidewalk around the corner. There was incessant weeping, and hundreds of inconsolable mourners came to say goodbye. It was undoubtedly the most heart-wrenching experience of my life to that point. Somehow I made it through the next four weeks at school to the summer break, but not without walking past that blood stain every single day.

Shakil's

My life was seemingly simple. I went to school, played with my friends, played baseball, and went to karate school. I say seemingly, because the turmoil at home intensified daily and no one, myself included, knew of the confusion and misery that was snowballing in my sub-conscious. I now realize that at some point in early childhood, probably third or fourth grade, I built a wall in my mind that automatically funneled pain and discomfort directly to my subconscious, what I have come to call my "depression file cabinet," because I was totally incapable of handling the hardships of my life. In my conscious mind, I buried myself in anything that involved my not being home and not having idle time to wallow in my misery. Athletic competition was actually my first addiction, it was just a healthy one. Baseball was always fun for me, but still left plenty of time for my mind to wander when I was not actively engaged in a play.

In August of 1990, I had begun training at Shakil's School of Martial Arts with Master Kevin Thompson. NJKA moved to another town in a bad neighborhood, but I still wanted to train and Shakil's was in Montclair. NJKA was a very good school, but when I started at Shakil's I entered a whole new world. The styles were in stark contrast to each other. Where the instructors at NJKA modeled patience and fun, Shakil's was militant and extremely intense.

I started over as a beginner, but was promoted to the advanced class in two months, instead of the typical six. I trained four nights a week, and never missed a class. Classes were an hour and a half of intense, brutal training in every sense of the word. Asatida, which means head instructor, was merciless. He only had one speed when it came to training and that was full steam ahead. Now don't get me wrong, this was not by any means a brutal man. Off of the dojo floor he was a kind, funny, charismatic person. But in his twenty plus years of training he had established a legacy of incredible work ethic and commitment to the art, and that was how he taught. His methods were beyond reproach as he has won numerous world championship titles and produced a number of national champions.

I never went to a karate tournament when I was with NJKA, but it was a big part of the training at Shakil's and I turned out to be pretty good. It didn't take long for me to find a second home in the dojo. I didn't want to be home anyway and I loved being there. Class started at five thirty on weekdays, and Asatida got there around four thirty. My mother got off of work at four thirty, and I was usually waiting for her on the porch when she pulled up. If she was going to be held up or had an important errand to run she would call to let me know and I would throw my bag over my shoulder and walk to the dojo.

I was usually the only one there with Asatida, and I enjoyed the personal time to train and focus on myself. Eventually he began giving me chores to do, but I didn't mind. I enjoyed his brand of discipline. He was always consistent and fair, which was a refreshing change from Jimmy. I would sweep up in the office and the sidewalk out front, and I would light incense. In the winter time I would shovel the snow out front if it was necessary. It didn't take long, and still left plenty of time for my personal training.

I began competing more and more, and I never came home empty-handed. My father was always miserly but I never shied away from asking him for the entry fee and surprisingly enough, it was the one circumstance under which he wouldn't bemoan giving me money. Those tournaments served three needs for me. The first and most obvious is that they allowed me to be out of the house all day. We competed all over the east coast. By this time Khalea had become an excellent swimmer and Amina was just beginning to realize her talent as a soccer player, so my parents didn't make it to many tournaments. We would be given a time to meet at the dojo in the morning, usually five or six depending on how far we were traveling, I would jump in the car with another student and their family, and off we'd go. Sometimes we'd even stay overnight. My father would bring me to the dojo, and give me the tournament money and a little extra for food throughout the day. It was usually between nine and eleven when I returned home at night.

Secondly, it satisfied my competitive nature and allowed me to gain tangible rewards for the extra hours and sweat I had put into my training. Thirdly, when I came home with trophies in hand my father was proud. He didn't have to say anything-- it was written all over his face. Making him proud, for all the difficulty I had achieving the task, always gave me a greater sense of accomplishment.

Our class was mostly composed of boys. There were but a handful of girls in my class, but we all got along well and eventually bonded. There were Tia, Bianca, and Alana, all of whom were a couple of years younger than me.

We alternated spending weekends at Tia or Alana's when we weren't away competing. Tia lived in an apartment with her mom Renee, who was also in training. Alana lived in a huge house with her younger brother Sinclair and their parents. They had a spacious backyard, a makeshift dojo in the basement, a fireplace where we roasted marshmallows in the winter, and even an elevator. At long last I had a few female friends that shared a major interest and weren't objected to by my father.

My First Angel

My other escape from misery came unexpectedly in the spring of my fifth grade year, but didn't really take hold until sixth grade. On April 1st, 1991 my brother's girlfriend Ranita gave birth to their first child, a baby boy named Jamal Jr. At that time they were living with us and I was immediately attached. I had been feverishly excited for the duration of her pregnancy and when the baby came I was overjoyed. I spent countless hours with him, and I always felt calm within when we were together.

Ranita moved out before he was one, but she never denied me when I wanted to see him. She frequently dropped him off on Friday nights and I would keep him until Sunday night. I was only eleven so I got a lot of help from my mother, but I knew how to do all the basics and whenever he was with me I put him to sleep on my chest. He was an escape from the real world for me, and was the first of many children that I would become emotionally attached to as a means of escaping my depression. If you accept that athletics were my first addiction, it then follows that children were my second.

Cries for Help

For all of my efforts at not being home, I was still there enough to dread it. Seventh grade came and my depression was really starting to manifest itself in my grades. I hated being in school, I hated being home, and I hated to do homework even more. I would scramble to do the previous night's assignment in the morning in my father's classroom, and got away with it more often than not. I knew that my parents and teachers were becoming increasingly frustrated, but I was ultimately screaming out for help from my subconscious; not for my schoolwork, but for my emotional agony. My math teacher would go so far as to stop class the instant he realized my homework wasn't done, walk me down to father's classroom, and pull him out of his own class to apprise him of the situation. I was incorrigible though. It was never about ability for me, but a deeper need for attention and empathy. I obviously failed miserably in my quest.

Things pretty much went on like this for the rest of middle school. I never received lower than a C because I always paid attention in class and performed well on tests. Aside from being in the house, another major reason I hated homework and papers was that I failed to see the point. I already understood just from what I had learned in class, so why waste my time with homework? I developed a cynical arrogance revolving around my natural intellect. Things had to seem logical for me to agree, and homework wasn't. "Because I said so," hasn't worked on me in years.

Bunny

In January of 1993, tragedy struck once again. It had only been nine months since Ms. Lance's death and the pain was still very fresh in my mind. It was early on the morning of the seventeenth and the phone rang. A few seconds later I heard my father's voice, "Naima! Come downstairs." I came down figuring there was some chore he wanted me to perform. The moment I set foot in the kitchen my chest tightened up. My parents were both sitting at the table. My mother was crying, and the look on my father's face flashed me back to that fateful morning in his classroom the previous May. I knew what he was going to say before he opened his mouth. Someone was dead, and it wasn't due to illness or old age.

"Have a seat, Naima."

"What happened, Dad. Why is mom crying?"

"Leon just called. Bunny was involved in a car-jacking last night. She was shot."

"Oh my God. How is she?" I already knew the answer though. I just didn't know what else to say.

"She didn't make it Naima. She was killed."

This spurred tears and confusion on my part, but it wasn't quite the same as when Ms. Lance was murdered. My sibling's and I had all been baptized at the same time three years earlier, each with a different set of godparents. My godparents, Joyce and Leon, and my parents had been friends for many years. My father and Joyce had known each other since early childhood. When I was baptized Bunny was eighteen or so, and in the process of moving out on her own. I have always been crazy about my godparents and spent the night with them often. I never really spent much time with Bunny individually, but I always admired her. She was Joyce's only child from a previous marriage. She was absolutely gorgeous, and an incredible testament to her mother's grace-- always smiling and bubbling, never with a negative word to or for anyone.

I knew that I had to go to the house. I had to see Joyce and be there for her, but I had no idea what I would say or do. We went to the house, and there were already a number of people gathered there. The house I had come to know as one of joy and refuge was eerily quiet. Joyce was up in the bedroom in search of some solitude, and I was concerned about bothering her. However, when Leon informed her that I was there she summoned me upstairs. I was terrified. I was twelve years old, and this woman I loved and adored was in pieces over the loss of her only child, yet she wanted to see me. I came in the room and sat on the bed next to her. I had never even seen her frown before and here she sat, shattered. I had no idea what to say, so I said nothing. I put my arms around her and didn't let go for what seemed like hours. I didn't want to.

Bunny had gone out to a club the night before with her friend Sheila. They were on their way home in the early hours of the morning when a car with three men passed them in the opposite direction, suddenly made a u-turn, and began chasing them. They rammed the car causing Bunny to lose control and strike a curb, resulting in a flat tire. A man then exited the car he was in, which turned out to be stolen, approached Bunny's door wielding a gun, and demanded her leather jacket. For one reason or another, he wasn't satisfied with her response and he fired a single shot into her head, killing her instantly at the age of twenty-two.

Her wake and funeral were similar to Ms. Lance's. There were hundreds of heart-broken people there to pay their respects, with lines again out the door, to the sidewalk, and down the street. As with Ms. Lance's funeral, there was incessant weeping and people collapsing in grief. I could barely bring myself to look at Joyce. Seeing her in such misery literally made my heart ache. She asked me to read Bunny's obituary at the funeral, and I didn't think twice. At twelve years old I didn't have any idea what I could do to ease her suffering, but I was honored by the request.

I can still remember the torment I felt that first Mother's day. I had always given her a gift on this day, but would she be okay today? Would I make the sorrow of this day worse by going to see her? I surely didn't want that, but then how would she feel if I didn't come by? What was the right thing for me to do? I asked my mother and she felt that Joyce might be comforted by my presence, so I went. She was awfully sad that day but she was happy to see me. When she came downstairs and saw me, she smiled through her tears and I knew I had made the right decision.

A Place of Refuge

At some point during my seventh grade year my grandmother, my aunt Claudette and her two sons Andre and Joe moved into the house next door. I enjoyed spending time with them all, but Andre was ultimately my favorite because he was a huge Knick fan and so was I. Patrick Ewing was a regular in the barber shop my father worked in, and once I met him I was a Knick fan for life. Andre and I often watched the games together and rooted with embarrassing enthusiasm. He also spoke to me like an adult and truly appreciated my intelligence. He showered me with compliments and accordingly I was drawn to him.

Not long after they moved in, Andre's five kids came to live with him. The oldest, Damian, and I were one year apart and because of the transfer he was put in the same grade as me, but we were totally different. He loved video games and comic books, but was never very big on sports. Even though we were different, we thoroughly enjoyed each other. We loved just hanging out together laughing and watching television.

Aside from the ongoing drama at home, the next year went by uneventfully. In June of 1994 I graduated from Glenfield, and made a drastic decision the day before. Over the years my hair had gotten shorter and shorter, and the day before I graduated I asked my brother to take it way down. I don't remember why I wanted that. I'm sure that upon deeper psychoanalysis it had to do with my sexual identity, but I digress. There was something even more important going on that night-- well to me at least.

That night the Knicks were playing in game seven of the NBA Finals against the Houston Rockets. I didn't want to hear all the speeches or take any pictures after graduating. I was ready to win a championship. We had a dinner dance outside under the stars, but that wasn't for me. I spent that night in the library with a handful of boys watching the game. That game has since become one of infamy in Knick history, as John Starks shot two-for-eighteen and we lost ninety to eighty-four.

Mrs. McKnight

This concludes the chapter on my middle school years, but in the summer before I entered ninth grade, tragedy struck once again. It was a warm Saturday morning in July, and once again the bad news came in the form of a phone call. It was Renee from the karate school. I was again up in my room, and my mother called me downstairs. As I did the day I learned of Bunny's death, I came downstairs unassumingly. Once again when I entered the kitchen and saw my mother, I knew something had gone terribly wrong.

She had that look. It was the exact same expression I had seen twice before in Jimmy. She was about to tell me that someone was dead. It was Alana and Sinclair's mother, Mrs. McKnight.

The night before, she had gone out to do some food shopping. Around eight-fifteen Mr. McKnight heard their two dogs barking wildly and he came outside to see what was wrong. The family car was in the driveway, but it was not his wife behind the wheel. She was nowhere in sight. There was a man he didn't know in the driver's seat, and two more standing next to the car. When the two standing saw him approaching they fled, and the driver backed the car over him. Still in the driveway he turned the car, ran over Mr. McKnight once again, and cut across the front lawn, stopping briefly to pick up his two cohorts before escaping. Mrs. McKnight's body was found three hours later with a single gunshot wound to the back of her head in the back seat of the car, abandoned on a dead end street in Irvington.

When I got to the house there was the same morbid silence I had experienced at my godparents' house. It seemed like the entire karate school was there, but you could hear a pin drop. Alana and Sinclair were stoic, obviously in shock. Once again I was in un-chartered waters. What do you say to your friends at that age immediately following the murder of their mother? I had no idea. Tia, Bianca, and I spent the night to keep Alana company, but we had no idea how to help her.

So there you have it. In twenty-six months I was shoved to the forefront of human indecency three times. I lost people I cared for in the blink of an eye, and watched people I adored suffer tremendous loss. I stated earlier that I felt I probably should have gone for counseling after Ms. Lance's death, but after enduring the losses of Bunny and Mrs. McKnight in such rapid succession there is no doubt in my mind. To every dark cloud there is a silver lining, right? Things could not possibly get any worse for me because there was nowhere else to go but up, right? Wrong. It would take only days for what was left of my life to come crumbling down.

Chapter 3
My Parents

On Christmas day in 1992, something happened that will stay with me for as long as I live. The day began like every other Christmas before. My sisters and I were awake around four, tossing and turning in bed waiting for the sun to rise. As soon as the sky began to get light we were beating on my parents' door so that we could open up our presents. They reluctantly arose, and we all made our way down the stairs. One of my favorite childhood memories has always been coming down the stairs to the soft glow of our blue Christmas lights. That is my fondest memory of home.

So we came into the living room and there were tons of presents under the tree. My mother always knew which gift was for which child without even looking at the tags, and she took great pride in handing them out. My father liked to sit back with his camera so he could catch our expressions right when we opened the gifts. Jay always came down a little later, as he's never been much of a morning person. After all the gifts were opened we would play with our new toys, and my mother would go and make a huge breakfast.

After breakfast on this particular Christmas, I resigned to my room to relax for a while. Before I knew it there was a huge commotion coming from the kitchen. I turned my stereo up a little and tried to ignore it as I'd become accustomed to doing, but it grew louder and louder. Eventually I couldn't take it anymore, and I went down to see what was going on. My brother and Jimmy had gotten into an argument, about religion of all things, and it was getting out of control. As I came down the hallway I heard my father say, "F--- this, I going to get my gun." Jay ran out in his pajamas and I ran out after him. I got outside just in time to watch him jump the four-foot gate in the driveway without even touching it. I yelled his name through my tears but he kept running.

My father had a number of guns throughout the house, and he went for the closest one which was in the closet. Thankfully, he didn't have any handguns there, only rifles in their cases. I guess he didn't want to waste time removing one from its case and loading it, so he grabbed a construction leveler. When I returned to the kitchen, I saw him standing with it in his hands. My mother was standing behind him in tears with her arms wrapped around his waist, pleading with him to stop and calm down.

He began rapping her on the knuckles with the leveler so he could get free, but she refused to let go. Her hand began to bleed, and I too began to beg him to calm down. Eventually he dropped the leveler and stormed off somewhere else in the house. I tried to comfort my mother, and after assuring me that she would be okay, she asked me to grab Jay's jacket and try and find him. I put on my jacket, then his, and jumped on my bike. I rode around for about an hour but I never found him

Shortly after I returned home, Jimmy told Khalea and me to go down to the basement and fold the laundry. We went down without a word and did as we were told. A good ten minutes passed as we folded in silence. Finally, I looked at her and said, "They're gonna get a divorce."

She looked back at me and said matter-of-factly, "I know." We went back to folding in silence.

The majority of my mother's duties at work involved writing and typing, and for three months she had to do so with a terribly bruised right hand, a constant reminder of my father's rage. She didn't even have anything to do with that argument. We figured the news would come down sometime in the next month or so, but it never did. Life went on as usual and we figured they had worked it out, or were trying to stick it out for our benefit. Khalea and I no longer wanted them to though-- we were tired. We were totally drained from years of arguments, terror, and heartache. Amina didn't really talk about it much but she obviously wanted mommy and daddy, together. She had not seen nearly as much as the rest of us, and I would imagine she had difficulty processing the things she did see.

My father has always lived within his own version of reality. He has never truly taken responsibility for any of his wrongdoings, seeking instead to explain them away or outright blame others. He bullies and intimidates people into getting his way wherever possible, and he lies to justify his actions so much that he often has no clue how to distinguish truth from fiction. On the other hand, he can be very charming and charismatic. He is no stranger to hard work and will give his friends the shirt off of his back. He worked two jobs most of his life to support his family, and has helped to educate thousands of children over his teaching career. He was never able to truly reconcile these two sides of himself, resulting in a confusing and absolutely frustrating man. His inability to ever find balance and self-discipline is what ultimately caused the demise of his marriage and legacy.

My Mom

So far there hasn't been much mention of my mother, but it has not been intentional. My mother has always been phenomenal, but her efforts were constantly destroyed or at the very least overshadowed by Jimmy's antics. I would like to take a little time here and focus on who she is in order to paint an accurate picture of the way their marriage worked.

As I mentioned previously, my mother has always been extremely petite. I don't think she has ever weighed a hundred and twenty pounds aside from pregnancy. She was born and raised in the Deep South, two blocks from the Gulf of Mexico in Mississippi, and is my father's complete opposite. Her mother is a devout Catholic and raised her children the same way, even sending my mother to Catholic school. My aunts and uncles have very strong Southern accents, but my mother's is mild. She was the baby, and was ultimately exposed to the most opportunities when they moved to New Jersey.

My mother doesn't like a lot of noise and very rarely raises her voice. She says what she means, and means what she says. If she promised me a reward for a good deed done, I could take that to the bank. She is one of the most nurturing women I have ever come in contact with. She does not like to scold children, but instead sees their mistakes as an opportunity to teach. No matter what she was doing, she never seemed to mind putting it aside so that I could show her what I learned in karate class or read her a paper I had written for school. She was never too busy for her children.

We were always the center of her world and she never left it up to chance that we knew solely by her actions. She hugged us and told us she loved us constantly, and she would sneak to comfort us after one of Jimmy's tirades. Her life was inundated with our activities, and when she got off of work she actually worked harder. She was our chauffeur, our cook, and our tutor. She somehow juggled everything we had to do daily and never missed a beat. It wasn't just picking up and dropping off either. Somehow she was always there for most of our games and meets. Her love was the constant in our lives. When I sought advice from Jimmy he told me what to do, but when I came to my mother she gave suggestions. She loved us enough to let us learn on our own.

So now I hope I have painted an accurate picture of both of my parents. This is how I knew them, but this marriage was rooted in a history that extended far beyond my birth. As I further illustrate these roots it will become evident to most of reasonable judgment that their marriage was doomed before it ever began. It was rooted in anger, hostility, irresponsibility, and fear.

How It All Began

Although he has never admitted it, I believe my father had a son before Juno was born, but that is unsubstantiated. I make mention of that because it was a factor that seriously affected how my family came into being. Juno was born on October 28, 1967, but my father always had problems with her mother and they didn't last very long. He went to California for a few years, and upon his return to Montclair he met my mother who was new in town. She had no idea that he was a maniac and a control freak, but it didn't take extraordinarily long for her to figure it out.

In the early spring of 1970, my mother found out she was pregnant with Jay. When she told Jimmy he was not happy at all. He was fed up with women getting pregnant and telling him what he was going to do with his life. He did not want my mother to keep the baby, but he knew that she was a devout Catholic and an abortion was out of the question. He visited my mother frequently, always trying to convince her to give the baby up for adoption.

Eventually his persistence paid off and she moved into a "home for unwed mothers" in Jersey City, where she would stay until she had the baby and then give him up. My father came to see her and they continued to date, although he was not being faithful. On December 26th, 1970, my mother gave birth to a baby boy and named him Gerard Anthony Mosley. She signed the appropriate paperwork and her son was taken away. She stayed a week or so at the home and then moved home with her mother and siblings.

For months she was haunted by nightmares and woke up in cold sweats constantly. She cried often and fell into a deep depression. She couldn't take it anymore, and had a long discussion with her mother. After their conversation they decided they would call family services and get him back. When Jimmy found out he was furious. He came and picked her up saying that he wanted to go for a ride. He took her out on the highway to west Jersey and put a gun to her head, saying he would kill her if she didn't call back and tell the agency she had changed her mind. She agreed tearfully and he brought her home.

Immediately she told her mother and they went to the Montclair Police Department to file charges, but things didn't quite turn out that way. The good old boys that had grown up with him were saying, "Nah, not Jimmy Tryman," chuckling as if this wasn't a serious matter. They didn't write anything down and nothing was ever documented. They simply sent an officer to go and bring him in to straighten things out, and they didn't have to go far. He had followed them to the police station and was lurking around outside. He came in and denied that any of it happened.

He said that he wanted his son and he wanted my mother to move into his parents' house because he didn't want him raised in her mother's household. Seeking an amicable solution, my mother agreed to move into his parent's home. He didn't live there and she wouldn't have to worry about him acting like a maniac. They went through the appropriate steps and the adoption was rescinded. Gerard Anthony Mosley became Jamal James Tryman and my family was begun.

My mother stayed there for a while and then moved into her own apartment in the neighboring township of Orange. Their rocky relationship continued and they argued constantly. One time my father became consumed with such rage, throwing chairs and turning over tables, that my mother fled clear to Mississippi for three weeks. When she returned they once again reconciled their differences. In April of 1972, my paternal grandmother died of an aneurism. The following month my mother moved back into the third floor apartment and shortly afterwards, so did my father.

Nothing about their relationship was ever romantic, not even their wedding. He didn't even propose out of love. My mother got pregnant in 1975, but had serious complications. She had an ectopic pregnancy which meant that the baby was developing outside of her uterus, and thus could not survive. She got very sick and emergency surgery had to be performed to save her life. My father was concerned that had she died, her mother would have gotten custody of Jay. He didn't want that, and to protect against it they were married in the living room of his parent's home on May 26th, 1975.

The Breaking Point

So from the very beginning my family seemed to be destined for dysfunction. Jimmy's deep-seeded control and anger issues stemmed from his own childhood, and were a theme in his marriage. Over the years my parents had numerous altercations, but there is one that stands out vividly my mind. On a Saturday afternoon when I was six years old, my mother took my sisters and me on a trip to the state fair at the Meadowlands. Jimmy was at work, and Al and his wife Nancy were taking their kids along with Meikel and her mother.

We all met up and car pooled to the fair, and when we got back Jimmy was waiting with Jay in the car. He was enraged with her for going without him and even more so because she had gone with Al and Nancy. I was too small to see out the window of the car but I could hear him hitting her, followed by her crying and pleading with him to stop. I could also hear Jay trying to break them up. He was so mad that he punched a tree out of frustration and severely sprained his hand. My mother had a black eye for months.

There had been many loud arguments in the five years from then until that particular Christmas, but those were the most terrifying for my mother. After the way he had jumped in her face and injured her that Christmas, my mother made a vow to herself and God that if he ever jumped in her face like that again she would leave him, and for a while it seemed like things were going to work out.

It was a year and a half later before my father dropped the final hammer. My brother had adopted a puppy named Major, but decided that he no longer wanted it. I didn't want him to be euthanized at a shelter, so I asked if I could have him and Jay agreed. I never had the money to get him any shots, so my father made him stay outside even though he was very young. One day Khalea decided to bring him inside for a while and that was when all hell broke loose. Worms started squirming out of Major's penis and we all started freaking out. Jimmy picked him up by the neck and threw him outside, but there was a trail of worms from the living room to the back door.

"Khalea get in here and pick up these worms!"

"Daddy please, I can't! They're nasty!"

"I told you all to leave that dog outside. Quit whining and clean up this mess before I get my belt!"

She was horrified and began to cry. As she bent down she began gasping and dry-heaving, but he felt no sympathy for her. I was miserable for her and felt guilty since it was my dog, but I was equally incapable of picking up the worms without getting sick. My mother pleaded with him. "Jimmy this is too much. She's twelve for God's sake!" That only further infuriated him, and he completely lost his temper. Once again he jumped in her face and called her names, which was the final straw. She couldn't take it anymore, and in that summer of 1994 she told him so. I imagine she had been fed up for years, but they had built a whole life together and her children were at such crucial stages in life. There comes a time when enough is just enough though.

Finally

A few days after burying Mrs. McKnight and the incident with Major, my father called for me and my sisters to come into the living room. "Your mother and I are getting a divorce. I want us to stay together and work things out as a family, but she doesn't want to." They had agreed to tell us together, but he went behind her back and broke it to us while she was at work. I have always had a problem with the way he did that, but I realize why. He wanted to put it all on her and get us on his side. We all began to cry. I ran out and went next door to see Damian. I knew he would understand how I was feeling as he himself was a child of divorce.

I'm not sure why I was crying. Lord knows I didn't want things to continue on as they had been. Ultimately, I guess I was just in shock. I didn't *really* want them to break up. I just wanted it to be better. I didn't want to make choices on holidays. I didn't want to move out. I didn't want to live in two different homes. I did want my mother to be happy though. She deserved it.

Since Jay's birth she was a loving mother and eventually a devoted wife. My father had successfully distanced her from her family, and she dealt with it for the benefit of her children. She had endured physical and mental abuse for close to twenty-five years. Amina held resentments towards her for a long time, but she was the only one. Jay, Khalea, and I were ultimately relieved because we knew it was for the best. Any resentment we held was towards Jimmy. He was the reason our family had become dysfunctional, and my mother was finally standing up for herself.

If my father had any hopes of saving his marriage, he put them soundly to bed with his actions in the next year. In my infinite teenage arrogance I tried to conduct a counseling session with them, but it wasn't very successful. My father admitted no wrongdoing and was not at all receptive about changing his methods. His home was his castle and he would run it as he saw fit, and no women or children were going to deter him. He stood firm in his assertion that he was doing an admirable job of running his household.

We stayed there for another year while my mother gathered the money to move out and start over, but she no longer wanted to sleep in the same bed with him so she began sleeping on the pull-out couch in the family room. In a supreme show of insensitivity and his need for control, Jimmy put a lock and chain on the rails of the bed so that she could not pull it out. His verbal assaults on her family became more and more frequent and vicious, and the house was always very tense. He did not want the divorce, but he was not willing to change in any way. Over the course of that year my father just continued to dig the grave for his marriage. Instead of seeking counseling or trying to be a little more patient, he became more belligerent. He constantly belittled my mother's family and initiated unnecessary arguments.

At some point, my mother found comfort in a fireman named Glenn. He was patient, considerate, and chivalrous-- three qualities that my father was desperately lacking. Jimmy has maintained that they were seeing each other before she asked for the divorce, and I truthfully don't know. I've never asked my mother because as far as I am concerned it's irrelevant. The bottom line is that either way, she deserved him. She had endured over twenty years of grief and was long overdue for some happiness. Although to this day Jimmy will say that Glenn caused the demise of his marriage, the sad truth is that he had been systematically dismantling it on his own for years.

Chapter 4
High School

In September of 1994 I entered the ninth grade. Needless to say I was thoroughly intimidated, and for the most part I stayed to myself. Somehow with all of my academic troubles in Glenfield, I landed in all honors classes. Well, I saw them as troubles, but I imagine there were a number of students that would've loved to trade report cards. I had never received below a C, but for me that was failure. I had Biology and Geometry, both tenth grade courses and both on the honors level, and I had honors History and Spanish.

That year I began systematically committing academic suicide. As usual I never did any homework, but now I couldn't get my mind to stop wandering. I began dealing with the divorce by not dealing with it. I daydreamed all the time, completely incapable of dealing with reality. I would sit and fantasize about being rich, being popular, having a boyfriend, being a national karate champion, and anything else that seemed dreadfully out of my reach. My classes were considerably harder than those in Glenfield, and my inability to focus doomed me. I barely took notes, and was therefore totally unprepared for tests and quizzes.

In my first quarter I failed Biology, English, and Spanish. I got a D in Geometry and I didn't care. I wasn't proud of it, but they were the worst grades I'd ever received and I wasn't terrified of going home. Looking back I'm sure I gave my mother an ulcer which was not my intent, but I had won a deeper victory. He couldn't hurt me anymore. I could fail every single class for the rest of my life, and there wasn't a thing that Jimmy could do about it. I now realize that I was proverbially cutting my nose to spite my face, but damn it felt good back then.

Things did not improve much for the rest of the year. By June I somehow managed to avoid failing everything except Geometry. We got seven grades per quarter, so at the end of the year I had twenty-eight individual grades plus the final grade for each class. Of those twenty-eight cycle grades I received nine F's. I did spend one session with the student assistance counselor during that year and I was able to release a lot of pent up pain and anger, but for some reason I never went back. Instead I continued to purge as much frustration as I could in karate class, and whatever was left over got shoved into the "depression file cabinet."

My First True Friend

At some point that fall, I became friends with a girl named Maleka. She turned out to be an extraordinary athlete, her specialty being softball. She had grown up only two blocks away from me, but our paths never crossed because we attended different schools and played different sports. As it turned out we also had Geometry together, and it was no coincidence that I failed. I got a D the first cycle on my own accord, but when we hooked up any chance of my passing that class went straight down the drain. It wasn't her fault though. She passed because she did homework and studied for tests, but neither one of us paid attention in class.

Our teacher had to be at least sixty years old. She was a relic, and totally incapable of engaging her students. She seated us alphabetically by last name, so Maleka (B) and I sat on opposite sides of the room, and we created nothing short of havoc with all of the space between us. It started out fairly harmless, but became increasingly menacing as the year went on. The teacher spent a good percentage of the class period with her back to us writing proofs on the chalkboard, so Maleka and I would throw things to each other every time she turned around. By springtime we were bouncing pennies off the board when she turned to write on it. That was by far the worst behavior I ever exhibited in school and it was way outside of my character, and most of it was my idea. I was in a rebellious and infantile mindset at that time.

By the time baseball season rolled around I was academically ineligible. *Damn.* My father didn't have to take anything away from me. In the process of trying to get back at him I'd managed to shoot myself right in the foot. I had no idea that I needed certain grades to play sports, but I sure found out the hard way. I came to realize that I was hurting my mother more than I was hurting Jimmy, which was the last thing I wanted. She had invested a considerable amount of time, money, and effort into books and computer programs for me in my childhood in order to nurture my intellect and feed my curiosity, and I was flushing that all down the toilet. I was disintegrating right before her eyes, and there was nothing she could do about it.

I didn't realize it at the time, but Jimmy was using my failures to denigrate my mother. He was going around telling anyone who would listen how my mother's decision was tearing his kids apart and that her selfishness would lead to our downfall, and I was proving it. I don't know what hurt her more, my failures or his using them to lay blame, but either way the pain I was trying to invoke in Jimmy was being diverted to her and it had to stop. This woman had devoted her life to us, and my antics were the emotional equivalent of spitting in her face. That spring I decided that I would have to find another way to make Jimmy feel my pain.

A Guiding Light

That year Maleka and I became incredibly close. I needed a friend, and she was always there for me. She was my first real best friend. We were alike in so many ways. I could talk to her about anything, I could cry to her if I needed, she could always make me laugh, we could watch a baseball game together and she even wore baseball caps. Being with her made me feel like maybe I wasn't a freak. Maybe there were even more girls out there that liked the things I liked. I finally had a friend that I truly identified with on every level.

I started hanging out with her all the time. We were inseparable. When our winter and spring breaks rolled around Maleka would spend the week at my house so that we could hang out even more. Somehow we had lived two blocks away from each other our whole lives without our paths crossing, and then God brought her into my life right when I needed a friend like her the most.

That year I began one other friendship that has truly sustained me for the past fourteen years, and I never saw it coming. It wasn't anyone new though. It turned out to be someone I had known my whole life. When my parents separated I began to see much more of my mother's family. My cousin Cindy and I are six years apart, and when I was nine that seemed like a lot, but when I was fourteen it was perfect.

She was so easy to talk to. The more time we spent together, the closer we got. We both assumed roles completely opposite those we were accustomed to. She was the baby of seven children, and I was the oldest of three girls, so she got to have a little sister and I got to have a big one. It began as her always giving me a shoulder to cry on, but I quickly came to realize that I could tell her anything. She never passed judgment on me, and she never said a discouraging word. I love all of my family dearly, but I soon found that I was not enjoying gatherings until she arrived. I was always anxious to see her and tell her what was going on in my life.

Our age difference made her the perfect confidante. She was old enough to give me sound advice, but not so old that she had forgotten what it was like to be my age. Many times at these gatherings I would pull her coattail about something that was bothering me, and we would end up somewhere behind a closed door for hours, me pouring my heart out and her intently listening and advising me. She was my savior in high school.

I was not handling the change that comes with divorce well at all. We moved out in August of 1995, and when I was home I was in my room. I became very reclusive and only came out to go into the bathroom or to get food, which I would eat in my room. We were two blocks away from the karate school, so I began walking to class. Karate was the biggest release that I had. Four days a week I could scream, yell, stomp, and sweat, which proved incredibly therapeutic for me. I believe one hundred percent that I would have fallen into substance abuse my freshman year if it wasn't for martial arts.

When my sophomore year began, I had a renewed attitude towards school. I was not going to let my resentments towards my father cause any more detriment to my studies, and things slowly began to improve for me. By this time we had developed a small clique and we would hang out every day after school. Maleka, Damian, Onaje and I would usually hang out on Maleka's porch for a while, and then migrate to Jimmy's. We would go down in the basement and shoot pool until seven or eight, and then we'd all go home. My father was still working at the barber shop, so we had the house to ourselves almost every day.

Basketball

When basketball season rolled around this time I was ready. I strode into the gym the day after Thanksgiving ready to raise hell. There was a new coach that year so I figured I had a great shot at making Varsity, but things didn't quite work out like that. The coach summarily placed all the upperclassmen on Varsity and the underclassmen on jayvee, and I was livid. Maybe I wasn't starting material yet, but I damn sure deserved a Varsity uniform. I was made captain of the jayvee team and started at point guard.

I never saw a great deal of the Varsity coach. We practiced in separate gyms and our games usually ran simultaneously. The jayvee coach was a nice man, but he had no clue what he was doing. It took four games for him to realize that he didn't have to burn a timeout in order to make a substitution. Our uniforms were made of 100% cotton and stuck to us when we played, but they were a tremendous upgrade from the blood-stained, undersized, polyester uniforms we had from the previous ten or so years. I began calling the plays and even timeouts if I felt we needed one. If I knew anything at all about myself back then, it was that I was not a loser. I couldn't stand to lose, and we wouldn't if I had anything to do with it. My temper got me whistled for seven technical fouls in the first half of the season.

One day I was beside myself with anger because I felt the head coach did not care about us. We were 9-0, and she barely even commented on our success. Our game finished before the Varsity, and I went on a tirade in the locker room. "I'm sick of this! We're undefeated and the Varsity sucks! How can Coach not realize that she needs to bring some of us up? She doesn't even realize we exist! She couldn't coach her way out of a paper bag!" I have no idea how long the Varsity coach was standing in the doorway listening, but when I turned around her face was beet red. She had an earful for me, but I must have struck a nerve because a week later she gave me the option to move to Varsity, and I jumped at the chance.

I loved leading an undefeated team, but it was jayvee and I had set out to make Varsity. I had worked hard for years practicing alone and playing against my brother. I would line up chairs and garbage cans in my backyard and dribble around them as fast as I could for hours. Apparently she had made the same offer to my friend Zakiyyah earlier that day, but she declined in the hopes of completing an undefeated season, never thinking that I would leave them. That year the Varsity finished eight and twelve, and without anyone that was comfortable handling the ball or a competent coach, the jayvee didn't win another game. From that point on I developed a fear of success because of the people I would leave behind.

As soon as the basketball season ended I had to shift gears to baseball mode. High school baseball was nothing like the town league. These guys were considerably bigger, stronger, and faster than I was. I was able to hold my own due only to sheer natural talent. I started at second base for the jayvee team, and I also pitched occasionally. I never really got along with the Varsity coach, but the jayvee coaches Fisher and Ferguson treated me like one of the guys. They saw me as a player and gave me the confidence to stick with it when I wanted to quit.

It was at some point that year that my relationship with Jimmy really began to hit the skids. We didn't see much of each other with my sports, his two jobs, and our living in different homes. I asked him all the time to take me camping or to the batting cages. Occasionally he would oblige, but more often than not he would grumble about not having the time or money. One day that May it was over ninety degrees out and I was hanging out with my Aunt Claudette. I went next door and asked my father for money to get ice cream, at which point he handed me five dollars. I went to the store down the street and bought a pint of ice cream, a Jet magazine, and an ice cream bar to eat while the pint softened.

My sisters were living with Jimmy at the time and he sent Amina over to get the change, but I didn't have any. I turned her away but she returned shortly. "Dad wants to talk to you."

I got up without a word, knowing exactly what was about to go down. I walked over and said, "What's up, Dad?"

He looked at me with a scowl and said, "Where's my change?"

"I don't have any. I bought a Jet and an ice cream bar."

"I didn't tell you to spend all that money! I guess that's all I'm good for these days, huh? I never see you anymore unless you're looking for money."

I couldn't believe my ears. My eyes welled with tears and I dropped my head and walked away without a word. How could he say that to me? All I ever wanted was to play baseball and go camping with him, but he constantly turned me away. I couldn't find the words to express my pain at that moment, but it didn't take long for me to get them together. I wrote him a searing letter and enclosed two dollars, which is what his change should have been. We didn't speak for months until my mother interceded and got us to sit down together, because she didn't like seeing me in unnecessary pain.

Improvement

Ending the basketball season with a losing record left a nasty taste in my mouth, and when the summertime came I vowed to do everything I could do avert ever having to feel that way again. We played in a local high school summer league, but that was not enough for me and Zakiyyah. We woke up early every morning that summer and worked out in the park together for three hours. We didn't understand a great deal about technique or mechanics, but we made up our own drills and executed them with all the intensity one could imagine. At the end of the season the head coach had given us all brochures for a summer camp in Pennsylvania. Zakiyyah and I had become close and we both wanted to go sorely, but we knew that her family could not afford it and I wasn't so sure that my mother could either. I'm not sure how she did it, but not only did my mother send me to camp; she scraped up enough for Zakiyyah to go as well.

That summer we spent a week at the Pocono Invitational Basketball Camp. It was non-stop basketball all day, and there were girls there from all over the east coast. Zakiyyah and I were in the same cabin and seemingly joined at the hip. One of the guest speakers that year was Carol Blazejowski, one of the greatest women's basketball players of all-time. She was second only to "Pistol" Pete Maravich on the all-time collegiate scoring list with a total of 3,199 career points, and she had done so right in our backyard at Montclair State College. She talked to us about the importance of repetition and work ethic, and we were all ears. We returned home with a whole list of drills, and made the most of them. Montclair High's Varsity girl's basketball team had not had a winning season in twenty years, and we were determined to change that in the upcoming campaign.

When my junior year started I had two agendas. By this time I was well aware of how important that year is both academically and athletically with respect to the college application process. It is the last full set of grades and stats that admissions boards and coaches see when considering applications. Obviously I needed to make a good showing academically, but there was also much work to be done on the basketball court. It's hard to get coaches to come scout you when your team sucks.

Academically, I loaded my schedule with classes that interested me, yet presented challenges. I also became close to two teachers that provided me with guidance and counsel. Ms. Barnes was my chemistry teacher in her twenties, and she seemed to be speaking an entirely different language than my previous Chemistry teacher. She had gone to school with my brother and my cousin Jewel, and was so down to earth. She called me on my shortcomings but was never stingy with praise. I hung out with her whenever I had free time. The other teacher was Mrs. Stewart, my African-American Literature teacher. I had her for English the previous year and I didn't really enjoy the course because I hated grammar work, but I was interested in this subject and she eventually became a friend and mentor as had Ms. Barnes.

I sought out a teacher that would be willing to supervise an after school open gym so that we could begin getting in shape and playing together. After seven or eight denials from assorted teachers, Ms. Barnes finally agreed. She didn't know much about basketball but she was willing to help with anything that empowered young women. I went to the athletic director and he referred me to the Montclair Community Intervention Alliance. He gave me the phone number of a man named Jerry Citro, who was in charge of it at the time. I contacted him but we ultimately could not make it happen for insurance reasons, so I began to condition on my own.

Mistake of My Life

At this point in time I was now a candidate for black belt promotion, and I was pushing myself especially hard. Sometime in October, three weeks before my test, I developed an infection in my lower abdomen. It started as a nagging pain one morning and I figured I was getting my period, so I popped a couple of Aleve and went to school. By the end of the day I could barely stand up straight. Somehow I made it to Aunt Claudette, who was a retired registered nurse. I curled up in a ball on her couch and cried uncontrollably. She called my mother and told her to meet us at the hospital.

To that point it was the worst medical experience I'd ever had. I was a virgin and had never been to a GYN, so needless to say the examination was extremely uncomfortable. They had to manually fill my bladder using a catheter in order to conduct an ultrasound. I was poked and prodded and ultimately diagnosed with an inflamed appendix. I had never undergone surgery before and was terrified, but not just about the prospect of going under the knife. If I had surgery I would never recuperate in time to test for my Black Belt! I would have to wait an entire year. The doctor decided to put me on intravenous antibiotics and keep me over night. Thankfully I did not need an appendectomy and, against the advice of my doctor and admonitions of my mother, I was back in the dojo the next night. Asatida kept an eye on me and told me to stop if I felt any pain, but I didn't listen to him. I was going to be ready. I pushed through the pain, completely focused on my goal.

With each promotion we were required to do more and more. For Black Belt we had to start with an extensive workout that included 1,000 jumping jacks, 100 sit-ups, and various calisthenics. We had to execute every single technique in the system ten times each from the right and left sides. We had to perform seventeen open hand katas and ten weapons katas. We had to break three boards and perform twenty self-defense techniques. We had to fight three and four people at a time, and we had to write a two-page paper on some aspect of the system. When all of that was done, we still had to undergo a question and answer period. On top of all that, for any and every mistake that we made over the two day period, we were penalized with push-ups. I was excited though. Back in those days I thrived on challenges like that.

Black Belt promotion was designed to be the most grueling two days one could possibly imagine. Anytime we went up for promotion we knew we were in for hell, but Black Belt was to be the end all, be all. We started with the jumping jacks and I was strong. We went through the entire workout and I was still okay. We did all the beginner techniques and combinations, and near the end I started getting shooting pains in my abdomen, but I kept pushing. As we got into the advanced techniques the pain began to escalate. I began to feel the way I felt the day I had to go to the hospital, but I obviously wasn't getting any sympathy. I began to cry, still executing techniques but very poorly, trying to do so while clenching my stomach.

Some of the Black Belts began to get on me, yelling and smacking me on the legs. None of them knew that I had been sick and it wasn't like I could stop and explain it to them, so I kept going. Not long after that Asatida walked up behind me, yelled at me to suck it up, and then smacked me on the behind, *hard*. That broke me. It wasn't the hit that did it though. Asatida had broken my heart. I knew what this day was about. I knew that it would be the hardest thing I'd ever done, but I had bent over backwards for this man for five years, showing up early and staying late, being an emotional leader in class, and always being a model of hard work and discipline.

I was suffering from a medical condition that was no fault of my own, and he knew all about it. Until that day, I had never quit anything in my entire life. When he hit me I stopped all together, briefly glared at him through my tears, and walked off the floor. The other Black Belts tried to get me out of the dressing room, but I was shattered. I sat and cried for about fifteen minutes then changed my clothes, gathered my things, and walked out of the dojo.

A week later Asatida convened a panel of all the Black Belts to discuss the situation with my mother and me. I had always been extremely astute and ambitious when it came to karate. When Asatida taught the higher ranks new katas and techniques I paid attention, and usually caught on faster than they did. When the previous class was preparing for promotion the year before, many of those students came to me for help even though they outranked me. Although I had only been there for four years, I felt that I should have been given the chance to test then on the merits of my knowledge and commitment. I didn't dare ask Asatida though, as that would have been taken as a sign of disrespect and arrogance, so I put in another year.

Based on all of this, I did not feel I should've had to wait a whole year because of a medical condition. I respectfully requested a period of three months to heal and prepare, followed by an individual promotion ceremony. I was willing to do everything all over again, which I felt would be harder because there would be no one to divert the attention. The panel did not see it that way, and decided that I would have to wait a year and try again with the next class. I was heartbroken, and could not accept those terms. I told them I quit as my eyes welled with tears, and walked out the door. I did not speak to Asatida for years. It would prove to be the biggest mistake I ever made.

I immediately went to see Master Hinton Kinsler who ran a shotokan karate school around the corner from my house. Our paths had crossed numerous times at tournaments and he was well aware of my skill and work ethic. I explained the situation to him and he accepted me with open arms. As soon as I learned the differences between the two systems and the new katas, he promoted me to Black Belt. Soon after that I began teaching classes and was given keys to the school. I brought a new energy to the school and it was well received. Enrollment at the school started to go up and I realized for the first time my talent for giving instruction. I was able to get kids to trust and work hard for me, because they liked but also respected me.

A Winning Season

There were only a few weeks left until Thanksgiving, and I was chomping at the bit. At some point during this whole ordeal I learned that our coach would not be returning. I wasn't really sure how to feel. She and I didn't have the greatest relationship and I was eager for a fresh start, but the season was fast approaching and we had no coach. On the Wednesday morning before Thanksgiving break, an announcement was made for all girls trying out to come to a meeting after school.

They had finally hired a coach, and it was none other than Jerry Citro, the man I had contacted earlier about open gyms. He briefly introduced himself, told us to be at the gym at seven-thirty on Friday morning, and warned us not to eat too much turkey because it would end up in the garbage can during tryouts. He wasn't kidding. I've never seen so much vomit in my life. We must have run a hundred wind sprints that first practice and I don't think he even took a ball off the rack.

There were two freshman girls that were having a particularly hard time, and didn't mind voicing their objections as they ran. The coach ignored them, and his only response was, "Shut up and run!" Shut up was a phrase that I had very little tolerance for. I felt it was very disrespectful and I was faced with a dilemma. Here I was fighting for a starting spot with a new coach, but he had used a term that I had come to take as highly offensive and, although he hadn't said it to me, I figured it would only be a matter of time.

We had double sessions that day, which meant we had a second practice at one o'clock. After changing my clothes I came and knocked on the door to the coach's office. I was pretty nervous but secure in the fact that I had a valid point. "Hey, Coach, do you have a minute?"

"Sure, honey. Come in. What can I do for you?"

"Well, when we were running sprints before you told a couple of the girls to shut up. I'm sure you didn't mean anything by it, but I found that to be very disrespectful."

"What's your name?"

"Naima Tryman."

"Okay, Naima. Listen, I didn't mean to be disrespectful. The truth of the matter is that I am very demanding, and I have nothing but respect for anyone that steps out on the court to play for me. My job is to motivate you girls and I got caught up in the heat of the moment. Thanks for being honest with me about your feelings. It won't happen again."

I was satisfied with that, but that wasn't the end of it. When everyone returned for the second session he sat us all down and apologized for his use of the term. I knew then that this was a special man that cared a great deal about coaching and teaching, but I never could have imagined the impact he would have later in my life. The previous coach's resignation was God opening the door for a man that would eventually prove crucial to my survival well beyond the realm of basketball.

Coach Citro came in and made an immediate impact on everyone and everything. He pushed us harder than most of us had ever been pushed. We finally had enough girls to field a freshman team and he got new uniforms for all three levels, as well as warm-ups for the Varsity. He hired a deejay to play music at the games and introduce the starting lineups. He taught us a number of new concepts, both offensive and defensive, and took the time to make sure we thoroughly understood them all. His leg was seriously damaged when he was hit by a car years earlier, but that didn't stop him from strapping on a bulky knee brace and banging us around to better prepare us for our games.

I became the starting point guard that year, and took that job very seriously. I have always idolized Dawn Staley and wanted to be just like her. She was a floor general, truly an extension of the coach. She could always be seen telling players where they belonged and controlling every aspect of the game. When the uniforms were handed out I made sure I got the number five, because it was hers. I was never a very good shooter by virtue of my tiny hands, so I also adopted her pass first, shoot second mentality. I usually agreed with everything that came out of Coach Citro's mouth, and made it my business to see that his expectations were met by the team.

One of the senior captains, Candyce, and I got very close that year. She had been the point guard last year, but now she was starting at shooting guard and she took it in stride. She always supported me and knew how to make me laugh. Every day after practice we would vandalize the telephone booth on the corner to get change, then walk to the pizzeria and buy French fries for the walk home. That season we went fifteen and nine and lost in the second round of the state tournament, but we had achieved our ultimate goal.

We had effectively climbed from the cellar of the conference and earned respect as a team to be taken seriously. Opponents could no longer write us off as an easy win on their schedules. Coach worked the sidelines with passion and intensity, arguing with officials and barking out orders. His pre-game speeches left us foaming at the mouth, thirsty for blood. He taught us to believe in ourselves, which was an incredible weapon for an upstart team that was sick of losing. That was the year that I truly fell in love with the game of basketball.

Chapter 5
Changes

When the season ended I had already missed the first two days of baseball tryouts, so I never got a day off. The day after we were eliminated from the state basketball tournament I was in the gym with the baseball team, as it was too cold to be outside. This was a big deal for me. The softball coach had been pleading with me to switch over, so I told him that if I was cut from the Varsity team I would come and play for him. He said it was all or nothing, so I told him thanks but no thanks. I hadn't spent my whole life playing with the boys to give it all up my junior year. As tryouts went on I thought I had fared well and deserved a spot on the Varsity roster, but it was not to be. I was assigned to the jayvee team and I was not happy about it in the least. I didn't expect to be a starter, but there were at least three players I was better than hands down that made the cut.

I went to the Varsity softball coach and told him that I was his if he wanted me. I expected him to laugh in my face, but he didn't. I would have to make some adjustments offensively, but defensively I was ready to go. Our first scrimmage I batted leadoff and hit a triple to right field, effectively announcing my arrival. Everyone was happy and I felt accepted. Of course when I came off the field Maleka immediately deflated my head, remarking that I was the slowest person she'd ever seen, and that on a ball hit that far she could have made it home running backwards. I guess that's what friends are for.

The Team

Playing on the softball team brought me into a whole new world socially. When I was moved to the Varsity basketball team I gained a few cool points. Students I didn't know would speak to me in the hallways and congratulate me on a game well played. My social anxieties had begun to ease, but I was still an introvert. I only went to one party when I was in high school, and on weekends could usually be found hanging out with Maleka somewhere or at home in my room alone. I had become quite close with my basketball teammates, but most of them were very popular and partied almost every weekend, which wasn't my scene. I got along well enough with the baseball team, but I was never invited to any gatherings or activities with them.

The softball team was a tight knit group, but they were all extremely accepting of me and didn't hesitate to take me in. I was obviously close to Maleka, and the starting shortstop and team captain was also my basketball teammate. It started with a team slumber party. I had missed school and practice that Thursday and Friday with the flu, and we were playing Passaic Valley High School Saturday morning. Maleka called and told me that there was a team sleepover and they were coming to get me, sick or not.

The girl that threw the slumber party had an open house because her parents had gone away for the weekend. The girls pooled all of their money and got someone to buy what had to be about a hundred dollars worth of liquor. I had fun watching them get drunk, but I respectfully declined to drink. A few doors down another boy had an open house, and he was having a huge party. We all walked down, but I didn't stay long. Everyone was drinking and I really didn't know that many of them.

A few of us drove down to the 7-Eleven and someone bought some cigarettes. I couldn't resist the temptation. I wanted to know what the big deal was and why so many people smoked. When we got back to the house I asked one of the girls to teach me, but she was rushing to go relieve herself, so she tossed me the pack and the lighter and said, "Just suck in some smoke and inhale!" That sounded easy enough so I tried it, and almost threw up right there in the backyard. I was determined to figure it out though, so when a girl named Allison came out, I asked her. It took a few pulls, but when I got it right there was this euphoric relaxation that came over me. It was already around one in the morning, and that put me right to bed. The other girls came in from the party an hour or so later and passed out.

We had to be at school at eight-thirty the next morning to go to Passaic Valley. I was still sick, and the rest of the team was hung over. This was not supposed to be much of a game. We were ranked as one of the top teams in the state in the pre-season, due largely in part to the sectional championship they had won the previous year. We swung the bat pretty well, but we were atrocious in the field. We made error after error and had terrible communication, eventually losing seven to six. We never made that mistake again, and from there on out saved our partying for after our games.

A few weeks later, seven of us ended up at one girl's house with three random guys from school. This girl had stairs in the back of the house that allowed us to come and go as we pleased without having to go through the house. She had a walk-in closet that probably could have fit ten people. Four girls and the three guys went into the closet to smoke some weed. I stayed out with the two other girls, but I might as well have gone in. In my infinite teenage wisdom I decided I was going to start chain smoking Marlboro Lights. They got high their way, and I got high mine. I literally lit one off of the other until I got light headed. I don't think my high felt as good as theirs though. I started to get nauseas, and the room started spinning. I didn't like that feeling at all, and it was the last time I picked up a cigarette for years.

I had so much fun that season. I was with the team or some faction of them almost every weekend. As the boys grew bigger and stronger than me I was merely an average baseball player at best, but on the softball team I became a leader. I ended up leading the team in extra base hits and the two errors I made all year came when I was playing out of position, but more importantly I finally came out of my shell. I was part of a group of girls that accepted me as I was, cared a great deal about me, and never pressured me to do anything I didn't want to do.

Confusion

Allison and I became very close over the course of the season. Maleka was my right hand, but this was somehow different. We were total opposites, but we got along famously. She lived in a beautiful house in the "rich" part of town. She was in all Advanced Placement classes and took her education very seriously, so seriously that I once found myself consoling her when she got a B on an her report card. Somehow we clicked on all cylinders. We would pass notes to each other in between classes, and actually made a game of finding long and complicated words and using them in our notes. She ultimately won with antidisestablishmentarianism.

She lived in a huge house and her mother was always cooking or baking something. Both of her parents were crazy about me, and before long I was spending more time there than I was at home. We would talk about everything and never had one argument. I was drawn to her, but I didn't know why. There was something very pure and comforting in our friendship. I was flattered that this popular, brilliant, elegant girl took so much interest in me. Although we were total opposites I never had to be anyone but myself when I was with her, but something else was going on here.

When I slept over I would usually wake up first in the morning, but I never got right out of bed. I found myself staring at her as she slept, but only for a few moments. Then I would get freaked out realizing that this wasn't normal, and I'd jump out of the bed and go downstairs to watch television. I became quite confused about the whole thing but I didn't tell anyone, not even my cousin Cindy. It terrified me, and I was terrified of what anyone would say to me if I told them this.

I had struggled with my gender identity for years, but now my sexuality was coming into play. *I'm not gay, what the hell is going on here?* I was never tempted to kiss her or even express these feelings, but they were hard to ignore. I definitely loved her deeply, but as my friend. I was not attracted to girls, and definitely did not want to damage our friendship, so I shoved whatever was going on within me into a dark corner in my brain, and behaved as though nothing was bothering me. That was the first time I realized my attraction to girls. The season ended, but our bond remained

My First Kiss

That summer Coach Citro entered us into two summer leagues, and he would pack us all up in his van and drive us to the games every night. My bond with Zakiyyah had become quite strong, especially on the court. We dubbed ourselves Stockton and Malone Jr., having learned to run the pick-and-roll to perfection. We had spent a great deal of time on the court together in the past few years, and we believed we had an extrasensory connection. She worked extremely hard that off-season, and we were thrilled about the upcoming year. Besides playing basketball, I didn't do much that summer. I hung out with Maleka and went to Allison's summer softball games. I spent a lot of time in the pool at my father's house and just enjoyed my freedom.

I threw myself a little pool party for my birthday. It wasn't anything formal, just some friends, the pool, and the pool table. When Onaje arrived with my friend JJ they had two cute boys with them. I recognized one of them but I couldn't place him. I was in the pool and Maleka was on the deck. Their names were Rasheed and Nate, and they were both athletes at a prestigious private school in Newark. Rasheed ran cross-country and Nate played basketball. When I was at Shakil's there were two dojos, the one in Montclair and one in Newark. Rasheed was a student at the Newark dojo early in my training, and he remembered me from the occasional joint training sessions we had.

Before the night was over I'd exchanged numbers with Rasheed and we began talking on the phone. I couldn't believe it. This boy was smart, sweet, articulate, and very cute, and he liked me! About a week later he came to visit me on a Saturday when my mother and sisters weren't home. We watched television for a while, and eventually he kissed me and asked me to be his girlfriend. I was ecstatic. I was seventeen years old and in the blink of an eye I had my first kiss and my first boyfriend.

I really liked him a lot, but the relationship only lasted about five weeks. He became harder and harder to get in contact with, and when I did reach him he was distant and made excuses about coming to see me. Then it hit me. The day of the party I was in a bathing suit and my hair was wet and flowing down my back. He didn't know me and didn't realize that I was such a tomboy. The day he came over I was dressed in my usual jeans, t-shirt, and baseball cap with my hair in a ponytail. The next time I saw him I was dressed the same, and that was when he started acting differently. He had realized that I was not by any means feminine, and he no longer wanted any part of me. I was crushed, but I wasn't about to change myself.

Rebellion

Senior year all hell broke loose. Actually it started a couple of weeks before school resumed, when I decided I wanted to try smoking weed. Nyerere was up visiting from Mississippi and Allison came over. We sat out on the pool deck and I smoked weed for the first time in my life. The feeling was incredible. This was a lot better than chain smoking cigarettes! Nyerere is one of the funniest people I have ever met, and when I was high he was hilarious. There was a mild breeze that night and every time a tree swayed I jumped, thinking someone was coming.

Although I had keys to the house, Jimmy was out of town and had locked every room, but we didn't realize this until it was time to go to sleep. The only area we could get into was the basement, so Nyerere curled up on the love seat and Allison and I slept on the pool table. I have always slept better with music playing, and I had a small portable tape player with me. There wasn't a whole lot of room on the pool table so I decided to place it on a stack of buckets next to us. I picked the radio up and reached out to place it on the buckets when Allison asked me what I was doing.

I replied matter-of-factly, "I'm putting the radio on these buckets so we'll have a little more room."

She didn't even get a chance to respond. All she got out was, "what buc..." crash!!! That was the end of the radio.

Two days before school started I had a back-to-school gathering. My teammate Kelli came by with her boyfriend Gus whom I'd known since early childhood. They had been drinking Bacardi, and she had about a shot left in the bottle. She offered it to me, and I figured it was my senior year, so why not? I'd never had a drink before, so that little bit did a lot for me. I wasn't drunk, but I felt great. I mentioned that walking out of Shakil's that day was the worst decision I ever made, and this was exactly why. In the nine months since I'd quit I had my first cigarette, I got high, and I had my first drink. My coming decision wasn't much better.

My days that fall were very simple. Maleka and I would go to school, and then hang out at Jimmy's as had been the routine all throughout high school. Our clique now consisted of me, Maleka, JJ, and Onaje, and Nate would come as soon as he got off the bus from school. We would shoot pool until eight or so, and then go home. Occasionally Allison would come over, but she was a lot more focused on her school work than we were, and her classes were a lot harder.

Sometime in October my father was out of town, and I once again caught the "naughty bug." I really liked the way that Bacardi made me feel and I wanted to feel it again, so I conveyed that to Maleka and Allison. They were thrilled. They couldn't believe that after all of my abstinence I was giving in, and they came over with a fifth of cheap vodka. We didn't know what to mix it with, but I had heard of vodka and orange juice, so I figured that was the way to go. Unfortunately we had spent all of our money on the liquor and all my father had in the fridge was orange soda, so we went with that but we had another dilemma. We needed to eat first. We needed to find something generally harmless to eat, because my father has an odd sense of nutrition and taste in general. Eventually we settled on turkey burgers, which I soon learned are not adequate to aid in the absorption of alcohol.

So now the stage was set. We ate the burgers and went down to the basement with the vodka. Man, they set me up big time. I'm sure that in their travels with different softball teams they had learned to play a number of drinking games, but the one they chose was geared towards getting *me* drunk. It was called "I Never," and is not a game you should ever play with your two best friends, especially when their primary goal is for you to be the drunkest.

It pretty much goes like this: everyone has their own cup and you take turns making "I never" statements. If you've done the thing that the speaker says they've never done, you have to drink. They hammered me with statements like, "I never had a pool in my backyard, I never played high school baseball, I never did karate," and so forth and so on. Needless to say by the end of the night I'd consumed at least twice as much liquor as they had. The evening ended with me trying to keep from falling off the sofa as I purged my turkey burger onto the carpet, after which I passed out. Although I felt awful in the morning I'd had a blast, and couldn't wait to do it again.

At this time there was an Indian man in his early thirties named Mike renting the second floor apartment, and he loved hanging out with us. On the weekends we would get him to go to the liquor store for us by agreeing to hang out in his apartment. He made his occasional passes, especially at Allison, but he was harmless. I began sleeping at Jimmy's more and more often so that I could drink. My mother gave me three dollars a day for lunch, but I would save it all week so I could get liquor on the weekend.

Senior Season

Before I knew it, basketball season was upon us, and I can't ever remember being more excited. That season was a remarkable series of highs and lows. Zakiyyah and I were voted co-captains, and we split the duties in half. She scored twenty-five points a game and anchored the team offensively and defensively. I was the vocal and emotional leader. I was constantly talking, helping coach to make corrections, praising my teammates for good play, and occasionally chastising a poor one. It was an arrangement that worked well.

Over the years I have had a number of teammates in a number of sports. I have never felt anything close to the bond I shared with Zakiyyah on the court. It was like we shared a brain. I hardly ever missed her when she was open and always knew right where she wanted the ball. I was always looking for her and it didn't hurt that she had the greatest hands of anyone I've ever played with. She scored the points and I ran the team, and that was exactly how we liked it.

Earlier that school year I found out that my karate classmate, Bianca, was coming to Montclair High. She had started as a freshman in a neighboring town, but her family had recently moved to Montclair so now she was playing for us. I was in the gym after school working out, and she came in to play. We shot around for a while and then I challenged her to a one on one. I had never seen her play before and luckily we were alone in the gym, because she destroyed me in a ten to nothing shutout. My pride was a little hurt, but I got over it quickly. I knew I wouldn't be able to help Zakiyyah with the scoring much, so this was great for the team. Bianca was excellent and went on to play at Wake Forest.

That season we really made some waves. Our arch rivals were Bloomfield and Ridgewood, and although we lost all four games they were all down to the wire, losing by margins of two, two, four, and seven. These two teams in particular had destroyed and embarrassed us consistently over the previous years, but this season they had to fight tooth, nail, and claw to walk away victorious. Although we weren't even supposed to compete with them, I didn't handle losing well at all. I would typically lose my temper after the games and punch the locker's, one time even busting my knuckle open.

We pounced on the rest of the league, often winning by more than forty points. I was geeked for the entire season. Zakiyyah and I would go around on game days and write the time, location, and opponent on the chalkboard of every class we had. We wrote the same information on paper and pinned them to our shirts and book bags. We were on top of the world.

I started having gatherings at my father's house every Saturday night after our games. I'd get twenty dollars from my father and buy donuts, soda, and chips, and Kelli would make a liquor run for anyone who had the money. I'd set up a card table in the front room of the basement for spades, and we'd shoot pool in the other room. It was never a big deal, just fifteen or twenty of us hanging out and laughing. There were a few girls from the team, plus my usual crew and a few others. We never had any problems or fights, and life was grand.

Not long after my brief relationship with Rasheed, I developed a crush on Nate. He came by with Onaje almost every day and was so easy to be around. I really wanted to say something but I was terrified. What if he didn't like me like that? How would I ever look him in the face again? I would be too embarrassed. He started coming straight to the gym after school to watch us practice, and I thought maybe I had a chance, but I was a tomboy and a virgin so what would he want with me?

In the middle of January my teammate Kisha came over to study for mid-terms, but all I could think about was Nate. Eventually she'd heard enough and I got her to call him for me. She told him I really liked him and asked what he thought of me. He wasn't quite doing back flips with the news but he didn't seem repulsed by the notion. We called him on three-way again when she got home and he said he would be my boyfriend. I was ecstatic. No more than two weeks later he transferred to Montclair High. When mid-terms were over I moved in with my father, putting me much closer to Nate, Maleka, and school. My schedule had changed and I didn't have to be at school until nine forty-five, so this way I could sleep in.

If Varsity basketball raised me from obscurity, Nate pushed me into all out popularity. Everyone was talking about the new transfer, his good looks, and his sense of fashion. Imagine their surprise when they found out I was his girlfriend. People were coming up to me asking about him, and if we were really together. Most girls couldn't fathom how someone like him could hook up with someone like me. I wasn't worried about them though. Between Nate and basketball, I walked around in a state of euphoria.

There had been so many fights and problems in years past that the administration had given up on dances but that year, upon the urging of the student government, they decided to let us have a Valentine's Day dance. I bought two tickets and was so excited, even though I didn't plan on dancing. We got the third seed in the county tournament and had a quarter-final game the next day at one. Coach had given us a ten o'clock curfew on game nights, and I honored it. Nate was with Bianca's boyfriend, Terrell, and we were all supposed to meet up and go to the dance for a couple of hours, but it didn't work out that way. They didn't show up at her house until nine-thirty, so when Nate called me I told him to go ahead without me. I was so disappointed.

Seven of the thirteen Varsity players were at the dance that night well after ten, and the next day they all looked awful. I got a sickening feeling in my stomach. Our opponents came in very confident, carrying their Valentine's Day balloons and flowers. You could see what little energy we had as a team completely drain from our bodies. We fell behind early in the game and never recovered. At halftime we were down by twelve, and to make matters worse, Nate wasn't there. He was always there for the jump ball. He arrived sometime near the end of the third quarter, but my mind was already gone. We were getting embarrassed by a mediocre team on our home court on Valentine's Day.

In the fourth quarter all of my emotions collided. The girl I was guarding had been pushing me on her spin move all game. I had complained to the ref, but she wasn't called for it once. This time I stepped back as she went to make the move and her hand swung around and smacked me right in the face. I went ballistic. I stopped right in the middle of the play, smacked the floor, and jumped in the official's face screaming, "What are you blind? She smacked me in the f---ing face!" I was two inches from his nose. I was whistled for a technical foul and the celebration began. The game was already out of reach but that put the cap on it. I was devastated over losing that game, and I guess Coach understood because he didn't even take me out. I'd managed to avoid getting one technical foulto that point in his tenure.

Although I wasn't in much of a partying mood, I couldn't wait to start getting drunk. Nate and I walked up to the house to relax and people started coming around seven. Maleka and I each had a half-pint of Bacardi Limon, and decided to see who could drink the most without stopping. I saw her stop around the halfway point, but I kept going. I drank the entire bottle in one big swig. It was all I could do to try and quell the agony of defeat.

A few weeks later I became very sick. My throat was extremely tender, I had a fever of one hundred and three degrees, and I was spitting blood. I wanted to practice, and coach had to tell me to sit down. I begged him to let me practice but he said no way. I saw a specialist and he told me that my tonsils needed to come out. I decided to play through it because I wasn't even considering surgery during my senior season. I had worked too hard.

We were playing Paterson Kennedy the next day. They were a team that was hungry, and played like it every game. They had an extraordinarily athletic freshman that went on to play Division I basketball at Auburn. To make matters worse, the back-up point guard didn't show up to practice because of menstrual cramps, and Coach's rule was if you missed the practice before a game, you couldn't play. It was a close and hotly contested game and I had to play all but two minutes of it, but we won. My thirst for victory was insatiable.

The end of the season came, and it was senior day. Senior day is usually observed during the last regular season home game in high school and college sports. Typically there is a small pre-game ceremony honoring the graduating seniors for their years of dedication. I will never forget mine, because it was special on a number of levels. The gym was packed, and we were playing Caldwell High, whose star player had amassed over 2,000 career points. Right off the bat this day was special to me for two extra reasons. The first was simply because my father came. It was the only basketball game he ever made while I was in high school. The second thing that made this day extra special was that Zakiyyah was twenty-four points shy of reaching the prestigious 1,000 career points mark.

The pre-game ceremony was quite emotional. Zakiyyah and I were both crying as we knew we were heading into the twilight of our playing days together. We were honored with one other senior named Heather. Coach said a few words about us and then called us out to half court where he met us and our families with flowers. We took some pictures, handed off the flowers, and got ready to play. Before the ball went up I came over to the manager and told her to let me know how many points Zakiyyah had whenever I looked over at her. I figured I would have to make a point of getting her the ball even more than usual for most of the game. I was wrong.

She was on fire. She missed her first few shots, but not many after that. At the end of the first quarter she had tallied twenty-two points. She scored on a soft six foot jumper a few moments into the second quarter and the gym went crazy. Coach stopped the game and brought out flowers and balloons for her. She wasn't done though. Zakiyyah proceeded to put on a clinic, scoring however she pleased. She was hitting three's, posting up, running the fast break, and scoring off of offensive rebounds. She ended up with fifty-five points that game, setting an all-time record for Montclair's boys and girls teams which still stands twelve years later.

The following week it was time for the state playoffs. We were sixteen and six, and were matched up against Randolph whom we had beaten the previous year. We had a half day and got out of school at twelve fifteen. I went home to eat and rest a little, and was back to the gym at three. Our game wasn't until six, but I wanted to shoot around. I wanted to savor every moment of my final season. At five thirty we were in the locker room and ready for battle. Coach had scouted them and given us all very specific directions. I was so excited after Whitney Houston's rendition of the national anthem that I didn't even want to do the starting lineups. I wanted to get straight to it.

We battled viciously, but were down by two at halftime. When we went into the locker room Coach made his adjustments and assured us that we would be victorious if we gave everything we had for the next sixteen minutes of play, and we complied. We came out in the third quarter with renewed confidence and fire. We ended up down by two with seven seconds to go on the clock. Coach called a timeout and drew a play for Zakiyyah to catch the ball and drive hard to the basket. In the opposing huddle the Randolph coach was telling his players not to let us get a clean shot off, and to foul before giving up a basket.

Zakiyyah caught the ball in the baseline corner and drove hard to the basket as she was told. She beat two girls, but as she rose towards the basket someone placed two hands squarely on her back and shoved her out of bounds causing the ball to go flying, and there was no foul called. I spent the next ten seconds trying to catch up with the referee that missed the call, but they both shuffled off the court as soon as the buzzer sounded. We cried in the locker room and Coach told us how much he loved us and how proud he was of us. I went back upstairs and sat in the gym until the lights went out.

The next day in school I was miserable. I walked around with a hat and headphones on, and defied anyone to tell me to take them off. I never broke the rules, but on this day I didn't care. Had it not been for softball practice I wouldn't have come to school at all. I could feel myself on the verge of tears the whole day. We had a new softball coach that year, and she and I did not see eye to eye. She was a nice woman, but she was trying to completely change my swing and get me to stand closer to the pitcher in the batter's box. I didn't like either one of the adjustments at all, especially during the preseason of my senior year. As it turned out, I wouldn't have to deal with it for long.

Surgery

On April 6th, 1998 I had surgery to remove my tonsils. I scheduled it that way because we were on spring break that week so I wouldn't miss school and very few games. I went to stay with my mother for the week because no one could care for me like she did. The week dragged by as I began to get cabin fever and wanted to play softball. I was supposed to return to school and softball the next Monday but when I woke up that morning I noticed I was spitting blood. My mother wanted to wait a while to see what happened, and it stopped after a while. We called the doctor a little later and he said that it was normal, that the scabs were falling off.

The next morning I awoke around five thirty with a stomachache and a nasty taste in my mouth. I covered my mouth and walked to the sink. When I removed my hand there was blood running out of my mouth like a faucet. I grabbed a plastic cup and ran upstairs to show my mother. She jumped out of bed and rushed me to the hospital. By the time we got there I had two cups full of blood. The scabs were falling off of my throat but my blood was not clotting, so I was scheduled for emergency surgery later that day to cauterize the veins. I was out of school and, more importantly to me, softball for another week.

That Friday was Khalea's seventeenth birthday. We had been out of my father's house for over two years now. My mother had been going out with Glenn for some time and was ready to introduce us. Khalea had met him once before, but this would be the first time for me. He treated all of us and Khalea's boyfriend to a steak dinner. He seemed like a very nice man and I liked him, but in the next few weeks he would show me how truly generous he was.

The next day the team was playing in a tournament so I went. I had so much energy that day, screaming and yelling like I didn't just have surgery on my throat. I wanted to be on the field so bad, and I couldn't wait until Monday came so that I could get out there. Little did I know, that day would never come.

Chapter 6

Trauma

April 18th, 1998 was supposed to be a joyous day. When I came home from the tournament, I packed my things to go back to my father's house and get ready for the basketball banquet that night. My mother's best friend was getting married to the deputy chief of the fire department. She was going to the wedding with Glenn, so she let me use her van and said she would meet up with me at the banquet. I gathered my things and drove back to Jimmy's.

I was so excited about the banquet. The whole team would be honored, but this would be the culmination of all the hard work that Zakiyyah and I had put in over the years and my father would know what kind of leader I had become. I showered and got dressed, and then fussed with my hair for a while. Seven o'clock could not come fast enough. Coach had rented a smoke machine and erected an arc of balloons for us to walk through while the DJ from our games announced us one by one.

It was a great night. Coach spoke about each player individually and really paid homage to Zakiyyah and me. I had recently given a verbal commitment to the New Jersey Institute of Technology to play on a partial Division II scholarship for Kim Barnes-Arico, who is now the head coach at St. John's University. She had gone to Montclair State with Coach and he asked her to speak at the banquet. She gave an inspired speech about excellence and perseverance in life. Coach then gave Zakiyyah, Heather, and I navy blue fleece pullovers embroidered with our names and a basketball. Finally, Zakiyyah was awarded the MVP trophy and I was awarded the team leadership award.

The night ended with music, hugs, and tears, but when I looked for my father he was nowhere to be found. I knew that I had seen him there, but he had apparently slipped out early. I later found out that he left sometime soon after my mother arrived with Glenn. To this day Jimmy let's his hatred for Glenn impede his love for his children. I didn't think much of it at the time, choosing to enjoy the night instead. When I asked my mother what she wanted me to do with the van she told me to keep it over night and we'd hook up the next day.

She then told me to stop by her house because I had left my medication and a few other things, so I rounded up five girls and off we went. We didn't know where we were headed, but we were going. When I got to my mom's house she had all of my things in a plastic bag and tied a get well balloon from a friend to the handles. She told me she loved me, kissed me on the cheek, and watched as I walked out the door. That's the last thing I remember. The following is a combination of witness accounts from the girls in the car, the firefighters that responded, and my family.

The Accident

We decided to travel to a neighboring town but I'm not sure where or what for. As I made a left turn the balloon drifted into to my vision. I raised my right arm to push it out of the way and in doing so took my eyes off of the road and turned the wheel with my left hand. Kisha was riding in the front seat and all she had time to say was my name. I turned a split second before crashing into a tree dead on.

Kisha always wore her seat belt, but had removed it in order to reach something in her coat pocket and subsequently went flying into the windshield. I smashed my face on the steering wheel and crumpled down by the pedals. My seat had tipped over and our manager Shana was thrown forward and got lodged underneath my seat. The three other passengers, Amirah, Khadijah, and Stacey were injured as well, but not as severely as Shana and I.

I briefly came to consciousness and realized I was trapped underneath my seat and the steering wheel. I'm claustrophobic and get very uncomfortable in tight spaces. I started freaking out. I was dripping with blood and in absolute horror. I began banging on the doors and trying to force my way out, but I was pushing my overturned seat back onto Shana's broken leg. When I got out of the car I began walking around, completely unaware that my knee was busted open. My body was in a state of shock and for the moment I didn't feel any pain. As the firefighters and paramedics tried to get me to lay down, I shook them off stating that I was fine. Then I collapsed.

Word of the accident traveled quickly, especially within my family. My grandmother's house was two blocks away and the whole family heard the crash. They all came out and stood horrified, not knowing who was in the car. My childhood friend Carla happened to be a few cars behind me and called my mother. A firefighter named Marc that cut hair with Jimmy called him. My brother was about a mile away when he got the news and sprinted the whole distance to the scene of the crash. Coach Citro got the call, picked up Zakiyyah from her house, and sped to the hospital.

Stacey and Khadijah were transported to Mountainside Hospital for their injuries, but Kisha, Amirah, Shana, and I were taken to the trauma center at University Hospital in Newark. The waiting room was a grim scene as my mother was informed that I wasn't expected to live through the night. As my family held a prayer vigil, my father walked around brooding because he blamed Glenn. He even tried to go after him. His half-baked theory was that I was so upset about Glenn coming to the banquet it caused me to run into a tree.

When I woke up I had no idea what had happened, but I knew I was in a lot of pain. My first question to my mother was, "What happened?"

She looked at me tearfully and said, "You were in an accident honey."

"Oh my God. Is everyone alright?"

"Yes, Naima. Everyone is going to be okay." That wasn't quite true because Shana was in a coma, but she didn't want me to be worried as I had a long road back to recovery myself.

"What happened?"

"Don't worry about that right now. Just rest."

Just as I began to fade again Kisha and Amirah stopped by to see how I was doing and let me know they were okay. I had annihilated the right side of my face. There were over twenty fractures in my jaw, cheekbone, and eye orbital. My right eye was swollen shut and my face was the size of a beach ball. My nose was broken in three places and I also had two holes in my knee, resulting from something under the hood going through it. Miraculously it passed through one side and out the other without damaging the tendons or ligaments, and the doctors had already done surgery to close the holes. I don't remember a great deal of the next two days because I was put on a morphine drip to help manage my pain. I spent ninety percent of that period sleeping.

My clothes were in a plastic bag in the corner of my hospital room. When I put them on, they were a black skirt and a green blouse. I had foolishly put on my new blue fleece as well, but now it was all a deep, crimson red. They were completely drenched in blood. In the next room Shana had come out of her coma, but had suffered a couple of seizures. She came to see me in a wheelchair when she was able, and was released that Tuesday.

On Monday news of the accident was all over the school. Although we had broken up a month ago, Nate was on the first bus to the hospital when school let out along with Onaje, and a friend of ours named Michelle. Onaje tried to make me smile by riding up and down the hallway in a wheelchair until he was reprimanded by a nurse. No more than half an hour after they arrived my room was overrun with visitors. The hospital only allowed two visitors at a time but the policy folded that day. Khalea and Tia made a system out of returning the passes to the visitor's desk and coming back up so that more people could visit. I must have had fifty visitors that day. Many people kept vigil over me during that period. My mother was there all day, every day and only went home to sleep and shower. Khalea, who took the week off from school, Cindy, and Aunt Claudette all took turns spending the night with me.

The Aftermath

I had tons of supporters, but no one would let me see a mirror. I wanted to know what I looked like, but everyone's face would drop whenever I mentioned a mirror, and with good reason. Eventually I realized that there was a mirror attached to the bottom of my tray, and I pulled it out. I was devastated. I looked like Sloth from *The Goonies*. I had never thought myself to be a terribly attractive person, but I had completely disappeared. My face was gigantic, there were dark circles around both eyes, cuts on my nose, and I looked like my mouth was full of marbles. *Would I ever be the same again?*

That week I received many visits from Dr. Rosen who was an ear, nose, and throat doctor, and Dr. Langer, said to be one of the best eye doctors in the state. They evaluated me and decided that I could not have surgery to fix my face until the swelling went down. They prescribed antibiotics, pain relievers, and muscle relaxers and sent me home. We hadn't heard from my father the whole week, so Glenn brought my mother to pick me up. Jimmy showed up just as we were about to pull off and made a commotion, so I ended up letting him bring me to my mother's house.

I remember that day like it was yesterday. I gingerly sat on the couch and didn't want to move, but my mother insisted. I was filthy, and needed to clean up. It was now Thursday and I hadn't been washed since before the accident. I felt sick and really didn't want to go up the stairs, but I was covered in dry blood and my hair was matted. She and Khalea brought me upstairs, undressed me, and sat me on a stool in the bath tub. Khalea held me up while my mother washed me. She turned the shower on to wash my hair and all I could see was red water running down my face. The smell of blood caused me to dry-heave, and it took everything I had not to vomit in the tub. It took her almost an hour to wash my hair and work through the tangles once all of the blood was out. They took me out and dried me off, then my mother put my hair in two braids and I went to sleep.

I was scheduled for reconstructive surgery on May fourth, and my mother took that two week period off from work to care for me. I was still sleeping much of the time, but when I was awake I was miserable. It was a tremendous effort just to switch positions on the couch, and I had this gnawing, ongoing ache behind my eye. It was considerably painful to even attempt to talk, so I communicated with my mother through grunts and hand motions. For the next month all I ate was ice cream and fried eggs mixed into grits. That was pretty much all I had been eating anyway because I was just coming off of the tonsillectomy. I lost twenty pounds over an eight week period.

Complications

The day of my surgery everything went well. I arrived early on that Monday morning, underwent the procedure, and stayed overnight for observation. The bones that made up my eye orbital had been shattered, so the doctors inserted four plates and four screws to reconstruct the area. The next day I was released and went back to my mother's house. My father had not been around much and my mother's van was totaled, so Glenn did an enormous amount of taxiing us during this time.

I thought that I had made it through the hard part and could now rest until I felt better, but I was wrong. It was an absolutely miserable week. It rained non-stop and I was in constant pain. I always had a compress on my face, sometimes cold but hot more often than not. The ice was probably more beneficial but the heat made it feel better. I spent all of my waking hours in agony. I wanted to cry but I couldn't, because the incision in the corner of my eye would sting excruciatingly.

That Friday Maleka wanted to get me out of the house, so our mothers arranged for me to go see the school play with her, and then sleep at her house. It was somewhat overwhelming. I was bombarded by people wishing me well and asking how I was doing. I appreciated the concern but really just wanted to sit down somewhere. I wore a patch over my eye and didn't have much strength. After the play Maleka asked me if I wanted to go to a diner with the cast and, not wanting to be a drag, I said yes. I had a good time though, and was glad I had gone. We went back to her house and I slept on an air mattress. When I woke up the next morning I knew that something was terribly wrong.

I went into the bathroom and removed the patch from my eye. There was a huge red bubble creeping up from the inside of my bottom eyelid. I called my mother and she came to get me. We went home and immediately put ice on it. I wasn't extremely concerned though. I thought the cigarette smoke in the diner may have irritated my eye. It hadn't gotten any better by Sunday, and on Monday it was even bigger, so my mother called Dr. Langer who told us to come back to the hospital immediately.

I was admitted when we got there, and the nurse came in my room to start an I.V. but could not find a vein. I was in enough pain as it was without her sticking me with needles, with which with I was already uncomfortable. After the second stick I began to cry, which only made matters worse. My tears were running directly into the incision. The tears caused the cut to begin burning which in turn led to more tears, so after the third poke my patience was gone and I told her to get me another nurse. It took me almost twenty minutes to get a grip from the vicious cycle of pain causing tears and tears causing pain.

Eventually the I.V. got put in and I calmed down. Dr. Langer came to examine me and ordered an MRI. I figured that would be painless enough, so my mother and I waited to be taken to radiology. When they brought me into the room, I saw a mechanical arm hovering over the machine that looked like the arm on the space shuttle. They laid me on the table and strapped me down. Then they moved the "arm" to mine and connected the head to my I.V. The tech told me that I might feel a little discomfort and walked out of the room.

The next thing I knew I felt like I was disintegrating from within. I don't know what came through that "arm" but it felt like a mixture of ammonia and bleach, and I could feel it working its way through my blood stream. I immediately began to scream. I twisted and turned as much as I could and yelled for them to come take it out. Again the tears started, putting me into even more pain. They told me to stop moving and I told them I would break the whole machine if they didn't take me out. My mother came in and eventually got me calm, but not before making them disconnect whatever they were pumping into my arm. Once I calmed down they were able to complete the test with the remaining chemicals in my body.

It was nighttime at this point, so once my mother got me back to my room and in some degree of comfort, she left. When Glenn came to pick her up, he brought me a bean pie and a strawberry milkshake. I pulled my tray in front of me and began watching *7th Heaven*. My arm was really bothering me from the day's events but I didn't want to be a baby, so I kept my eyes on the television and refused to touch my arm. About fifteen minutes later I couldn't ignore the pain anymore and went to rub it, but when I touched my forearm I realized it was twice its normal size! It was the size of a log, and my hand was turning blue because the hospital band was now cutting off my circulation.

I was overwhelmed with fear, to the point that I could not speak. I pressed the nurse's call button, and she replied with an agitated, "What is it?"

"Arm... swollen... pain..." She made some nonchalant reply and I screamed out, "Help!"

She strolled into the room, in no way altered by my tone of voice and said, "What's the problem?"

I raised my arm and said, "Look!"

"Oh my God!" she replied, and went running out of the room. Not liking her attitude in the least, I called my mother. Luckily she was just a block away at Checkers and said she was on her way. The nurse returned with a warm compress and scissors to cut the I.D. band. After removing the band, she disconnected the I.V. and wrapped my arm with the compress. By the time my mother returned I was calm, so she kissed me and said she'd see me in the morning, but not without some choice words for the nurse. Apparently when I was kicking and screaming during the MRI, I had shaken the needle out of the vein, but not out of my arm. The fluid was pooling up in the arm itself, which was what caused the swelling.

For the remainder of the week, I saw Dr. Langer three times a day. When I told him that my veins had to be cauterized after the tonsillectomy, he knew exactly what the problem was. The blood around my eye orbit was not clotting and was putting pressure on my eyelid, causing the red bubble. He kept constant watch on the eye pressure and prescribed some medication for me to get intravenously. Eventually the bubble began to shrink and I was discharged that Friday.

More Tragedy

I stayed at my mother's house for another week or so and then decided it was time to go back to school. I was still on crutches but I was going stir crazy in the house. I could open my eye but the impact of the crash had jarred the muscles holding it in place, so it was no longer pointing the same direction as the left one. I was told that nothing further could be done until the swelling had gone all the way down, so I covered it with a patch and went to school.

School was a little weird the first day back with everyone welcoming me and asking how I was doing, but after that it was business as usual. I only had three classes, and my teachers were all willing to work with me with regard to making up my schoolwork. The weather was nice and I was soon off of my crutches with the help of some physical therapy. No more than a week after I returned to Jimmy's, tragedy struck once again.

I was at home and my phone rang. It was my mother. She was crying and everything inside of me clenched up. She told me that Glenn's son Eric had been hit by a car while he was out riding his motorcycle, and did not survive. I had never met him, but I was instantly saddened. I had only known

Glenn for a little over a month, but he had been so gracious in my time of need. In middle school I had learned firsthand of the agony that comes with tragic death and I cringed with the knowledge that Glenn would now have to endure it.

Eric was Glenn's pride and joy. He was a 1989 graduate of Montclair High school and held the NJ record for high-jumping for years. He was named an all-American and went to Wheaton College in Massachusetts. While he was there, a White female teammate of his accused him of sexual misconduct and he was suspended from the team and arrested. His trial had ended about two weeks prior and he was found not guilty. He was riding his motorcycle in Newark and an unmarked van blew a red light and hit him. The driver and passenger got out and ran away, never to be found. Although I did not know Eric, I went to his funeral in support of Glenn. There were tons of mourners and Glenn looked miserable.

Four days before I was scheduled to graduate, I got a phone call from my mother. "Hey, Naima. What are you doing?" Immediately I got that feeling in the pit of my stomach. I didn't need to see her face. I could hear it in her voice.

"Nothing, Ma. What's wrong?"

"Are you sitting down?"

"Yeah, Ma. What's wrong?"

"Meikel was in a car accident last night. She didn't make it."

I couldn't believe my ears. I somehow put the phone back on the base and numbly walked down to the corner store to buy a paper. Meikel and her mother had moved to California when we were in Glenfield. They had just moved back to town following her high school graduation and she was preparing to attend the University of Virginia. She had gone out the previous night, and was on her way home in the early morning.

Something caused her to cross over the median and strike an oncoming car. The car bounced her back to her original side of the highway, but spun her in the opposite direction. Before she could right the car she was hit by a Mack truck and killed instantly. The car was so mangled that she was taken to the morgue still in the car which was mounted on a flatbed. This was the hardest I had ever been hit by tragedy. Granted, I was very sad when the three murders occurred in middle school, but this was different. I had never lost someone my age before, much less a friend. I was sad, but somehow I didn't have the tears to cry.

Her wake was scheduled for the day of my high school graduation. My mother picked me up and we went to the funeral home. There were a ton of people. I couldn't believe my eyes when I went inside. There she laid peacefully, as if she were sleeping. I could still see us in my mind, sitting on her computer making banners for our parents. I wanted to reach in the casket and wake her up. The tears began to stream down my face. As the reality of the whole situation set in, I began to sob. I saw so many friends standing and sitting in grief and shock. I couldn't believe this was really Meikel.

I left the wake and went home to prepare for graduation. *I can't do this. How can I go smile and celebrate when my friend was lying in a coffin, robbed of everything we were in anticipation of?* I couldn't-- not without a little help. I had to find some liquor. I rummaged through the house until I found some Jack Daniel's. There wasn't much left but I took the rest of it, desperate to take the edge off.

I walked down to the high school with a slight buzz and tried to talk myself into a state of happiness. Although the dress code specifically said no sunglasses I wore a pair anyway. I had already planned on wearing them because I was still cock-eyed, but now I needed them even more as my eyes were bloodshot from crying. We walked outside into the amphitheater and over the bridge to our seats. As I sat listening to the different speakers, I couldn't help but think of how Meikel had been sitting at her own graduation just a month ago, filled with excitement and joy. What did my future hold, and why was my life spared?

When my name was called, I received a tremendous ovation. I knew it was more appreciation of my surviving the accident than popularity, but I enjoyed it just the same. It was a far cry from the courteous trickle of applause I had received upon my eighth grade graduation and it felt good to be recognized. When the ceremony concluded, we all spilled out onto the front lawn of the high school to accept congratulations from our loved ones and take pictures. I changed my clothes and prepared to board the bus to Project Graduation. Project Graduation was a parent and community sponsored party that was intended to provide a safe, fun, substance-free environment for the graduates. It was held in a different, secret location every year.

Ours was held at the Essex County Country Club in West Orange, about ten minutes from Montclair. It really was a nice set-up. There were two swimming pools, a roller skating rink, and three basketball courts. In the racquetball rooms they set up inflatable obstacle courses and a karaoke machine. There was an unlimited amount of food and they even brought in a hypnotist. I had a decent time, but I could not get my mind off of Meikel. The entire night had a completely surreal feeling to it.

We returned to the school at six the next morning, and I walked home. I slept for two hours, then bagged up some clothes and walked to my mother's house, where I then showered and got dressed for the funeral. It was held in the same church that held the ceremonies for Bunny and Ms. Lance. I arrived an hour early and sat three or four pews back from the casket. I just sat looking at Meikel and crying nonstop. I don't ever remember a time in my life where I cried so hard for so long. I cried so much that the muscles in my face were sore the following day.

In a matter of twenty-four hours, I had viewed Meikel's body, graduated from high school, "celebrated" all night, and then buried her. At the end of it all I was physically exhausted, but not as much as I was mentally and emotionally. I had made it though. I had somehow pulled myself up by my bootstraps, gotten on track academically, and earned a Division II basketball scholarship. I had managed to avoid total self-destruction in the wake of a violent childhood, severe identity issues, a terrible divorce, five tragic funerals, and a near-fatal car accident. It was now time to face the next phase of my life as I moved slowly towards adulthood.

Chapter 7
NJIT

A few days after graduation my father bought me my first car, a white 1984 Dodge convertible. It was a cute car, but he accidentally damaged it before he got it home. He rode his bike to the dealership and after buying it he put the bike in the backseat and then decided to put the top down. The bike got wedged in between the back window and the seat and shattered the glass. The only other problem with the car was that it was a struggle to get the top all the way closed. It was as if the canvas had shrunk and was too tight for the frame. I could never get a decent seal on it, so I couldn't go over forty mph without the top starting to come up. I even used duct tape to hold it down, but it didn't help much. I never went on the highway with the top up for fear of pulling a Mary Poppins!

I didn't care about the minor defects though. I had a car, and therefore the freedom to do anything I wanted. My father and I had developed a cold distance ever since I gave him that letter, and we barely interacted with the exception of quick greetings in passing. For all of the venom he had spewed about Glenn and my mother, I suspect he was aware of the damage he had done over the years. He had ceased trying to rock the boat when it came to me, so he didn't really interfere with my daily affairs. I was preparing for college and had become very independent over the course of the previous few years. I hadn't been behind the wheel of a car since April 18th, but I wasn't scared one bit. Although my vision was still severely impaired, I couldn't wait to jump in the driver's seat.

I put a patch over my right eye and sped off to go show Cindy my car. Now that I had transportation I spent more time with her than ever. That summer our relationship reached a new plateau. It had been a great relationship, but it was mostly unilateral. She was my big cuz, so it was always me confiding in her, me seeking her advice, and her keeping my secrets, but that summer she had a secret to tell me. She was pregnant and she hadn't told anyone. I was in shock. I was happy that she was having a baby, but even happier that she had chosen me to tell first.

That summer was mostly very mellow. I spent it working out at NJIT and strengthening my knee, working at the local summer basketball league, and hanging out with Cindy. *The Miseducation of Lauryn Hill* came out that year and I almost wore the tracks off the tape by the summer's end. I also began drinking whenever I got the chance. I would get Jay or Mike to buy me some liquor and hang out on the pool deck in the evenings. My only problem was that I could not seem to get my wind back, even though I was working out about two hours a day. I had never been out of shape before and I didn't like the way it felt.

I was scheduled to have surgery about two weeks later. A great deal of the swelling and bruising had gone down, but my eyes were no longer aligned. When my left eye was looking straight ahead, the right one was looking about thirty degrees off to the right. As a result I had severe double vision with both eyes open, so most of the time I covered the right eye or tried to keep it closed. The surgery was going to adjust the muscles so that my eyes were once again aligned. Although my eye was not positioned properly, it had decent range of motion and vision clarity, so Dr. Langer advised me to use it whenever I could deal with the double vision for a little while in order to exercise the muscles, specifically when I watched television.

A Miracle

At this point I feel it is appropriate to take time out to explain what my faith was like to this stage of my life. Although my mother was Catholic, my father got his way as usual and we were raised in the Methodist church. Church was always an obligation in my eyes. I never really heard Jimmy actually speak about God or having a relationship with Him. We only prayed before meals on holidays, and we were never really encouraged to pray at bedtime.

My sisters and I were in the choir at St. Mark's Methodist church, and we went to rehearsal every Thursday. We sang every third Sunday which was the only day we went to church. We were not baptized until I was eight years old and we went to Sunday school sparingly, so we didn't retain much. We stopped going to church altogether when we left Jimmy's. None of us really wanted to go anymore and my mother was never really comfortable there. I never liked the fact that you had to get all dressed up for church. I don't think you should go disheveled, but it's not the prom either. It was nothing more than a waste of time as far as I was concerned.

I believed in God, but I did not understand the difference between religion and spirituality. I saw Him as a supreme being that I had to try and be good for. I had grown up feeling the constant pressure to prove myself to my father, and that was where I derived my understanding of my Heavenly Father. In high school I started watching *Touched by an Angel* every Sunday night. During that time I didn't answer the phone, return pages, or have company. That was my spiritual time. It was that show that changed the way I perceived God, and it ultimately led to my return to church a few years later. Watching that show gave me peace, and it gave me hope that life would get better. It created in me an image of a truly benevolent, forgiving Father, slowly doing away with the overseer and disciplinarian image that I had.

After the accident my grandmother had given me some Padre Pio oil and a pamphlet about him. In 1918 he became the first stigmatized priest in the history of the church, and spent his entire life suffering for the benefit of others. I rubbed it on my eye every morning and every night. I was scheduled to have surgery on a Wednesday, but on the Sunday of that week I was the recipient of a medical miracle.

All of my mother's family was next door at my aunt's house cooking out. I had been enjoying myself, but the time for my show was fast approaching. I went home and settled in the living room. I decided I would try and watch with both eyes open for a while as Dr. Langer had suggested. Near the end of the show, my vision suddenly came together. I was incredulous. It was as if God Himself had reached down and adjusted my eye. My vision wasn't perfect, but it was much better. I felt like I had on 3-D glasses.

I jumped off of the couch and ran out the back door. I shot across the back yard and catapulted over the fence. I went running up to my mother, whom I had terrified by jumping the fence, and she looked at me and said, "Hey, what's wrong?"

I stared right in her eyes and yelled, "Look Ma! My eyes are straight! I don't need surgery!" She jumped up and hugged me and joined in my enthusiasm as we proceeded to tell the rest of the family. I was especially happy when I told my grandmother how I'd been using the oil.

College Life

On my eighteenth birthday I cleaned out my bank account of three hundred sum-odd dollars and went to the tattoo parlor. I had always wanted a tattoo, but my mother refused to consent to it so I waited. Before my accident I had resolved to get Snoopy spinning a basketball on his finger and wearing a uniform with the number five on it. Afterwards I decided I wanted something with more meaning, and when Meikel died I decided that I wanted a memorial. I decided to get praying hands on my right shoulder and then had Terri, Bunny, and Meikel's initials placed around them. It came out beautifully although my mother didn't like it, and it helped me to cope with my grief.

At the end of August I moved into my dorm at NJIT. My roommate was an architecture major and we were like two ships passing in the night. I chose to be a business management major because I knew I didn't have the work ethic to study architecture or engineering. I met all of my teammates on the first day, and was so excited to be in college.

The other point guard was a junior transfer from south Jersey named Kerri Ann. Her roommate Tennille was also a transfer player. Their room was directly above mine, one floor up. Kerri Ann and I clicked from day one. She didn't let anyone get over on her. She always did what she wanted and stood up for herself, and that was how I wanted to be. A month into the semester we were joined at the hip. I was almost never in my room, and we didn't make it to classes often either. She became my best friend at school.

I had a hard time with conditioning. We had to be at the track at six thirty on Tuesday and Friday mornings to run a mile, and the best time I was able to record was ten minutes even. I couldn't understand it. No matter how hard I tried, my conditioning would not improve. I had been in the gym all summer, and I didn't smoke. Coach Barnes rode me hard. She continuously tried to motivate me, but motivation wasn't my problem. My problem was my knee and my lungs. I would even run extra sprints in the gym, but nothing seemed to help. I automatically assumed that my problems stemmed from my accident and I began to fear that I would never play basketball again.

There was one factor that I failed to realize at the time. I'd never had problems with physical conditioning, but I had always taken good care of my body. I hadn't had a cigarette in a year and a half, but I was now drinking every night without fail. I didn't have much money, so I drank cheap. I had been shown a liquor store not far from school that served minors, and every three days I would buy a half-pint of Everclear. Kerri Ann drank almost as much as I did, so she would get her drink and we'd go back to the dorms. Kerri Ann was a very pretty girl, and as such was constantly getting invitations from the baseball and men's basketball players to come hang out. I had good intentions when I went to school, but every night there seemed to be something better to do than studying. We became good friends with a guy named Ryan and he drank just as much as we did, so I figured this was normal college life.

My First Breakdown

That year I developed a literal allergy to alcohol. Whenever I drank, especially when I consumed a large quantity in a small time, my face became extremely red. It was beyond flush, and even looked to be painful. I could always tell when my face was getting red because it got incredibly hot as if I had a fever and I became short of breath. This had never happened to me before, but it didn't stop me from drinking. My grandmother has the same affliction, and I am the only one of her offspring that inherited the trait.

At the end of September I had a minor meltdown. I found out that a girl named Joelle that befriended me early in high school had died in a motorcycle accident. I came home the day of the wake intending to sleep at home, go to the funeral, and then return to school. I went to the wake and was overcome with emotion. This was the third accident-related death in the five months since my accident, and they were so young at eighteen, eighteen, and twenty-seven. I couldn't deal with my grief. I decided I would go back to school and drink. There was no way I could handle the funeral.

I went home and got my bag then headed towards Newark, but I had to make a stop first. I needed to see Cindy. Once we got into her room I broke down, but my grief was not just over their losses. It was the product of confusion and fear. Why had God spared my life? It had been one of pain and sorrow, so why did He leave me here to suffer more? I obviously had a purpose, but what was it? I was a shell of the person He had created, so what did I still have to offer?

I spilled my guts about the fear of not fulfilling my destiny, of falling short of God's grace. I had endured so much, but where was I headed? I didn't really know what I wanted to do for the rest of my life. I liked sports and helping people, but was studying business in school. We spoke about adversity and spirituality on a very intense level and I felt much better when we were finished, but I still had no clue as to my purpose in life.

Doubt

Our conversation was not enough to stop the psychological plunge I had begun. By the time the season started, I was already beginning to give up on myself. It seemed like no matter what I would not be able to come back from this accident. My physical struggles continued, but there were mental ones as well. I had always been good at math, but I was becoming confused in class. It wasn't coming to me the way it always had. I had similar struggles in accounting and business class. My thoughts always seemed clouded and jumbled and the harder I tried to concentrate, the more difficult the task became.

My motivation to go to class began to dwindle. Maybe college wasn't for me. Maybe this was just too hard. I'd never had these thoughts before. I had never doubted my physical or intellectual abilities and if I quit, who would I become? I was always the athlete, and I was so smart although my grades didn't always reflect that, so what would I be left with if I gave up on school? Although I was scared of my impending failure, I was even more scared to drop out, so I stayed.

I didn't deliberately miss class. Most of the time I was just too hung over to get dressed, or Kerri Ann would talk me out of it. There were times I'd be in my room studying and Kerri Ann and Tennille would be banging on the floor with free weights to get me to come up. I usually didn't have to be tempted away from my studies, but when the occasion arose, they would get the job done. The temptation of a bottle was usually all it took for me to drop my pencil and go upstairs.

In the gym, I felt that I had the talent to be a starter, but I was never able to get it together. No matter how well I played, I was never able to go a stretch of more than two minutes without tugging at my shorts and breathing heavily. Our first games were Thanksgiving weekend at a tournament in Washington D.C. We left early that Friday morning in two vans. I really had no expectations with regards to playing time, and I only ended up playing about two minutes in each half. This was not something I was used to. I had never come off the bench in any sport in my life. I had become completely inadequate in both academics and athletics.

When the time came around for final exams I studied hard. I needed to make a good showing so that I could transfer after the spring semester. This school was obviously not for me. For three days straight I studied for my math exams, shaking off Kerri Ann's requests for my company. I had struggled my way through the semester with decent grades, but I wanted to do well.

The morning of my exam I went to breakfast and then back to my room to review my notes, but when I tried to do a couple of problems I couldn't remember any formulas. After I wrote the problem I would draw a complete blank. What was I going to do? After an hour I figured I was screwed anyway, so I went to the liquor store and bought a pint of rum. Alcohol was quickly becoming my refuge. When the time for the exam came I was ripped. Needless to say I failed the exam, but somehow passed the course. I failed accounting but passed all my other courses. I had done enough to remain eligible for the second half of the season, about which I wasn't sure how I felt.

I began to develop a severe distaste for my coach. I resented her because she continually pushed me to improve, but I no longer believed I had the capacity. I had completely lost all faith in myself and wished she would just leave me alone. I didn't think she liked me as a person and just wanted the season to be over. For the first time in my life, I hated basketball. I dragged myself to practice and didn't even want to get into the games. I wanted to quit, and I continued to bury myself in liquor.

Coach Citro taught me that once you quit something, it will be easy to quit anything for the rest of your life. I mentioned earlier that walking away from Shakil's that day was the worst decision I ever made, and that is another reason why. I had quit on myself altogether since that day. I had ingested various toxins, I'd given up on my intelligence, and now I was ready to walk away from basketball. It was not a decision I came to lightly, but after careful consideration I bagged up all of my basketball gear and uniforms and went to her office. Kerri Ann tried to talk me out of it but I was miserable.

I sat down with Coach Barnes and told her that I didn't want to play anymore. I told her that I wasn't happy at the school and wanted to transfer. She caught me totally off guard. I had built up a belief that she didn't like me and figured she'd be happy to see me go, but she wasn't. She handed my bag back and told me to sleep on it. She told me she had high hopes for me and that I just needed to get in shape. That was enough for me. I was thrilled that she believed in me and that she didn't dislike me. I wish I could say that was a turning point for me, but it wasn't. Nothing else in my life changed, including my playing time, and I was still very depressed so I continued drinking daily.

Why Me?

January 29th, 1999 was a very disappointing day. That morning I met my parents at the Essex County Courthouse. Jay had been convicted on drug and weapons charges and was set to be sentenced. This wasn't the first time I'd been here. When I was nine or ten, I had been there as he was arraigned on assault charges, but that was for less than a year, and it was five miles away at the Caldwell County Jail. We visited all the time and it didn't seem that bad. This time he was sentenced to three years in south Jersey, two hours away.

I began to cry as I had the first time, but these tears were different. The first time I was a young child and cried because I thought maybe it would change the judge's mind, but this time I was truly sad. I was sad because I would miss him and because he was my role model. He was my hero when we were growing up because although his life had been hard, he always had a plan. I knew the extent of his childhood circumstances and admired his perseverance through many hardships. It seemed so unfair to me.

I went to the liquor store and back to my dorm. I changed my clothes and was just sitting down on my bed when my pager went off. It was Cindy 911 from a number I didn't recognize. I called back and she told me that she was at the hospital in labor. I jumped up and ran out the door. She had decided she wanted me to help coach her through the delivery so I ran out to my car and threw it in reverse when I heard a loud crack. I tried to put it in drive, but it just rolled backwards a bit. The engine revved but the car didn't move. The universal joint had broken. A couple of security guards helped me to push the car back into the parking space, and then I went upstairs and got drunk. It was the perfect end to a perfect day.

I got up to the hospital the next day, but I had missed the delivery. Cindy had a little girl and named her Cerrina. When she left the hospital she moved in with her boyfriend's family. They already had a son together, Nigel, so now they could all be together as she finished up her bachelor's degree. The house was only a five minute drive from school and I went there every day. I loved spending time with Cindy anyway, but I was totally engrossed with Cerrina. I would hold her in my arms most of the time I was there, and I rarely left without putting her to sleep. Once again, in a time of heavy emotional turmoil, God sent an angel of peace in the form of a child.

A few months later something else happened to further complicate my inner turmoil, and left me feeling helpless. Amina was living with my father and they got into one of their usual fights. She suffered from a chemical imbalance for which he had no tolerance. I still fail to understand how an educated man could be so cruel and callous towards someone suffering from something beyond their control. She occasionally went into episodes of rage that he spurred, and he could never bring himself to walk away. We've all had our arguments with him and he never prevented Jay, Khalea, or I from walking away from a fight, but he would literally chase Amina to perpetuate one. He got a sadistic pleasure out of seeing her explode, and took equal pleasure in using those explosions against her in future discussions.

On this particular day he decided to throw her out of the house. He began bagging her clothes and tossing them across the front lawn. She called my mother to come get her, and when she arrived with Khalea everything escalated. Amina hit him over the head with a picture frame, and he yelled for his wife to call the police. My mother and Khalea were just trying to pick Amina up and possibly defuse the situation, but when the police arrived Jimmy told a twisted story.

He said that my mother had hit him with the picture frame and that they'd come to attack him in defense of Amina. Khalea walked over to

Jimmy and the police officer because she knew that he was lying, but the police officer told her to go away. She rolled her eyes as she turned around, and no sooner than she'd taken the first step, he grabbed her and informed her that she was under arrest. She asked him what he was doing as she had been trying to walk away and he got very nasty with her. She shoved him onto the hood of the cruiser and Amina came to help. When a second cop stepped up Amina punched him square in the face. They both went to jail, and so did my mother because of Jimmy's lies.

When I found out about the fight I was furious. I was sick and tired of him acting like that. Although he and I had our problems he treated me far better than he did my siblings and, instead of them coming to resent me, I came to resent him. I loved my family too much to ignore the way he treated them, regardless of how he treated me, and it wasn't as if he treated me that great either. I called to talk to him but it was pointless, because he never does anything wrong. In Newark I was riddled with guilt, believing that everything would have been avoided if I was home.

The end of the school year came and Kerri Ann went home to Florida. Over the course of the year I had actually gotten closer to Kelli although she was a year behind me. She and Gus would come to my basketball games and afterwards we would get high. I would make as many of her games as I could and we would do the same thing afterwards. That summer the three of us hung out every day. I helped Coach Citro run his summer camp and became his assistant coaching the games. After the games I would call them and they'd pick me up. We would go to the liquor store and the weed spot and then figure out what we were going to do. At the end of the semester I moved back with my mother. I'd had my fill of Jimmy's shenanigans. Every night I would sneak in the house drunk and high and go to sleep.

Investments

At the end of the school year I was going to transfer schools because NJIT was just not a fit for me, but Coach Barnes left first. I figured that maybe I could get a fresh start with the new coach, so I stayed. When the new semester started I was in a new dorm and Kerri Ann had not returned. I saw some familiar faces but I didn't really have any friends. The new coach and I did not see eye to eye at all. I perceived an intense arrogance about her and instantly wished I had transferred. I had already wasted one year, I would not do it again. A few weeks into September I withdrew from school.

Over the summer I had made mention of the fact that I was unhappy and wanted to leave NJIT to Glenn. He told me that the fire department was giving a test soon and that I should take it. I laughed at him and told him that although I was a little down I wasn't desperate, but he was serious. He even offered to pay for me to take the written exam, so I figured what the hell? There were over eight hundred applicants there, and not many women. They invited the top one hundred applicants back for the physical exam, and I was number thirty-three.

The physical exam consisted of two parts. The first part was to simply climb to the top of the aerial ladder on top of the truck. They extended it almost straight up in the air and attached a harness to us. There was no time limit, only a pass or a fail. It didn't make much sense for anyone to proceed with the testing if they were afraid of heights. I have always been afraid of heights, but I couldn't turn back now. Everyone that passed that portion was given a return date for the remainder of the physical exam.

The physical exam was not easy, but I received some help. Glenn had spoken to John Sterling, the first African-American firefighter in Montclair, who had retired as a deputy chief. He showed me the best way to carry a ladder alone and gave me some other pointers. I wasn't incredibly sparkling in comparison to the muscular men I was competing against, but I held my own because I had been working out feverishly trying to ensure a better season at school. I would not hear anything for a while, but six months later I learned that I'd come out number three on the hiring list.

I had no idea what I was going do, but I wasn't going to do it at NJIT. I had liked coaching in the summertime and wanted to help out during the season. Coach Citro welcomed my help and so began my mentorship. I had kept in touch with Kerri Ann and she was able to get me a job. Her father was the vice-president of a glass company and there was temporary work available at a factory in Carteret.

My job was to sit on a crate and count how many bottles broke as they were filled. That was all I did for twelve hours a day. During the week that was all I had time for. The commute was an hour so I woke up at six and tried to get in bed by ten. That job ended when the basketball season began, but in those six weeks I realized how much I needed to return to school.

I loved coaching basketball. I was only in my second year out of school, so I still knew all the players. I didn't have many responsibilities but I was a sponge soaking up information from Coach Citro and his new assistant, Coach Bittner. I was incredibly eager to learn as well as to teach. Maybe this was it. Maybe this was why God spared my life. I was good at coaching and thoroughly enjoyed it. Maybe I could be a coach and a school counselor. Coach Citro was my mentor and the idea of following in his footsteps made sense. It seemed right. I had found my destiny.

Chapter 8
The New Me

One day on the way to a game Coach Citro mentioned that we needed to create a feeder program. We had become successful on the high school level but there was too much work to be done in order to reach the next level competitively. He had heard about a bunch of middle school girls in town that were talented and enthusiastic about the game. I told him that I didn't know much yet but I would try and put an AAU (Amateur Athletic Union) team together. He gave me the names and numbers of an AAU program director and the local basketball guru who had control of the gym at Glenfield.

I held tryouts and kept five girls from Montclair: Monica, Jennifer, Denise, Erin, and Rayna. We practiced three days a week at Glenfield and Zakiyyah helped out some when she came home from school. We did the same drills we ran at the high school and emphasized defense. I thought we were fairly talented, but we were no match for our opponents. We lost eight games and only won one. I coached with all of the intensity and passion I could muster, but we were all terribly inexperienced.

That season was rough, but I learned a lot about coaching. The first thing I learned was that I had a lot to learn. There is a great deal of thought that goes on mentally before a coach speaks, and a great deal of planning before each practice and game. I also had to deal with a number of personalities and it wasn't easy. Monica was a quiet little eighth-grader that was an excellent point guard. She was easily the best player on the team, but she was shy and reserved. Jennifer was a vibrant, energetic eighth-grader that played the shooting guard position, worked tremendously hard, and hated to lose like I did. Erin was a five-foot-eleven seventh-grader that was skinny and timid. Rayna was a quiet seventh-grader and a shooting guard that was extremely strong and quick. Last but not least was Denise, a loud, sassy, emotional seventh-grade guard with an incredible shooting touch.

Denise became one of the biggest challenges I've ever faced as a coach. She had incredible potential but her attitude was awful. She hated running and defensive drills, and would roll her eyes or suck her teeth every time I assigned something she didn't like. We butted heads for much of the time I knew her but she worked hard and wanted to win. I can't say that I ever got her completely in line but we developed an understanding that endeared us for the duration of our years together.

Something magical happened over the course of those three months. I bonded with those girls. They would come over my house and call me all the time. Although I was a drill sergeant in the gym, I was fair and I cared about them. I was only nineteen at the time and they liked hanging out with me. I enjoyed having a bunch of little sisters that played basketball, and they became "my girls."

I became especially close with Monica. She was quiet and precocious and everyone took that as arrogance because she was so good in basketball, so she didn't have many friends. She began coming over my house all the time and I started calling her my little sister. Being a point guard myself, I was able to give her a lot of little tips on getting better. She was incredibly funny too, and we spent much of those days laughing and having a good time.

Now What?

That was a time of confusion for me on many levels. I didn't know what I was going to do about school, I didn't have any money, and I was lost spiritually. I knew that I loved coaching though. I had a tryout with the basketball team at Zakiyyah's school, Felician College, and arranged one with the softball team. After showing both coaches what I could do, they put together a package that allowed me to attend school there for free, so that was resolved. I began umpiring softball games for the town middle school league, so that put some money in my pocket. But what was I to do about this spirituality? I did not want to return to the Methodist church. My mother's family was Catholic, so I started going to their church.

I liked it for many reasons. The biggest was that you could wear whatever you wanted and no one looked at you sideways. I could go however I was comfortable and that was a big plus, but that only got me in the door. The service was only an hour and I liked that, but there was more. I enjoyed the excitement of Baptist churches but there was something intoxicating about the sense of peace I felt when I left the Catholic church. Ultimately I decided to convert to Catholicism because of the sacraments of penance and communion. Understanding forgiveness would prove to be a huge theme of my life. I enjoyed the fellowship that I felt with God when I was there.

The priest was a man named Father Nickas and he seemed nice enough. He tended to drone somewhat which gave me doubts about joining that particular church, but I went ahead and told him that I wanted to convert. We started meeting in his office every Tuesday night and we would talk for a while, then he would give me literature to take home and read for discussion the following week. Over the course of our meetings I came to appreciate the way he spoke because I realized that he was not droning, but speaking patiently and thoughtfully. Often times I stayed for hours, because he was so easy to talk to. We became friends and kept in touch even after his retirement a few years later. I also went to church every Sunday. This went on for about three months, and I was Confirmed during the evening service on Holy Thursday.

By the end of May I had temporarily sifted through all of my confusion-- then I got a phone call. There was an opening on the fire department and I was next on the list. I went in for an interview and a week later a police officer was assigned to perform a complete background check on me. I was about to become Montclair's first female African-American firefighter! But wait a second. I took that test as a back-up plan. I had successfully procured a full Division II scholarship and I wanted to play sports. I never really wanted to be a firefighter. I wanted to get my education and be a coach.

I also wanted to have money in my pocket though. Getting money out of Jimmy was like getting a bone from a pit bull, and my mother was struggling. I knew that the last thing Jimmy wanted to see me do was join Glenn's profession, so I made him a proposal. Fifty dollars a week while I was at school worked out to be around two thousand dollars but I didn't trust him to keep his word, so if he gave me two thousand dollars in cash up front I would return to school. He agreed and I turned down the fire department job.

Bonding

That summer was great. I ran workouts for both the high school and middle school girls in the morning. I was playing against them every day and felt like I was back in shape. I also worked at a town pool as a lifeguard with Khalea after workouts and on weekends. We played spades and generally had a blast there. Monday through Thursday I coached the B team in the summer leagues. After my games or when I got off of work I would go home, shower, and call Kelli. She and Gus would pick me up and we'd get smashed as we rode around looking for something to do. Sometimes we played cards or went to the movies, but we were always inebriated.

My little sister taught me a valuable lesson that summer about kids and trust. I loved them and they loved me, but they were also a little scared of me. I knew all of their private business and I lectured them about respecting themselves in their dealings with boys. If I heard a rumor about one of them doing something promiscuous I would berate and scold them. They came over so often that Khalea had gotten close to them as well. One day she told me something about Monica and I was crushed. I was supposed to be her big sister. How could she confide in Khalea before me? If it wasn't for me they wouldn't even know each other!

Khalea said to me, "Naima, she's scared. How can you expect her to confide in you when you yell at her? She's a teenager and she's going to have experiences with boys. If you want her to trust you, you have to be her friend. She already has a mother." She was absolutely right. Cindy never did that to me, and I was aiming to create the same bond with them. From then on I vowed to be a good friend and mentor to them, and saved my yelling for the court.

When I started at Felician I had the intentions of a champion. I took six classes and had a double major in Math Education and Sociology. I was going to be a high school math teacher while I got my Master's degree in counseling. Zakiyyah and I were roommates. I played with the softball team and worked out by myself playing basketball for two hours a day. I was focused and knew what I wanted to do in my life, but no matter what I accomplished during the day things always ended up the same way-- with me and Zakiyyah getting drunk in our room. Jimmy had given me twelve hundred dollars of the money he'd promised me, and I wasted no time in putting it to use. Sometimes people joined us and sometimes it was just us two, but all we needed was each other and some liquor for a good time. Our door was always unlocked and our room became the party room.

Myrna

I was having a rough fall softball-wise. I was very rusty and considered myself average at best. After one game early in October I was especially frustrated. I had a fifth of Bacardi Limon waiting for me back in my room, and I was anxious to get started. One of the things I loved to do while I drank was play spades. There was one girl in particular that I really enjoyed playing with named Myrna, and when I got back to my room there was a voicemail from her saying that she wanted to play. When I called her back she said she had changed her mind, but five minutes later she called again and wanted to play. I poured half of the Bacardi into a Gatorade bottle and went to play with her and two boys.

After the game I was going to say hi to some girls that lived by her, so we headed towards her dorm together. As we began to part ways I got the inclination to ask her if she was okay because she hadn't seemed like it on the phone, and she began to tell me about a fight that she'd had with her boyfriend. We ended up in her room talking and looking at pictures until about one o'clock, and then went back to my room for the rest of the fifth. We stayed up until seven talking and drinking, and from that night on we were best friends. We spent all of our free time together and got drunk every night. Zakiyyah moved off campus a few weeks later and Myrna all but moved in.

Little by little I began slacking off in my classes. I missed almost all of my morning classes because I was too hung over, and attending the afternoon ones was a matter of energy and motivation. On the outside I was a confident, happy-go-lucky, outgoing athlete, but on the inside I was crumbling. The depression file cabinet was getting full, and I didn't even realize it because the drinking had me completely numb to it. My issues were not going away though, and day by day I dug myself a little deeper into a hole that would eventually become a crater.

October fifteenth is the first day that college basketball teams can practice, so many of them kick the season off at midnight on the fourteenth with a pep rally. My cousin was getting married in Long Island earlier in the day, so I rode out with my mother and cousin's. There was an open bar and I took full advantage of it. I drank nonstop until it was time to leave. Although I was well aware of the fact that I had to play later that day, I could not curtail my alcohol consumption. I slept the whole ride back, but I was still drunk as I slightly staggered into the locker room. All things considered, I didn't play too poorly. I made all of my shots, but I threw the outlet pass to the coach during lay-up lines.

Aside from that one error, the rest of the night was uneventful. Practice started the next day and I was ready. I worked hard in the off-season and it had paid off. I wasn't finishing sprints first, but I wasn't last as I always was at NJIT. I felt that I was the obvious choice to become the starting point guard. Practice was usually at six which I wasn't crazy about, but to make matters worse I had to arrive early to receive treatment for my back. Every morning I sat in the dark at five waiting for the trainer. I had to get electro-stimulation and heat before every practice or game to avoid as much discomfort as possible.

The weekend of November 3rd, my cousin Reggie wanted to go to Hampton University for Homecoming weekend. My other cousin, Russell, was a student there and had an apartment off campus, and he said he would take care of us but we had to get down there first. Zakiyyah, Myrna, and I had obliterated the money from my father and I had nothing left. We were able to scrape up eighty dollars and I convinced the coach to move Saturday practice to Sunday evening. Reggie, Myrna, and I gathered some clothes, said a prayer over his beat up car, and headed to Virginia.

When we got there Friday evening the campus was a hotbed of activity. There were cars and people everywhere, horns honking, and people yelling. Russell lived right across the street in an apartment complex mostly inhabited by students, and we started partying as soon as we arrived. Reggie and Russell were never big drinkers, but Russell provided more than enough for Myrna and me. We freshened up, poured some liquor in a soda bottle, and went to a step show. The next afternoon we went to the football game and then planned on relaxing for the rest of the day. Myrna and I were drinking all day and by the evening we were three sheets to the wind.

Something had been bothering me for a while and I really needed to address it. The greatest effect that alcohol has is that it significantly diminishes your inhibitions. The euphoria is nice, but my ability to shirk my self-consciousness was what eventually addicted me to alcohol. Myrna and I had become very close, especially in Zakiyyah's absence. There was something stronger than friendship going on here though.

Maleka and Zakiyyah were my two best friends, but somehow Allison, Kerri Ann, and now Myrna invoked a different feeling in me. I had been stifling it for four years, which I'm sure added to my depression. Ultimately I realized that they were different because I was attracted to them. Earlier that week Myrna had mentioned to me that she'd kissed a girl once. That opened the door for me to draw the courage to speak about what I was feeling. I figured that even if she was not attracted to me it wouldn't destroy our friendship and she wouldn't be repulsed by my feelings, which was a major fear for me.

Eventually I mustered up the nerve to tell her, so I asked her to come out on the balcony with me. "Myrn, I have something to tell you, but I'm really nervous about it and I'm not quite sure how to say it."

"What's up, Nai?"

"Well, I've had something on my mind lately and it's really been bothering me. In the past month or so we've gotten really close, and I feel like I can tell you anything, but this is hard, because it has to do with you."

"Don't sweat it, Nai. Whatever it is you can talk to me."

Although I was drunk, it was still hard for me to believe that I was about to say these words. She waited patiently as I beat around the bush for the next ten minutes, explaining how I'd never done anything like this before and how I hadn't planned it before blurting out, "I think I'm in love with you."

I had developed a very skewed understanding of love to that point in my life and believed my words. I think that believing I had fallen in love also eased my discomfort in that I had no choice in the matter. Although I think she knew those words were coming, Myrna paused for a second to compose herself and then said, "Okay. Let's take this conversation inside," so we went into Russell's room and locked the door.

She was so incredibly understanding and easy going. We sat and talked for around an hour about my feelings, confusion, and fears. Then she caught me off guard and said, "So can I have a kiss?" I was stunned and didn't know what to say. I was curious about how it would feel, but was I ready for this? I knew I was a tomboy, but did that mean I was gay? I struggled with the idea for another ten minutes, and finally agreed. I was scared out of my mind, but I had created this whole situation so I wasn't going to back down now.

She leaned over and kissed me ever so gently on the lips. Now, for some reason I expected either fireworks or disgust on my part, but interestingly enough neither occurred. It was a normal kiss, and felt no different than the few times I had kissed boys in the past. *Wow, now what?* Moments after the kiss Reggie and Russell came knocking on the door and we went back to drinking and playing cards as if nothing had happened, although I was even more confused than ever.

We headed home on Sunday morning and Myrna and I never got the chance to talk any further. Practice was at six that evening and I was late because we hit traffic on the way back, so Reggie dropped me off at the gym and Myrna went back to "our" room. I caught a cold over the weekend but I was late as it was, so I didn't say anything to the coach. I was still fighting for a starting spot and I didn't want him to think I was a punk, so I practiced hard as usual. Even though I was laboring through practice, I didn't want it to end because I knew that Myrna and I were due for a talk.

When practice ended I begrudgingly made my way back to the room. Myrna was sitting on the bed watching television, so without a word I undressed and jumped in the shower. When I got out I went and sat at my desk with my back to her and started playing solitaire. She let a couple of minutes go by and then said, "Can I have some sugar?" I was pretty sure that she was talking about a kiss, but I didn't want to concede anything. I had stockpiled a number of condiments in my top desk drawer, so I pulled out a sugar packet and tossed it on the bed. She chuckled for a second but was undeterred saying, "Thanks, but that's not what I was talking about."

I went and sat on the bed next to her. I was still very unsure about this entire situation. I could always use inebriation as an excuse for the first kiss, but this one would be for real. I'd struggled my whole life with being a tomboy and had banished every thought of my sexuality to the far recesses of my mind, but now I was face to face with it. As if in a movie scene, right as we leaned in to kiss the fire alarm went off, so we grabbed our jackets and went outside.

Myrna and I eventually kissed again and began to explore the possibility of a relationship. I was terrified of anyone finding out and she had a boyfriend, but what we felt seemed so magical and special. I felt connected to her spiritually. We talked about everything and thought we had a big secret from the world. After a few days we pushed the beds together and she moved the rest of her clothes in.

We rarely went to class, almost never leaving the room. I only left for practice, liquor, and a couple of times a day one of us would go to the cafeteria and load a tray with enough food for three people and bring it back to the room. She spent time with her boyfriend occasionally but they had a rocky relationship and I was happy to pick up his slack. We were best friends in every sense of the phrase. The only time we argued was when I got sad because she was leaving me to see her boyfriend. We ate our meals together, slept together, and were miserable when separated.

Basketball Struggles

Ever since I returned from Virginia I had trouble breathing in practice. The cold I caught in Virginia turned out to be Bronchitis and I'd put considerable strain on my lungs by playing in that condition. When the Bronchitis cleared up, my difficulties breathing in practice remained. I began falling behind during sprints and wheezing during drills. The trainer deduced that I had developed athletic asthma when I was sick. She got me an Albuterol inhaler but I was never the same. No matter what I did I could not regain my conditioning.

We opened up our season at a tournament in Shippensburg, Pennsylvania on Thanksgiving weekend. It was an overnight trip and I roomed with Zakiyyah and Myrna, who was responsible for videotaping our games. I started the first game, but was incredibly winded and came out three minutes into the game. I only played maybe ten minutes that game and we got blown out. I was so disappointed. I had worked so hard to get here and couldn't help my team at all. We went back to the hotel to shower and then the coach took the team out for pizza, but I declined. I was miserable over losing and didn't even want to think about food. Myrna brought two slices back to the room but I still had no appetite.

The next day we ate breakfast, dressed for the game, and checked out because we were supposed to be going home directly after the game. I started again, but I sprained my ankle early in the game and had to come out. This was the consolation game and I felt we could beat this team. I sat at the end of the bench with a bag of ice on my ankle, itching to get back in the game. We were losing, but not by much and I wanted to be involved. I did not want to go home winless. At halftime I went to the trainer's office to be evaluated and she said I was done for the day. I argued with her and convinced her to tape it and then test me. I walked gingerly out to the gym, trying not to limp. She had me perform a series of exercises and I did my best hiding my pain. After a few minutes she reluctantly cleared me to play.

I ran to the bench and told the coach hoping he'd put me right in, but he didn't. I sat on the bench for about three minutes and then he called my name. Within seconds of entering the game I was so excited I dribbled the ball off of my foot. I went running after it and dove, but as I did so another player came out of nowhere and kneed me right in the face. I collapsed instantly and momentarily lost consciousness.

When I came to I was writhing in pain. She got me just below my right eye, right where the plates are. I was helped off the court and an ambulance was called. Five seconds after the final buzzer Myrna had packed the camera up and was by my side. The coach rode in the ambulance with me but Myrna came into the hospital as soon as the bus arrived. The whole team sat on the bus while the doctors x-rayed my face, and I was diagnosed with a concussion.

Myrna held me in her arms for the entire bus ride home, and woke me up every hour through the night as the doctor had instructed. I could not practice for three days which didn't do much for my conditioning. I spent at least an hour with the trainer every day trying to speed my ankle recovery. I wasn't even allowed to travel with the team for the next game. My first game back I was no longer in the starting lineup and again became very frustrated with basketball. When I got in the game I played for about a minute and a half and then had to come out because I couldn't breathe. When I got back in I was dribbling when a girl tried to reach in and steal the ball. She was very strong and her shoulder collided with my jaw as she was running full speed. Again I crumpled on the floor in pain. I was dizzy and disoriented, and headed straight for the trainer's office as I was helped off the floor. I had sustained my second concussion in nine days.

Failure...Again

At this point in school I had dropped two classes and was struggling miserably in the remaining ones. It was almost time for final exams and any chance I had of last minute cramming went out the window when I got hit in the head. Between school and basketball I was becoming increasingly depressed.

I was able to play one more game after returning from the concussions before being declared ineligible. It was just as well though, because I had given up on basketball. I walked my way through practice without much effort. Between my frustration and my lack of respect for the coach, I was useless. I was put on academic probation and informed that I would not be playing softball either. I only passed two of the six classes I began the semester with.

Myrna hadn't fared much better academically and we were both facing expulsion if we didn't get it together. Right after New Year's a friend came to pick us up and we went to Delaware for a few days. One of her best friends, Marissa, lived there with her mother and daughter. Everyone called her mother Mommy, so that's what I called her. Marissa was very perceptive and it didn't take her long to figure out what was going on with Myrna and me, but she was accepting of us which took a load off of my mind. We eventually became good friends ourselves.

When the next semester started we were anticipating a fun spring, but things didn't quite turn out that way. Three nights into the semester we found out that because of her low grades the previous semester, Myrna's financial aid was being yanked. She had forty-eight hours to withdraw from school and move out. We were devastated. We both started crying, me more than her. I did not want to be in school anymore and I called Cindy to come pick us up. Myrna did not want to go back home so after spending the weekend with Cindy, Marissa came to pick her up and she moved to Delaware.

I was miserable. I couldn't play sports, I was failing out of school, and Myrna was snatched away from me in the blink of an eye. I knew that I was probably going to lose my scholarship, but I had to try and save face. I took seven classes and began to get focused. I still drank every night, but I made it to every class. I took notes and did all of my homework.

All I cared about was school and Myrna. I used money from a refund check to pay for bus tickets to Delaware. Every Friday morning I would get a bus to Port Authority in New York, and then catch another bus to Delaware. I would stay for the weekend and catch a five o'clock bus back to school on Monday morning. When I was at school I was always either in my room or in class. I could never be reached by phone because I was always talking to Myrna.

One weekend she came up to school and stayed with me. Although we thought we had some big secret, everyone suspected the nature of our relationship, including her boyfriend. We were drinking in the room and he came to see her. They started arguing and things got out of hand. The police were called and I lost my temper. It took Myrna and three other girls to hold me down as I tried to get to the door. I never felt that he treated her the way she deserved and the liquor had me ready to fight. Since Myrna was no longer a student there and the police were summoned, she was banned from the campus. A few weeks later she came back and was caught in my room. I couldn't bear to be without her and didn't care about her being banned or any resulting disciplinary action.

Myrna broke up with me on April 12th. Although she loved me, she also loved her boyfriend and I had become an emotional victim. I was always sad when she was with him and had always treated her so much better. She hated that I was going through so much and she knew there was no way I was going to break up with her. I pleaded with her to change her mind, saying that I could handle my issues with her having a boyfriend, but she held her ground.

I was heartbroken. I'd never had a real relationship with anyone, and she was my first girlfriend. I loved her, and I cried for months. I didn't eat for a week and I drank heavily. We remained friends but I always hoped she'd come back to me. I made every effort to turn my life around. I was convinced that I wasn't gay and that Myrna was an exception. I needed to figure out how to move on, and I even went and confessed my relationship with her to a priest, but it didn't do much to ease my pain.

That semester I earned a three point two GPA, including courses in Physics and Geometry, but when I met with my coaches it didn't help much. The softball coach was leaving and his assistant was taking over. We'd had our differences in the fall and she was not inviting me back. The basketball coach said that I could have a spot but no money, and that if I proved myself in the upcoming year he would restore my scholarship for my senior season. I couldn't afford to go to school there without aid, so I applied to be a Resident Advisor. I felt that I was the best candidate, but because I had gotten caught with Myrna in my room they turned me down. I could not pull the money together and could not enroll for the next year, so I returned home with my tail between my legs.

When I left for school I was full of confidence, but I had embarrassed myself and lost my scholarship. I applied to Montclair State University and was accepted for the Fall 2001 semester. The previous year I had decided I didn't want to have a relaxer in my hair anymore, so I wore my hair in cornrows the whole time I was at Felician. When I got home I had my brother cut all of the hair that was straight leaving about two inches, and I colored it strawberry blonde.

When Kelli returned from school, she announced that she was transferring to Montclair State. We spent yet another summer coaching basketball in the daytime and getting bombed at night. We were inseparable. When I told her about my sexuality she took it in stride and nothing ever changed with us. The only time we were apart was when I umpired a softball game or was working at the pool. We rode around every night listening to Eminem's new album, totally unaware that that while I loved his lyrics, they were soothing the demon that was growing inside of me.

Chapter 9

Disappointment

Transition

I became devoted to the basketball team. Aside from coaching practices and games I spent a lot of time just hanging out with them, Monica in particular. They came to the pool a lot and we often went out to eat or to the movies. I spent all of my days with my girls and all of my nights with Kelli. I always felt that my drinking was normal because no matter where I went I could always find someone who drank as much as I did.

Not much changed when I started at Montclair State. Kelli was taking a semester off, but we still hung out every night. I was okay for the first month at school but soon started to slack off in my classes. I had a big gap in my schedule and often times did not return for the afternoon classes. I would catch the bus to the high school and monitor the girls as they ran and trained for the season. Being with them became more important than school, and I paid dearly for it. The only class I passed was Calculus I with a C-.

Kelli and I were both assistants that year and she took on the same role with the girls that I had. We had become mentors, not only coaching them, but talking to them about their problems and helping them with school work. I worked from five to eight every morning as a lifeguard at the Y, and again from five to eight every evening giving baby swim lessons. Cindy and her husband Nick had bought a house and were expecting their third child, so I agreed to come and help out. She didn't really need me, but it was an excuse for us to spend time together.

I had been procrastinating and was still living at home when she went into labor. She called me in the middle of the night and I met her at the hospital. Throughout the night I talked with and comforted her as she prepared to give birth. When the time came for delivery her husband and I helped to hold her legs up as she delivered. She had a daughter and named her Cayla. It was the first time I had ever seen a baby born. I moved in with them a few days later and became somewhat of a third parent. Nick worked on Wall Street and was not home much, so I helped Cindy with the kids. On countless nights we sat up talking until one or two in the morning.

During the two months that I stayed there, Jimmy and Amina had another argument and he kicked her out. I needed to move back home because the basketball season was starting, but my mother's house had become crowded and there was an open room at Jimmy's. My mother had gotten to be very concerned about my drinking and hated that I smoked weed. These issues began to create a strain on our relationship, so between the small amount of space and the tension with my mother, I decided to move in with Jimmy. He had gotten soft since the divorce and let me do whatever I wanted. He was renting a three bedroom apartment on the second and third floors of a house, and he didn't care when I had company or if I drank. I began smoking Newport's when I lost my scholarship, and I could smoke in my room as well.

Everyday Monica's cousin Rachel and I would hang out. We would get high and drunk in my room, and sometimes we would climb onto the landing outside of my window and do so under the stars. She lived right around the corner and was beginning to butt heads with her mother. It was her senior year and she didn't want to be in school anymore. I didn't mean to enable her but she was going astray anyway, so I thought that maybe if we hung out enough I could get her on the right track. She was way beyond that point though, so we just hung out. Audrey, my basketball teammate from Felician, came by pretty often to hang out, but Rachel and I were inseparable.

If my drinking was not yet out of control, it became so at that point. I drank every single night whether I was with someone else or not. On the weekends my girls would come over, and they saw me get drunk night after night. Zakiyyah had transferred to a college in Jersey City, but I could always count on her to come and drink with me. I was learning to be a good coach in the gym, but I was becoming a terrible influence at my house. I constantly provided a deleterious example for the girls that totally contradicted the lessons I taught them in the gym.

I felt incomplete without liquor. Going a night without it was incomprehensible to me. I didn't drink in the daytime, but I never missed a night. If I treated the girls to dinner I would drink openly, and I always made a trip to the liquor store before I went home. Aside from liking the way it made me feel, I liked the feelings it hid. I never really felt like I fit in anywhere. I looked White, but always surrounded myself with Black people, subconsciously trying to live up to the standards my father had set. I looked, dressed, and felt like a boy, and was totally confused about my sexuality. I missed Myrna terribly and when I drank our situation seemed a little more tolerable. She lived thirty minutes away and I didn't get to see her very often. When I did see her I longed to hold her, but we never got back together.

I thought I'd never get over her. I cried a lot at night and thought of her constantly. I listened to Alicia Keys' *Why Do I Feel So Sad?* over and over again. I must have written Myrna over fifty letters, but I never had the heart to give them to her. Ultimately I knew that she did not want to be anything more than my friend, but writing the letters helped to ease the pain a little bit. We were slowly developing a friendship but we also argued a lot, because we wanted two different things. Burying myself in my team was all I could do to help deal with my feelings, and mentoring those girls became my fourth addiction.

I sat at the scorer's table and did the scorebook during the games. Monica and I had a pre-game handshake and she would come to the table for it just before tip-off for good luck. I occasionally yelled things from the table or made a comment in the locker room, but my contributions as a coach were largely behind the scenes. After almost every game I would talk to Monica at her house about how she played and sometimes we'd watch the game tape at my house. I had done significant work with Denise on her shooting, and whenever she missed a shot she looked to me for instruction. Being with those girls became my sanctuary. No matter how bad everything else in my life was, when I was with them I was at peace.

That winter I was given a puppy by a friend of Kelli's. She was a tiger-striped pit bull and I named her Dutchess in honor of my heavy smoking habit. I was crazy about her at first, but eventually she became a burden. Caring for her was inhibiting my drinking, so I became very neglectful. I beat her when she made a mess in my room, because that was what I'd seen my father do. She was a responsibility that I was not ready for by any means.

Kim

One night we were playing a parochial powerhouse and Zakiyyah came to the game with a friend named Kim. I was engrossed with the game and didn't have much time to talk, but I did introduce myself briefly. She was a pretty girl but I didn't really pay much attention to her because of the game. A week later Zakiyyah and her boyfriend came to pick me up with Kim, and we all went bowling. There was a bowling alley in Union City that offered a special on Monday nights. Each game was a dollar per player, Bud Lights were a dollar, and shoe rental was free. For ten dollars we could bowl five games and get a pretty good buzz on.

I had so much fun that night. The four of us laughed all night and had more fun than usual. Zakiyyah and Kim spent the whole night trying to distract each other, even going so far as knocking the balls out of each other's hands or throwing balls down the gutter right before the other one bowled. Something clicked that night. There was something very special about Kim. There was an innocence in her that was pure and refreshing. She was beautiful, but her personality made her amazing.

When I got home that night I could not get her off of my mind, and I could see her smiling face every time I closed my eyes. This was the first time since being with Myrna that I had feelings for a girl, and my confusion came back full strength. I went to pick Khalea up from a party a few nights later and I ran into Kim again. I was in a rush and couldn't really talk to her but she did hug me, and when I left she was all I could think about.

The next weekend Zakiyyah's boyfriend and some of his football buddies threw a hotel party in New Brunswick. I took the van and met up with them in Jersey City. When we arrived at the hotel we started drinking and smoking. Kim and I played Zakiyyah and her boyfriend in spades and then I got hungry, so she went with me to Burger King. I felt a really strong vibe with her but I was scared to say anything to her, so I didn't. She eventually left with her boyfriend who was also a football player.

Zakiyyah came to our next game and she had a piece of paper for me. It was a note from Kim! It was a simple note, really. She'd realized that she didn't say goodbye before leaving the party and wanted to apologize, but she took the time to draw pictures and used a highlighter. I was flattered. I wasn't sure what to make of it, so I just put it in my night stand. I hadn't told many people about my sexuality, and I was still very much in love with Myrna.

The following Monday we went bowling again, and had just as much fun. I felt a strong attraction to Kim and even thought that she might be flirting with me a little bit. She and Zakiyyah began staying at my house on the weekends and we would drink and laugh into the wee hours of the morning. Eventually we exchanged numbers and began having brief phone conversations. I started spending more and more time in Jersey City, but whatever was going on between us remained unspoken for weeks.

After two weeks of phone conversations and more bowling excursions, they were at my house again. Jamal was performing in a talent show so we went, but not without having a few drinks first. Afterwards we went out to Felician for a party, and then came back to my house. They were going back to Jersey City for another party, but I wanted Kim to stay. My brother wasn't home so I asked Kim to come and talk to me for a second. When we got into the other room I said, "Don't go to the party. Stay here and chill with me."

"Naima, I can't tonight. I have to meet up with my friends at this party."

Undeterred, I replied, "Man forget that party you can see your friends tomorrow. Please stay here with me tonight."

"I really can't tonight. I'll come and stay with you tomorrow night."

I got on my knees and asked once again. "I'm begging you. Please?"

"Tomorrow, Naima. I promise."

I got off my knees and said, "Okay, well can I at least have a kiss before you go?"

That was my drunken logic. We had not discussed any aspect of her sexuality or my feelings for her. I'd never even told her that I was gay, but I just decided to go for it because as usual, I was drunk. All of the color drained from her face and she muttered, "I have to go" as she scampered out of the room.

When I woke up the next morning there was a long voicemail from her. She said that she needed to speak with me immediately and to call as soon as I got the message. Although I remembered everything from the night before, I said that I didn't because I wanted to hear it from her point of view. She recounted what I said to her, at which point I became instantly apologetic, saying that the liquor was talking and I really didn't want to destroy our friendship. She said that it was not the first time she had been hit on by a girl, but it was the first time she'd ever considered saying yes. I was floored. Even though I thought I was getting a flirtatious vibe from her, she was gorgeous and had a boyfriend. What would she want with me?

We talked for over an hour, and made plans for her to come to Montclair later on. She and Zakiyyah came over that evening, and we began drinking as usual. When the time came for Zakiyyah to leave, Kim said she was staying. After taking a moment to process her confusion, Zakiyyah said okay and left. Kim and I talked for a while, and then I asked her for a kiss. She was still very uncomfortable and said she wanted it to happen in the natural flow of things. I turned the lights out and we watched television in my bed. When we eventually kissed, I felt fireworks. There was something really special about this girl and the way I felt whenever I was with her. I did not want to pressure her or make any drunken mistakes, so I held her in my arms and we went to sleep.

Over the course of the next few weeks, I was living a dream. In my eyes, Kim was perfect. She was an A student, she was funny and sweet, she was beautiful, she was athletic, and at the heart of it all, she was innocent. Physically our affair never progressed past a few kisses, but spiritually I felt a bond. Our bond was based on how well we communicated. Whenever I went to visit her, we would take a walk before I left. It was my favorite time of the day. We would go walking around Jersey City in the middle of the night but it felt like Eden to me.

Every night that we were not together we spoke on the phone until we fell asleep. One night we even slept on the phone together. We wrote each other notes like we were in high school and loved to play fight. She loved little kids and at times acted like one. When we drove to Hampton with Zakiyyah and Reggie for Black College Weekend, she drew me pictures with crayons and we played connect the dots. While we were down there we took a walk by the harbor and I told her I was in love with her. She didn't say anything back, and I didn't care. I just wanted her to know how I felt. I loved everything about her, and believed that we were soul mates.

Cindy and I had become very, very close and I felt like I could talk to her about anything. We didn't agree on everything but we were constantly debating and when we didn't see eye to eye, we agreed to disagree. I eventually resolved that if I was ever fortunate enough to share that type of bond with anyone else, that I would pursue them with all of my might. I believe the nature of our relationship is ideal for the basis of a happy relationship, and I found that with Kim. We were attracted to each other, but at the core of everything was a mutual appreciation for happiness and a healthy respect for each other.

A month later Kim began to grow apprehensive. People at her school were beginning to talk and it was causing problems with her boyfriend. She came to spend the night with me, but I knew that something was wrong. That night she told me that she thought I was really nice, but she only wanted to be friends. I was crushed, but I tried not to show it. I was head over heels for this girl, and the last thing I wanted was to push her away. We agreed to just be friends, and then watched television until we fell asleep.

She was a tremendous Sacramento Kings fan, and they had a playoff game the next day. We watched the game, but it went to overtime and she had to get back to school, so I borrowed Jimmy's car and we listened on the radio as I took her back. When we reached the school the game was in triple overtime and she didn't want to miss a second, so we listened to the rest of it in the car. When the game ended I walked her inside and headed home. I had no idea that that was the last time I would ever spend time with her.

For the next two weeks Kim avoided me, stating final exams and job interviews as the reasons she had no time. Although I called her often, I only spoke to her a couple of times. Halfway through the semester I had given up on school. I didn't withdraw from my classes, I just stopped going. I still managed to get a C in history, but I failed everything else. I was already on academic probation from the fall semester, and at the close of the spring I was dismissed. The only things that really mattered to me were my girls, Kim, and drinking, so I was devastated when I lost contact with her. I remained very naïve, and refused to believe she was blowing me off. We hadn't had an argument, so I figured she really was that busy.

I must have written her thirty letters that summer, but I didn't know where to send them. I knew what town she lived in, but I didn't know her address, so I just filed them away in a folder along with pictures of her, letters she had written me, and the phone bills from our numerous conversations. I even had an article that she had written for the school paper. I couldn't figure out what I had done wrong. Had I pushed too hard? I was in love with her and had told her so, but was that a mistake? Had I said something in a drunken blackout that offended her? I had no idea, and was left to wonder and lament alone for the whole summer.

Monique

I had been depressed for years, but I didn't realize it because I was stifling my emotions with liquor. When I realized that Kim would not even be my friend though, my depression came to the forefront. Kim had helped me to get over Myrna, but who was going to help me get over her? Coach Citro entrusted me with the Varsity team that summer, as I was becoming a very capable and knowledgeable coach. I coached their games and worked with them every morning but I found myself yelling more and more, releasing my frustrations on the team. We were winning games, but I was a perfectionist and was never satisfied. I was their buddy off the court, but on the court I was becoming a tyrant.

After one game I lost it. We were playing a game, and once we had the win secured I looked to get some of my weaker players some game time but one girl, a senior, declined to play. She was disappointed that she hadn't played to that point, and didn't want to go in. I was already aggravated from coaching an intense game, and could not deal with an ungrateful player, so I snapped. I sat down and didn't say another word for the rest of the game. After we shook hands I took them into the hallway and berated all of them. They had all done things that were spoiled and selfish over the summer and I made it my business to point out each and every one. I had completely lost it and was even letting the f-word go. I ended my rant in tears and walked away from them without a huddle.

Zakiyyah coached the B team that summer and they were playing right after us, so once I composed myself in the bathroom, I sat in the bleachers by myself and watched them play. I usually did some supplemental coaching when I watched them play, but on this day I just sat in silence. I did not want to be bothered and hoped that was evident in my facial expression, but I got a pleasant surprise. My childhood friend, Monique, had taken custody of her sixteen year old sister Tina, who was playing on the B team. I had seen her once in passing during the regular season, but aside from that I hadn't seen her since we were kids. She noticed that I looked sad and we spoke briefly, but I didn't want to elaborate in the gym so she invited me to her house.

As it turned out she lived right around the corner from me, so I bought a pint of rum and went to her house. That night we sat on her porch and talked until the sun came up. I hadn't spoken to her in over ten years, but that night it felt like we never missed a beat. For the next month, that was how things went. I would coach and work in the day time, and then sit on the porch and drink with her all night. I told her about Myrna and Kim, and she talked to me about her relationships. She had two children and custody of her sister, and they all lived together with her boyfriend. I began hanging there on the weekends and she even let me drive her car around.

Things went on like this for about a month, and I began to feel an attraction to Monique. I got the impression that she was attracted to me as well, but I wasn't sure. She had made mention of having previous attractions to females, but that didn't mean that she liked me. I had again become close to someone that I could talk to endlessly, but was I supposed to act on my feelings? I decided to keep to myself for a while and see what happened.

All summer I had been planning a camping trip, and I scheduled it to take place following the championship game. I collected money from everyone and made all the arrangements for a campsite in the Pocono's. Nyerere had come to visit and came on the trip with us, but we hit a snag. For some reason the playoff schedule was pushed back and the championship game fell right in the middle of our trip. Aside from my needing to be there to coach I had four or five players with me, so the day of the game all eleven of us piled up in the van and made the two hour trip back.

We battled against Paterson Eastside and their star, Essence Carson, for all four quarters. I don't remember what the problem was but Monica and Denise began yelling at each other in the middle of the court, and I had to call a timeout to calm them down. I told the rest of the team to get a drink as I walked onto the court to meet them. Through clenched teeth I told them that if they let their relationship cost the team that game they would pay for it, and they knew I meant it.

They composed themselves, and at the end of the game we were down by three with nine seconds to go. I called a time out and drew up a play for Denise to shoot a three. They ran the play perfectly, and against most teams it would have worked, but this wasn't most teams. Carson fought over the screens and came seemingly from nowhere to just tip the shot. It almost went in anyway, but instead bounced off of the back rim as the buzzer sounded. Carson clobbered Denise in the aftermath, but the official called no foul and the game was over. I was a little bit down but we had played well and battled, so I gave my post-game speech and dismissed the team for the summer.

We did some minor running around before leaving for the campground again, and one of those stops was at my house. After the game Monique handed me a letter and after reading it I asked her to meet me there. In the letter she had expressed her feelings for me and that she wanted to explore them. I was overjoyed, but I had the whole camping trip waiting in the van, so I briefly confirmed that my feelings were mutual and told her I would call her when we were settled in at the campsite.

We spoke for over an hour on both nights and decided to see where our feelings led us. We had to be careful though, because she had a boyfriend and a family. After about a week or so we told Tina who was okay with it, so everything seemed good. We didn't get a whole lot of time alone, but we enjoyed any time that we were together. I had plans to go to the Bahamas with Jimmy, Khalea, Ranita, and Jamal, but Khalea backed out at the last minute. My father told me I could invite anyone, but none of my friends were available. I knew that if I took Monica I would never hear the end of it from Denise, so I ended up taking Tina. She was thrilled and we had the time of our lives.

Another Accident

While we were down there I was approached by a flaming gay man who had assumed from my clothing that I was gay as well. After I confirmed his suspicion, he invited me to a gay club on the island. He gave me the directions and I told him I would see him there. I was so excited as I got dressed because I'd never been to a club before, and I was curious. As I gelled my hair back into a pony tail, I contemplated leaving my helmet in the room so that I wouldn't mess up my hair. It was only a scooter and I wasn't going far, but I'd been drinking and decided not to take any chances. I left the hotel around ten o'clock, ready for a good time.

When I got close to the club, I made an errant left turn that put me on a dark road. I had misunderstood the man's directions and was now on a road with no street lights. My lone source of light was the headlight on the scooter, and I hadn't realized that I was going the wrong way. I came around a curve at about thirty-five miles per hour and hit a speed bump. There had been no sign or source of warning and I didn't even have time to slow down. I went flying over the handlebars head first and landed about fifteen feet away, but

I rolled another ten feet or so. I was in pain, but even more so I was scared. I was off the main road and injured, so I got up as fast as I could, picked up the bike, and headed back in the direction I had come. As I rode on the scooter I could feel my body throbbing, but I wasn't stopping until I reached the hotel.

When I reached the hotel I got a chance to survey my injuries. I had numerous abrasions on my shoulders and knees, but they were mild. I had split my left elbow wide open though, and it was bleeding profusely. I also had a fairly deep cut on my right palm and my head was pounding. Had I been in the States I definitely would have gone to a hospital, but I was uneasy about doing so in the Bahamas so I decided I would care for myself.

I went to the front desk but they didn't have much, so I bought first aid supplies in the gift shop for some obscene price and made my way up to the room. Jamal, Ranita, and Tina stared at me in shock as I walked in oozing blood. Ranita helped me as I tried to wash off the gravel imbedded in my arm. I cleaned all the cuts with hydrogen peroxide, applied Neosporin, and wrapped them in gauze. I poured myself a glass of rum and crawled into bed, which is where I stayed for the rest of the trip.

When we returned home, I resumed my relationship with Monique, but only for a couple of weeks. Although I wanted to continue on, she was frustrated with her personal life in general. People around town were beginning to gossip about us and our relationship was bringing her more stress than joy. She had also decided to break up with her boyfriend of seven years, so I really didn't have much of an argument. Once again, I found myself heartbroken.

Despair

In August of 2002 I was completely broken. Although I was sad about breaking up with Monique, I was still in mourning over Kim. I was never able to get any closure on the matter and was very confused. I still thought about her daily and longed to see her. I had failed out of school and even coaching was a burden at times. I needed a change, and I needed it bad. There was nothing left for me to screw up in New Jersey. I would miss my girls, but I hadn't been much of a role model lately anyway.

I reached out to Kerri Ann down in Florida, and she invited me to come live with her. Monica took it especially hard, but I told her she could spend the following summer with me. Khalea also had her share of disappointments and was ready for a change. We were going to move to Florida and get a fresh start. Kerri Ann even had a job lined up for me as a bartender in a gay club. I would be in my glory.

Khalea and I were set to move in a few weeks, when I got a phone call from my mother. "Are you still interested in joining the fire department?" she asked. I asked her why and she said that I could write a letter requesting that my status on the list be reinstated, and after careful consideration, I agreed. I wrote the letter and not long after that a police officer was again assigned to perform a background check. I cancelled my plans with Kerri Ann and stopped smoking weed. This was it. I was finally going to do something with my life. I was really about to become a firewoman. It seemed like an unbelievable blessing, but it would also turn out to be a curse.

Chapter 10
My New Career

The process of becoming a firefighter was long and tedious. The written and physical exams and the interview were only the beginning. The background check was extensive in itself. The detective had to interview everyone in my immediate family, I had to supply my school transcripts, I needed three letters of reference, I was fingerprinted, my credit was run, and I had to list every job I ever held.

The next step was a psychological exam. I had to answer over 800 multiple choice questions, some of which were repeated in different forms, and then I did a few worksheets. I left for lunch while the psychiatrist went over my tests and then returned for a one-on-one session with him, and upon reviewing my information he declared me fit for duty. A few weeks later I was scheduled for a full medical exam, including a stress test and a drug test. I passed that part as well and was all set to join the department.

During this process I had a lot of free time. It was fall and school was back in, so maybe Kim would have time for me now. Her cell phone was disconnected so I looked up her soccer schedule online and drove out to a home game. I brought Dutchess with me because Kim had been crazy about her, but I had to watch the game from a distance so that she wouldn't annoy people. After the game I walked towards the bench and let Dutchess go. I knew she was harmless and I thought she'd run up to Kim who would be so happy to see us, but it didn't quite go like that. When Kim turned around she gave me a nervous half-smile and began to pack up her things. I only spoke to her for a moment and she rushed off. I was dumbfounded.

All I had to do now was wait to be sworn-in. There was no telling when that would be, so I went to Atlanta for a week. My cousin Jewel was pregnant with her fourth child, but her husband Chris was being sent out of the state by his job for promotional training. Since I wasn't doing anything and always enjoyed Jewel's company, I went down to help her with the kids and to be there in case she went into labor. In the daytime I read and watched television, and in the evenings I hung out with Jewel and the kids, and even picked up a couple of recipes from her. Chris came home after two days because he was going crazy with worry, so for the rest of the week we laughed, talked, and drank heavily. While I can't say I was with him shot for shot, I was close, and he outweighed me by at least a hundred pounds.

While I was down there tragedy dropped in on my life, once again. Although Monique and I had broken up we were still friends, and I spoke to her everyday that I was down there. Early on in my trip, she informed me that a guy we had grown up with had been shot and killed. "Butter," as he was called, was trying to ease a tense situation between an arguing couple that was becoming dangerous, and the man pulled out a gun and shot him. In the blink of an eye his life was wiped out, because he had tried to help someone he didn't even know.

Training

I was sworn in on Friday, October 25th, 2002 in the town council chambers of the Municipal Building. It was a small affair but was fairly well attended. My parents came as well as a few other family members and friends. Monique and Maleka came, some members of the fire department, Chief Sterling, and my little league baseball coach who was now a councilman. After the swearing-in I went to human resources to fill out some paperwork, and then the deputy chief took me to the uniform store in Jersey City to be fitted for my gear. I would spend the next six weeks in training, four in Firefighter I and two in Firefighter II. I was given the keys to one of the department SUV's for transportation and instructed to be at the fire academy by eight o'clock sharp Monday morning.

On the following Monday I woke up at six o'clock, showered, and got dressed. I took Dutchess outside and fed her, and then I drove Jimmy's van up to the fire headquarters where I switched to the SUV. It took me about thirty minutes to get to the fire academy without traffic, but I left by seven just to be safe. Since I did not have any equipment yet I was loaned the back-up set of one of the other two females in the department. I was also issued a helmet, a mask, an air pack, and a spare air bottle.

There were about thirty people in my class, and I was the only female. About half of them were on a task force from Puerto Rico, and did not speak much English. The other guys were from an assortment of townships, mostly volunteer departments. We usually met from eight until around twelve or so, broke for an hour for lunch, and then resumed with an afternoon session until four. Although the guys were nice, I didn't really feel comfortable with them, so I ate lunch by myself. Khalea had a Nextel in Reggie's name but it got to be too expensive, so she gave it to me and I took over the payments. The incoming calls were free, so I'd grab some Chinese food or pizza, call Monique, and then she would call me back and keep me company for lunch.

I was given a seven hundred page book entitled *Essentials* about the basics of firefighting and a syllabus. Every night I was assigned a chapter or more to read and be prepared to discuss in the next class. I learned about the chemistry of fire, ventilation, water pressures, collapse hazards, building construction, and a host of other things. I had no idea there was so much to firefighting.

The first two weeks we did mostly classroom work, but we did some practical exercises also. We were taught everything from scratch, starting with how to properly put all of our gear on. We had to negotiate a pitch black maze in full gear so that we would understand how to get around in a room blackened by fire. We learned how to hook up hydrants, raise ladders, and tie knots. We learned how to perform a victim search and then practiced with a cold smoke machine. We also learned how to cut open a roof, force a door open, and the different modes of attacking a fire.

We didn't actually see fire until the last three days of Firefighter I. We were separated into teams and given different assignments, such as water supply, attack hose line, search and rescue, and back-up hose line. They had a few different buildings made of concrete that had numerous racks for hay, which they set on fire. They also put dummies in hidden places for us to find. We ran a number of scenarios, rotating assignments and buildings. The instructors were in the buildings with us in full gear, watching us with thermal imaging cameras. After every scenario we were critiqued on our mistakes.

To pass the course we could not miss one class, we had to pass three written exams and three practicals, plus we had to take the state exam and pass a final physical test. I did well on all of my tests and quizzes. I passed the practicals and although I wasn't totally satisfied with my performances, my instructors assured me that I had done fine. The last day of Firefighter I we took the written state exam, and then the final physical. In full gear we had to drag a length of three inch hose to a hydrant and hook it up, climb to the top of a ground ladder and back down, drag a hand line into the building, and drag a one hundred and fifty pound dummy fifty feet in under six minutes, and if we could not do it we failed the course.

The test was rigorous in itself, and I was already at an obvious disadvantage due to my size and strength, but to make matters worse I had come down with Sinusitis. When I dragged the dummy over the finish line I collapsed in exhaustion and laid there for a few seconds. The instructor informed me that I had made the time and a wave of relief came over me. I had passed the course. That afternoon they were going to have us practice a basement fire, but seeing my condition the instructors sent me home to rest.

If you look for them, you will find many times in your life where it seems things have been aligned just for you, by a supernatural force. Whether you believe in God or not, most will admit that some things are a little too coincidental to be a coincidence. I have had it happen numerous times in my life, and I choose to call that force God. One such example of this occurred at the end of Firefighter I. Typically the fire academy ran the two courses right after one another, but the week following my course was Thanksgiving, so Firefighter II was to take place after a week off.

As I mentioned, we could not miss one class, and my sickness on that last day was only in the beginning stages. That weekend I got much worse, and was still feeling awful on Monday. I was assigned to ride a rig from eight to four for the three days preceding Thanksgiving since I wasn't in school, but I was not to enter any buildings until they had been checked out already. Had I been required to perform the physical activities required of us in the academy I would not have fared well, but since I had a week off I was able to recover before returning for the second course.

Since I started at the academy I didn't have much time for myself. When I got out of school I would race home to switch vehicles and get to Glenfield by five, where I was running preseason workouts four days a week from five to seven. After that I'd go buy a pint of dark rum, grab some dinner, and go home to drink and go to sleep. I spent all of Thanksgiving weekend in the gym for tryouts and Sunday evening prepared to begin my final two weeks of training.

Firefighter II was a lot more fun than Firefighter I. We were outside everyday and learned about the secondary duties we had as firefighters. We learned how to extricate people from car accidents and remove victims from confined spaces. My last day in the fire academy was December 13th, and when I returned to headquarters I was given a letter with my assignment. My group happened to be working that day, so my first day of work would be the seventeenth.

Starting Work

At that time there were four fire houses. Headquarters was centrally located in town, was in the same building as the police station, and housed the battalion chief and truck one. Station one was also centrally located and housed engine one. Engine three was in the south end of town and in Upper Montclair there was a dual company that housed engine two and truck two. The engine companies primarily handled fire suppression and carried a lot of different hoses. The trucks had hoses as well, but the responsibilities of their companies were to force entry, perform search and rescue, and ventilate. The major difference in the vehicles is that trucks have aerial ladders, but the roles are completely different.

It is standard practice for most paid departments in NJ to carry at least three people on each rig at all times. Although the letter I received had assigned me to engine three, I was used as a floater depending on where I was needed based on vacation and sick time taken by other members. Sometimes I moved to numerous houses in the same shift when there were guys that needed to take a couple of hours off. I had been told to report to engine one for my first tour, but when I got there the battalion chief had left word for me to go to engine three.

Our schedule is to work a twenty-four hour shift, and then we are off for seventy-two hours, which basically means we work once every four days. My first night in the firehouse I barely slept. I was so worried that I would sleep through an alarm. I was very apprehensive about making mistakes. The local newspaper had made a big deal about me being the first African-American female firefighter in Montclair, and I felt a lot of pressure. I was especially nervous around the battalion chief.

I had known a number of firefighters before coming on, just from growing up in town. Many of them either knew me or someone in my family. I had been warned that my battalion chief was a jerk by a number of people, but I decided to form my own opinion. He is a very smart man and taught me a great deal about the job, but I didn't quite trust him. Just as easily as he could make you feel confident about your knowledge and abilities, he could make you feel stupid and incapable. I didn't have any real problems with him in my first year. There were things he could have done to make my life a little easier, like letting me know where I was going the night before work instead of when I showed up at the wrong station, but I figured that was just his way of making me pay my dues in my probationary year.

There were other little things that he did as well. He was, as I mentioned, very smart and well aware of what he could get away with. For instance, following a heavy snow every crew usually spends at least an hour looking for buried hydrants. When they find one they jump out of the rig and dig it out so that it is accessible in the event of a fire. It took over a year for me to realize that entire crews usually did it, because that first winter it seemed as if it was a task specifically reserved for me. He had me grab a shovel and drive around alone digging them out. It was well within his rights as the boss, but unnecessary just the same.

Shea

In February of 2003, Glenn's grandmother passed away. I had never met her, but I was off the day of the funeral and decided to go as a show of support. When I came out of the funeral home I saw an unexpectedly familiar face. It was that of a girl named Shea who I had trained with over fifteen years ago at NJKA. I had run into her at a town festival a few years back, but besides that I hadn't seen her since we were kids. I walked up to her and we exchanged pleasantries. I have always been leery about eating food cooked by people I don't know so I skipped the repast, but asked my mother to give her my phone number so that we could keep in touch. They exchanged numbers but we didn't speak right away.

I was in the habit of throwing hotel parties for my players as rewards for hard work or good grades. I had scheduled one near the end of the season and when I was getting ready Shea called. She asked what I was doing for the night and I invited her to come to the hotel party. I went to pick her up in the van which was pretty much my car for the time being, then we rounded up the girls and made our way to the hotel. While we were talking, she mentioned the name of a gay club in Newark and I instantly became more interested in the conversation.

We began dating for the next month. Whenever I wasn't working I would come to visit with her and her two year-old daughter. We loved to go out to eat, but more often than not we ended up watching television in her mother's apartment. Shea lived down south and was in the Air Force, but was on leave and visiting her mother. I liked her, but I was crazy about her daughter. She was standoffish at first, but once I gave her a stuffed animal she was all mine. Although I came to visit Shea, I spent most of the time engrossed with her daughter. I would read to her and play with her for hours. Eventually her leave ended and she returned home, soon after which we lost touch.

My First Fire

I had been working for three months and hadn't gotten a fire yet. I was beginning to think we didn't get them in Montclair. I had initially been jumpy every time the radio started beeping, but I now assumed that every call was a false alarm until March 15th, 2003. It was a particularly busy Saturday afternoon, and it seemed like the radio didn't stop all day. I was on engine one which was dispatched on every report of an alarm activation. By early afternoon we had already answered around fifteen false alarms, and I had no reason to believe the next one would be any different.

When the tones came over the radio I began to make my way to the engine to put on my gear. Then I heard the dispatcher say the address and that there was a report of a working fire. Immediately my adrenaline began to kick in. I started putting on my gear faster and turned on my air tank as soon as I climbed in. This was it. I was going to my first fire, and it was right up the street. It was actually on the same street as station one, so I knew that we were going to get there first and I was going to be on the nozzle.

When we pulled up there was smoke pouring out of a third floor window. I was with a guy named Dave, and when we stepped off of the engine he turned to me and said, "Stay right here. Let me see what we have!" Seconds later he emerged from the building and said, "Grab the 200!" By the time I climbed up, grabbed the nozzle and some of the 200-foot hose, and stepped back down, he was standing right next to me. He grabbed the nozzle and I began following him in.

By that time the battalion chief had arrived and assumed command of the scene. He yelled to me, "Let's go, Naima. Grab some hose and get in there!" We pulled the line up an exterior staircase and into the house. As we got to the second floor landing the smoke was getting heavy. Dave turned to me and said, "Okay, let's mask up here!" We squatted down and put our masks on. When we were both ready he handed me the nozzle and said, "Okay, here we go! Stay low and just listen to me!" We went into the fire room and got the fire under control in a matter of minutes. It was a mild fire as they go, and we were able to keep it contained to the room it started in.

When we came out of the house I had such an incredible feeling of accomplishment. Although it had taken a few months, I finally got the chance to show what I could do. I knew that I hadn't done anything particularly special, but I hadn't messed up either and that was a relief by itself. Although it amounted to less than ten minutes of labor intensive work, I was exhausted. After we picked up all the hose and reloaded it on the engine I remember thinking to myself *I hope we get to go home for the rest of the night*, but it was not to be. After you fight a fire you go back to the firehouse and finish out your shift, so that's what I did.

Slummin'

At this time Rachel had moved out of her mother's house and into an apartment in East Orange with Monique's younger sister Alnissa, and another childhood friend named Mariah. Alnissa's twin sister Inez lived upstairs in the building with her boyfriend "Thud" and their son. I had temporarily lost touch with Rachel when I was in the fire academy, but we reconnected right before her birthday which was in April.

I had known Mariah for years because she was friends with Amina, but this was the first time I had ever realized how pretty she was. I started coming over every day and we would all drink together. Before long Mariah and I were dating, even though she had a boyfriend. A few weeks later I picked Mariah up from work and brought her home. We didn't have anything in particular planned aside from the usual drinking and playing cards, but we were not prepared for what happened when we got there.

As we walked up to the building Rachel came out in tears and collapsed on the sidewalk. Mariah and I ran up to her to find out what was wrong, and she informed us that Alnissa's boyfriend had been shot and killed. I comforted Rachel for a second and then brought her inside so I could see Alnissa, who was not taking the news well at all. I had only met him once before but he'd seemed nice. I felt terrible for her and stayed by her side as much as possible.

I continued to hang out there all hours of the night getting drunk. I knew that it wasn't a great neighborhood but back then I thought I was invincible. The four of us even traveled to the armpit of Newark one day and hustled up a card game for money with some guys we'd never seen before. We played on the trunk of a car, and Alnissa and I lost forty dollars. In hindsight I realize how stupid I was back then. There were drug addicts and thugs all over the streets where they lived, and I thought nothing of staggering out drunk at three in the morning, stumbling to the van, and driving home. It's amazing I was not robbed at the very least.

Car Trouble

In July my father helped me get a loan through the teacher's union for a car. I got a manual '93 Pontiac Grand Am, and although I didn't know how to drive a stick shift, I learned quickly. The backyard was huge, so I asked Audrey to teach me there. We had become good friends since our playing days at Felician and she agreed. Reggie had taught me when I was at Felician, but I wasn't very comfortable and hadn't done it since then. Once I got the hang of it I was off to the races, but in the first month I ran into two problems.

The van was very low on gas and I didn't have any money, but I'd promised to pick Mariah up from her job at the mall. I took the Pontiac, although it was unregistered and uninsured. I had plates on it though, so I figured I could get away with it, but I was drunk and therefore making stupid decisions. I came flying down a stretch of road near the mall at seventy-five miles per hour, well over the posted limit of forty, and got pulled over. The officer had the car towed, and I probably should have gone to jail, but I mentioned that I was a firefighter. He took me to pick Mariah up and then drove us home although we were in another town. Mariah was pissed and was walking home when we saw her, and not long after that we stopped seeing each other.

I had also been talking to a girl in South Carolina at the time and I had vacation time coming up around my birthday. I decided to drive down south by myself and planned on visiting a number of people, but it was not to be. I was about an hour from her house when I got into an accident, but this one wasn't my fault. As I exited route ninety-five south to get onto route twenty, there was construction and traffic had come to a standstill. I was looking down at my cell phone when I heard the loud sound of tires screeching and I looked back up just in time to see a pick-up truck barreling down the ramp. I barely had time to brace myself before he pushed my rear fender right through the backseat, totaling the car less than two weeks after I got it on the road. I sustained whiplash and was taken to the hospital. To make matters worse, the girl I was visiting said she wasn't coming to get me, so my brother had to drive four hours from Atlanta to come and pick me up, and I never spoke to her again.

Twin Killing

A few weeks after the mall incident Mariah and I stopped dating and I stopped hanging out over there. That summer was no different than any other. I spent it coaching, working at the pool, and drinking. I began throwing cookouts in the backyard and my house became a popular place for many people. Although the basement was dirty and poorly lit, the pool table was down there so I opened the bilko doors and we would shoot pool. I missed hanging out with Mariah a lot, but what was new? As usual I'd thrown myself into someone searching for acceptance, and once again I was left heartbroken.

I have come to realize that I am truly a child of destiny, and when I look over my life I can see numerous times where God removed me from danger without my even knowing it. The summer had passed rather uneventfully and Kelli and I were in the pharmacy on August 21st when her cell phone rang. Seconds later I heard her exclaim, "What!" and instantly I felt my heart drop. I knew what that expression was for. I walked over to her and stood there anxiously while she finished her conversation. When she hung up she looked at me in shock and muttered, "Thud got shot last night. He's dead." Damn. She didn't have much information, and I asked her to drop me off at Monique's house.

When the details started to come to light the story was one of tragedy, but Flynn "Thud" Myers had died a hero. Apparently there had been an argument outside of their building earlier in the day, involving a guy named "Lucky." He left the area but vowed that he'd be back. Later on that night a lot of people, Thud included, were outside the buildings enjoying the hot August night when shots rang out from a passing vehicle. There was a spray of bullets from a sawed-off shotgun and he dove to protect a little girl, but took a bullet himself. He saved that little girl, but a four year-old girl was also hit and killed, and four months after her twin sister buried her boyfriend, Inez did the same.

The day of Thud's funeral they had to shut down the entire block. Mourners flowed out of the church and into the street. People solemnly waited their turn to view his body and sign the nine-foot canvas that had been erected in the church vestibule. Many attendees took the opportunity to comment on his life during the service; so many in fact, that eventually the line had to be severed. He was truly honored as a hero. I was very sad that day, but not just because of Thud's death. I felt guilty and pressured, because it seemed that I had once again averted death. If Mariah and I hadn't stopped dating a few weeks prior, I would have been out there that night. Why did God keep sparing me?

The Fire Department

Things at work were going as well as could be expected. I had been in a couple of fires and done well. I was beginning to feel a little more comfortable around the guys, but I was still terribly afraid of making mistakes, and I knew that I didn't really fit in. I was also afraid of saying something stupid so I didn't usually talk much, but I did laugh a great deal. I grew up in the barber shop and knew how funny guys could be, but this was even better than I had imagined. There were tons of funny guys on the job, but I specifically enjoyed being at station two. I found the truck crew to be absolutely hilarious. Aside from their jokes in general conversation, they made firehouse life fun with various pranks and juvenile antics.

I was coming to the end of my probationary year, and was subject to evaluation by each of the six officers in my group. One by one they went over my evaluations with me and critiqued my performance. Overall I got good remarks, but the recurring theme was that I did not exhibit enough initiative. I tried to work on it, but I didn't know what to work on. I guess I was supposed to be more inquisitive about the rigs and the equipment, but I honestly just wasn't that interested. I knew I had a lot to learn, but I wasn't in any particular rush.

I was given my dress uniform and sworn-in at a town council meeting. My first swearing-in was a small ceremony in the daytime, but this was the real deal. The council chambers were overflowing with supporters. I asked my grandmother, who was eighty-seven, to hold the Bible for me and she agreed. I had made it through my first year and was now officially a firefighter. Typically the person being sworn-in or promoted throws a party at a bar following the ceremony, but I didn't have much money and my group was working. I'd worked in the daytime, but my battalion chief gave me the night off. It was the only nice thing he ever did for me.

My mother bought me a cake and everyone gathered in the conference room to congratulate me. Between my family, friends, co-workers, and other well-wishes there were about fifty people there. Somehow I had become a minor local celebrity. I was featured in the African-American Heritage Day Parade and another article was written in the local paper following the second swearing in. I began to dread going to the supermarket because I was always bombarded with questions about the job or someone in my family. The community I loved as a child had become too small for me, but I couldn't get out for years because of my drinking.

That night I went out with Khalea, Rachel, and Tiffany to celebrate. Although my father tried to keep me from Tiffany and Monique in childhood, I'd been able to resume my friendships with them both as an adult. The next morning my phone rang around nine o'clock. It was Dave from work, the same guy I got my first fire with. Dave had always been especially nice to me and went out of his way to make me feel comfortable. I answered the phone groggily and he asked me what I'd been drinking the night before. I told him Bacardi Gold and he said he'd be right over. He came with a fifth of rum and a twelve-pack of beer. I cooked him breakfast and we sat in the kitchen for hours drinking and laughing.

At the end of the last chapter I mentioned that coming onto the fire department was a blessing and a curse, but I never elaborated. Actually it's quite simple. It was a blessing for many obvious reasons. For starters, it saved my life. I was totally lost before joining and had no idea what direction I was heading in. There is no doubt in my mind that had I gone to Florida I'd be dead right now. I would've made a number of poor decisions based on drunken thinking, and one of them would've killed me. Secondly, it wasn't just a job, it was a career, and I would be able to retire at the age of forty-seven with sixty-five percent of my salary and full benefits. Thirdly, although I started pretty low on the pay scale, the top salary was quite generous and I'd never have to set foot in a classroom again.

It was also a curse in many ways. My depression was constantly deepening, and it manifested itself in excessive drinking. Alcohol is a depressant though, and the more I tried to drown my sorrows, the more sorrow I felt. I was caught in a vicious cycle. The discomfort I felt at work surely added to my growing depression, but that was not the primary issue that working for the fire department created. As my drinking progressed, everything else paled in importance. Because of my schedule I had a great deal of free time on my hands. Having no real responsibilities, I was often times at the liquor store promptly at nine every morning and I would drink the day away. The only time I didn't drink in the daytime was basketball season. The fire department gave me the time and the money to become a complete lush.

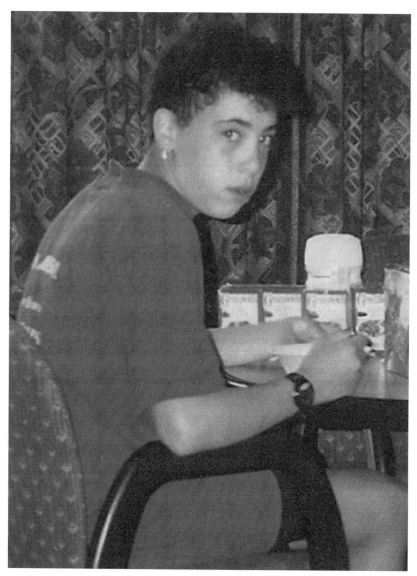

My hair cut the summer following 8th grade.

One of many self-sustained childhood black-eyes.

Me at the training academy in November, 2002.

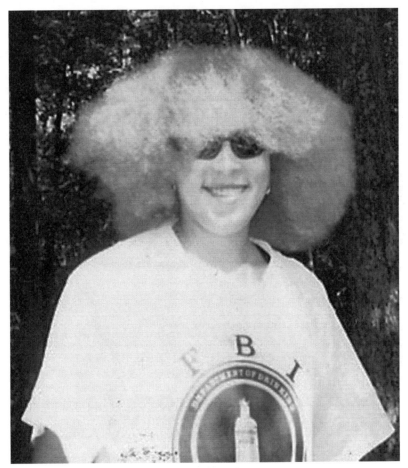

No that wasn't a wig.

17 years old

5th grade

Summer of 2007, 105-pounds

My mother, myself, and Father Nickas the day I became a firefighter.

121

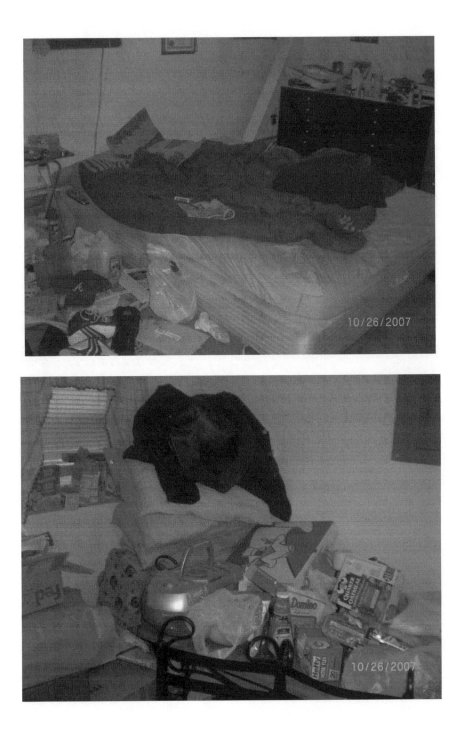

Chapter 11
True Love

Chasing Love

For the next year I was completely out of control. I was always hung-over at work, and sometimes I was still drunk. I was full blown in my sexuality and just about everyone knew I was gay, although I still hadn't told my parents. I didn't think it was any of their concern. I didn't pay any rent or car insurance, so I had the money to constantly take different girls out and drink daily. I'd had very few relationships to that point, but when I joined the fire department it seemed like girls were coming from all directions. My father stayed out of my affairs so I had a different girl in my bed every night.

During that time I did become involved with one girl that meant a lot to me. My cousin Christine was a student at Spelman and I asked her to hook me up with someone. Eventually she came up with the phone number of a girl named Jade. Jade was a senior and special in many ways. She was very intelligent, easy to talk to, and had a vibrant spirit. The first night I called her we talked for hours. The next day we spent a good percentage of the day on the phone and I felt an instantaneous connection to her, as if I'd known her for years. After practice I called her numerous times but got no answer. I did not hear from her until the next day, from a hospital bed. She was epileptic and subject to violent seizures. That Monday she'd had over twenty seizures which ultimately amounted to a stroke.

I felt like I couldn't breathe and wanted to see her immediately. I arranged to take the next day off and armed with *The Diary of Alicia Keys* to keep me company, I jumped on a bus to Atlanta. Christine met me downtown and we went to her room at Spelman. She didn't have a car and Jade was partially paralyzed, so I spent the night with her. The next day Jade made arrangements for me to get a ride to her apartment and we met for the first time. Even as she lay on the sofa ill, she was beautiful. I could only stay for two days, but seeing her was worth every second of the sixteen hour bus ride.

I returned home and for the next month we continued to be in constant contact. We spoke for hours a day on the phone, and when we killed the batteries we emailed each other. I thought for sure that I was in love. It didn't matter to me that she was in Atlanta. I believed that God had brought us together. I was totally absorbed in her spirit and felt that we could make it work. Maybe she could come to graduate school in New York or New Jersey. Then everything changed.

I called one night and Jade was clearly drunk. I was shocked because she was not a drinker, but on this night she was ripped. Then her best friend got on the phone and broke some horrible news to me. Jade had been to the doctor earlier that day, and was diagnosed with brain cancer. It was deemed to be inoperable, and she was given six months to live. Her best friend's next words to me were, "You need to get down here ASAP," and that's exactly what I did.

I called my battalion chief and requested the next two shifts off, which he was able to grant me. I bought a bus ticket and was on my way to Atlanta, but things didn't quite go as planned. I had planned on surprising Jade, expecting to bring her some cheer. I didn't tell her I was coming until I got to town. When I got to her house she was less than enthusiastic about my arrival, and spent the majority of the next two days in her room alone, while I was left to camp out in the living room.

Eventually she summoned me into her room and we had a talk. She felt it was disrespectful for me to come down unannounced, and didn't particularly want me there. Once again I was crushed. I had planned to stay with her for over a week, but that didn't seem to be ideal. Jay and Khalea were sharing an apartment about half an hour away, so I asked them to come and pick me up. Jade had stated that maybe I could come back in a few days, but she didn't answer the phone for the rest of my trip.

Once again I had extended myself and opened my heart, and yet again I was left heartbroken. I was beginning to get frustrated with the whole idea of finding love. I certainly had no idea where to begin searching. I was beating myself up for intruding on her privacy and felt like a fool. Eventually we spoke again and she apologized. She was overrun with fear and emotion and could not process my coming there. She was terrified of her impending death and had treated me poorly, for which she was sorry. I forgave her, she beat the cancer, and today we are close friends, but back then I was shattered.

My self-esteem was diminished every time I tried my hardest to make a relationship work and failed. I couldn't win. I became obsessed with companionship and tried to create love, which I now realize is impossible. No matter how nice or generous I was, I constantly came up short. I wasn't denied by all girls though, just the ones that had something to offer. Every girl I dated that had a high school education or better managed to push me away, but the ghetto girls loved me and eventually I began to seek them out.

Meeting My Son

Since I couldn't seem to find a girlfriend of decent caliber, I started scraping the bottom of the barrel. I just wanted someone in bed with me at night, and after a while it didn't matter who it was. Although I always had a bedmate, I never had a partner; someone in whom I could confide. I'd had that with Myrna, but I was sharing her with someone else, which was also the story with Kim and Monique. I was beginning to believe that I had missed my shot at true love when I lost Kim, and therefore had no reason to hold high standards. Ultimately I just wanted to be accepted, regardless of where that acceptance came from. That pattern led me into a relationship that would eventually bring me joy, love, anguish, and heartache in staggering quantities.

In the summer of 2004 I began hanging out with a former high school teammate. She knew I was on the prowl and told me she had a girl for me. Her name was Sharon and she was best friends with the girl my teammate was dating, Tanya. She was visiting with her best friend so we went to go see them. When she came out she was carrying an adorable little boy on her hip. He was her fourteen month-old son and his name was Sha-Quaan. I asked him to give me five but he turned away.

She was a sweet, cute girl and we hit it off right away. I gave her a ride home and sat on the porch with her for about fifteen minutes. My teammate and I returned to my house for a while, and then decided to see if we could get the girls to come over. She made the call, and Sharon was able to get someone to baby-sit her son. We went to get them and brought them back to my house. I could tell from that night that she was no different than any of the other girls I'd been dating, but I had no idea that love was about to knock me on my ass.

Over the course of the next month, Sharon and I spent a great deal of time together. Although she had never graduated from high school, she seemed very intelligent to me. Her lack of a diploma had nothing to do with ability. She and Tanya had been expelled for numerous fights, but she showed me a book of poems she had written and I immediately recognized her talent. I wanted to help her realize her dreams and achieve her potential, so I started tutoring her from a GED prep book she had.

In the course of that month I'd also grown quite attached to her son. It only took one visit after that first meeting for him to take to me as well. He was born premature and consequently was slightly behind developmentally, so at fourteen months he still was not walking. I took his hands and led him around step by step. I made a point of doing that with him every day and within two weeks he was walking. As a matter of fact, he took his first steps walking to me.

I started wanting to see him just as much as her, and eventually more so. They began spending more time at my house than at hers, even staying there when I was at work. Sharon was one of four children, but was the only girl and constantly butted heads with her mother. From what I could tell, it seemed that her mother treated her particularly unfairly without any real reason. I felt sorry for her and wanted to protect her, so sometimes she'd be at my house for weeks.

Eventually I began to lose interest in her. She was cute and full of potential, but she wasn't Kim. We didn't have much to talk about because we didn't have much in common. I said that love knocked me on my ass, but it wasn't her. Although I felt really bad about her situation at home, we didn't have much of a relationship and I just wanted to be friends. I didn't want to lose Sha-Quaan or hurt her feelings though, and when I told her how I felt she began to cry, so I reneged. They continued staying with me and her feelings for me continued to grow. She told me that she was in love with me and I felt guilty because I didn't feel the same way. I wanted to be in love; I just wasn't. I was however, in love with Sha-Quaan.

I started spending more time with him than I did with her. I quit smoking because I was around him so much, and I didn't even mean to. I became so consumed with him that smoking just didn't cross my mind. Sharon and I drank every night and more often than not she didn't feel like taking him to nursery school in the morning, so I would get him dressed and take him by myself. After a few weeks my name was on the list to pick him up and I went more than she did. When I picked him up from school, sometimes I would take him to basketball practice and games with me.

On the way home from basketball I would pick up some take-out and make a stop at the liquor store for the both of us. I got a pint of rum and I usually got her a pint of Alize. Sometimes Sha-Quaan would eat what we had, but I began buying him Gerber meal cups so that he received his proper nutrition. Man, did that boy have an appetite. Although he was fairly slim, I dubbed him "Fat Boy" because he ate like he weighed fifty pounds. He wasn't finished eating until everyone was finished eating. After I put him to sleep I'd usually go out for a while by myself.

As time went on, our bond grew immensely. He cried whenever I walked out of the room, whether I was leaving or just going to the bathroom, but he didn't do that for Sharon. She would joke about it, but a resentment began to grow that would eventually lead to my doom. I promised her that no matter what I would always be there for him, and in turn she promised that she'd never keep him from me. I always regarded my time with him as precious, and he obviously appreciated my attention. We'd watch Nickelodeon together and sing all of the songs. I bought him toys and never minded taking him places with me. Sharon and I were only dating for five or six months, but in that time Sha-Quaan became my son. Not only did he love being with me, he listened to me and saw me as an authority in his life.

He was only two pounds and three ounces at birth, and spent a great deal of time with doctors as a baby. As a result he hated doctors, but he got sick in November so we had to take him. He was cool in the waiting room, but as soon as we walked into the exam room he went berserk. He started crying and clinging to us as we tried to take his clothes off. We were finally able to calm him down a bit, but when the nurse tried to put him on the scale, he started screaming again. He'd had some pretty rough experiences with doctors, so I understood his fear.

When Christmas time came around Sharon couldn't afford to get Sha-Quaan any gifts. I took her to the mall and gave her a hundred dollars to buy presents for him, then we separated so I could find her gift. Although I felt great sympathy for her and wasn't in love with her, I did love her. She had been a good girlfriend and had a hard life, so I wanted to make her feel special. I went to Zales and bought her a four hundred dollar diamond tennis bracelet. I knew she couldn't afford to get me a gift but she cried when I gave it to her, and that was gift enough.

Coaching Woes

My only other concern at that time was the basketball team. The previous year we'd lost in the sectional semi-finals, due largely in part to Monica developing a stomach virus the day of the game. Although she had graduated, I thought we still had very good chances that year. We had a multitude of well spread talent and a wealth of experience. We were starting four seniors and a very talented sophomore. Our only issue that year would be team chemistry, which was great overall, with one major exception.

The season got off to a rocky start with us losing two of our first three games, but we were undeterred. We believed in our team and knew that with a few minor adjustments, we would be very successful. There was one girl in particular that was driving the other players and the coaching staff nuts.

Since we'd graduated our leading scorer in Monica, our method of winning was a well-balanced attack of offensive execution and defensive intensity. This particular girl intended on becoming a big time scorer and consistently forced inappropriate shots and ignored our set offense, which was tearing our team apart. The other players began to resent her and I could see the season, and five years of hard work, slipping down the tubes. When this class graduated we would virtually be starting from scratch, so if we could not win a championship that year all of my year-round efforts would go to waste.

We were playing in a very competitive Christmas tournament and in the second-round game she made a number of particularly ill-advised plays that essentially cost us the game. After the game the other girls were highly upset, and so was I. They came to me crying and I made a terrible, immature decision. Coach had driven his car to the game in order to scout another team, and had Zakiyyah and I ride with the team. I felt horrible for the girls that were being devastated by her actions, and I wanted things to change. I told them that when we got on the bus I would sit in the front and close my ears, so they could air out their concerns.

What started off as a slightly agitated discussion evolved into a full blown shouting match and everyone was ganging up on her. I should never have allowed the unmediated discussion to start, but I definitely should have stopped it when it got out of control. I didn't, and when we got back to the school her father was waiting. He didn't say a word to me. He just asked the bus driver for his name and took his daughter home. She'd called him during the screaming match and left the line open without saying anything so that he could hear what was being said.

I was particularly upset that night, and made my way to the liquor store (as if I needed an excuse). Practice was at seven thirty the next morning, and when I got there I was still drunk. I knew that I was going to have to answer for my actions the previous night. The girl's father was sitting in the gym and I asked him to step into the foyer. I admitted that I had made a poor decision the night before and apologized, but I also wanted to tell him why everyone was so frustrated. His daughter was disrupting the whole team with her play, and I wanted him to understand so that we could get back on track. After speaking with him, I still felt terrible that I had subjected her to that ridicule and wasn't quite sure that anything had gotten accomplished, aside from heightening her already existing belief that no one liked her.

Coach was holding a team meeting in the gym and I asked to speak. He was a little apprehensive since he didn't know what I was going to say, but he hesitantly said yes. Tearfully, I apologized to that player in front of the team, and then forfeited my position as a coach. As I began to walk out Coach jumped up and cornered me. When I was playing for him he was a gym teacher, but over the years he had worked for his Master's degree in counseling. When he tried talking to me I said, "Stop it, Coach. Don't handle me. I'm not one of your students." This was a man for whom I held the utmost reverence, but at that particular moment he was standing between me and the door which made him my enemy. He let me go and told me to sleep it off and call him later on.

I went to his house that night and we had a long talk about the responsibilities of coaching and controlling the occasional temptation to choke a player. Over the years he had become my mentor and taught me many lessons. That night he also expressed his concerns to me about my drinking. He had Amina when she was in middle school and was well aware of our turbulent upbringing. He made mention to me that I might be self-medicating and that I should probably curtail my drinking some. I told him I had it under control and he didn't press the issue, but it would only take a few more weeks for me to reach my breaking point.

Sacrifice for Quanny

A week or so later, death struck in Sharon's family. Her cousin had died suddenly from an untreated infection. Her cousin was only a year or two older than her and she was devastated. The day of the funeral Sha-Quaan woke up with a fever. She wanted to care for him, but she really wanted to pay her respects as well, so I came up with a solution. If she could get picked up by a family member, I would take the baby to the doctor. I had a game that day, and it was at four instead of the usual seven, so I just needed for her to come back before three-thirty.

I took him to the doctor and once again he was fine in the waiting room, but when we went into the exam room he got upset. His chest was sore and it hurt for him to cry, which made him cry more, similar to my predicament after the car accident. I was able to calm him down, and eventually I even got him to laugh. He had never so much as grinned in a doctor's office so I took a picture of him with my phone so that I could show Sharon. I figured that would cheer her up. I got his prescriptions, bought him a vaporizer, and took him back to my house.

It was around one o'clock when we got back, so I gave him his medicine and laid down with him. Sharon called and told me that she was working on a ride, and I told her to take her time. I took a shower while he was sleeping and got dressed for the game. When she got back it was well after four o'clock and I had no chance of making it to the game. Ordinarily I'd have had no problem taking him with me, but he was miserable and that would've been unfair. When I opened the door her first words to me were, "I am so sorry."

She knew what basketball meant to me and she knew I had missed my game because I was caring for her son. I told her not to worry about it and asked her how she was feeling. Since I considered him my son, I felt my sacrifice came with the territory. I showed her the picture of him in the doctor's office and sure enough it cheered her up.

Jerry Citro

To this point I haven't made great mention of Coach Citro or the role he played in my life after high school, largely because I didn't know where to put it. He'd been a constant mentor to me since my playing days, and although I had come to him crying on numerous occasions, I couldn't quite fit those talks into a time frame. At this point I feel it is necessary for me to further elaborate on his remarkable story and why he was able to provide me with so much guidance.

Gerard T. Citro was born to a poor family in Hoboken, NJ. He grew to become a phenomenal basketball player, eventually earning the nickname "Jerry The Gun." He was sixteen when he graduated from high school and decided to spend a year in prep school in Vermont. He was named all-New England and earned a scholarship to the University of New Hampshire. He was very talented, and had aspirations of playing in the NBA, but when he came home for Thanksgiving his freshman year he got into trouble. He was introduced to heroin and alcohol, and as a result was late returning to school.

He had to hitchhike from the airport as he had missed the shuttle, and that's when his life changed forever. He had just passed an on ramp and was hit by a car that was entering the highway. The driver never even saw him and hit him so hard that the impact literally tore the clothes from his body. His leg was shattered and his basketball career was over, forcing him to return home.

When he got home he became very depressed. His entire life had revolved around basketball, and now he was lost. He fell in with a bad crowd and tumbled through years of drug and alcohol abuse. After reaching his breaking point, he went to rehab and began to straighten his life out. He eventually opened his own real estate company and was making more money than he knew what to do with. He had all the material things he'd ever dreamed of, but he felt terribly incomplete.

He closed his business and decided to return to college. His passion had always been children and he wanted to devote his life to them. He enrolled at Montclair State College to study physical education, and at age thirty-nine decided to go out for the basketball team. The coach thought he was crazy and told him that there were a lot of young, talented players coming out that year, and his chances of making the team were very limited. Nevertheless, Citro began to train. He had to wear two braces on his right leg, one of which was considerably cumbersome. He would go to the gym and run sprints by himself.

When tryouts came he gave everything he had. Although he was at a monumental physical disadvantage, his intensity was undeniable. He earned the last spot on the team through sheer determination. He knew that he would never play in a game that was still in the balance, but he took pride in making his teammates work harder. He became the oldest person to ever play collegiate basketball, and was even featured on *Good Morning, America*.

Upon his graduation he taught and coached in Wallington, NJ for a year before taking the position at Montclair High School in 1997. He earned two Master's degrees and became a middle school counselor in town. He is a model of hard work and discipline, and hasn't picked up a drink or a drug in over twenty-one years. He specializes in substance abuse counseling and has helped hundreds of children in his tenure.

The further apart Jimmy and I grew, the closer I got to Coach. At least once a year for the previous five years I'd called him in tears and he would tell me to come see him right away. He walked with me step by step through my depression and became the father I dreamed of. He never told me any lies or half-truths, and I knew that I could count on him much more than I could my own father.

Chapter 12
I Have a Problem

On January 25th, 2005 my relationship with Sharon ended quite dramatically. The day started like usual, with me going to practice. I came home with dinner and liquor, and after putting Quanny to sleep I went out with a former player. It was her twenty-first birthday and I had been promising her for years that I would take her out on this day. When I picked her up I had already drunk the better part of a pint. I took her to a bar and ordered three shots for her, plus one for me. After she downed them I paid the tab and we went to a pool hall. I finished off the pint and was ready to call it a night.

When I got home I was extremely drunk, so I woke Sharon up and started an argument with her for no reason. Realizing that I was drunk she tried to ignore me, but eventually she got fed up and told me to get it together. I exploded. I told her that if she didn't like it she could get out. She made a phone call and gathered her things, but when she went to wake Sha-Quaan I told her she wasn't taking him out in the middle of the night. She told me she wasn't going anywhere without him, got him dressed, and left. I was in a blackout and still don't remember that night. I only know this because she told me.

When I woke up in the morning the only evidence from the night before was her bracelet laying on my nightstand. I'd woken from a deep sleep to the sound of my father's dog barking. I dragged myself out of the bed and went into the other room to see who was outside. When I looked out I saw Coach walking back to his car. I couldn't imagine what he wanted, so I ran downstairs to let him in. He asked me what was going on and I didn't know what he was talking about, so I invited him in. I blacked out almost every time I drank, but I'd never woken up that way. Apparently he had come to my house because I'd left him a message at work that morning saying I wanted to kill myself, but I didn't even remember waking up. I guess I wasn't strong enough to reach out for help, so God interceded.

We sat in my living room and talked for a while, and for the first time in my life I admitted that I had a problem with alcohol. He persuaded me to let him call a guy we trusted in the fire department named Mike, and we went to go see him. After assuring me that it wasn't a big deal, Mike called the head of human resources and I went to go see her. She had me go to the hospital for evaluation and found an inpatient facility for me in Summit, NJ. I got an appointment for the following morning.

The next thing I had to do was figure out how I was going to break it to my girls. Coach offered to do it for me but I wanted to tell them myself. I met him at the gym at three o'clock and he called a team meeting. He sat the girls down and told them I wanted to talk to them. Through pouring tears I told them that I was severely depressed and had been trying to numb myself with alcohol for years. I explained to them that I was very sick and needed to go away for a while to get better. When I finished talking they all came and hugged me, some fighting back tears.

Summit Hospital

The next day I went for evaluation and was assigned to begin intensive outpatient group therapy, but that wasn't what I wanted or felt I needed. No matter what I accomplished in therapy, I knew I would not be able to resist the temptation of the liquor store when I got home. The admissions counselor told me that if I failed a breathalyzer I would be admitted, so the next day I had a few shots before I came in. I was admitted the same day.

When I mentioned in my evaluation that I was gay, the woman told me they had a separate section of the hospital called the "Pride Institute" that was dedicated to GLBT (Gay, Lesbian, Bi-sexual, and Transgendered) individuals. It wasn't mandatory, but was a viable option for people that feared scrutiny from the other patients. The idea was to create a comfortable environment for us suitable for healing. I liked the program and decided that I wanted to be a part of it.

There were seven people in the ward, and we all got along incredibly well. I grew particularly close to three people. The first was a girl named Elaina. She was your typical "poor little rich girl" and she came in for an addiction to heroin. She was a few years younger than me and we hit it off right away. The second was a man named Jon from New York that was there for an addiction to crystal methamphetamine. The third was a man named Mike from Rhode Island who was being treated for an addiction to prescription drugs. Jon and Mike became very close to me in that week, but Elaina was a whole different story.

I was desperate for affection from anywhere I could get it, and for the time being she was the best choice. We began hooking up after lights out. One of us would sneak into the room of the other and we would sleep together. I don't know what was more prevalent, my personal desire to be needed or the state of vulnerability we were both in, but either way I once again allowed myself to be drawn into an unadvisable situation. We became attached and you never saw one of us without the other. It didn't take Mike and Jon long to figure out what was going on, although they waited for us to tell them.

I learned more about myself in that hospital than I had the entire three years in college. I had never taken the time to evaluate my feelings. I blamed my father for a rotten childhood and diverted everything else to my "file cabinet," but I was going to have to do a lot more work to find the source of my disease. Although we got a good amount of free time, we also did a lot of workshops.

We learned about the science of depression, the symptoms of relapse, and the stages of recovery. We also learned about the detriment that denial and resentment could cause personally and to those around us. We began to study the specific types of change that would be necessary for successful recovery, and there were many. Changes would have to be made in our physical, emotional, social, familial, and spiritual climates. We did everything as a group and even had the cafeteria to ourselves. The only time we saw the other patients was at eight o'clock when we'd all get together for a twelve-step meeting.

My experience at Summit was both frustrating and surreal. I cried a number of times during my stay because for the first time in six years I felt my feelings. Numbing my feelings had become automatic for me, but now that was no longer an option. Anytime I became frustrated with the staff I resigned to my room in tears, but on the other side of things something special was happening. Our therapy sessions were very productive because we all liked and trusted each other. We were able to open up fully and be honest with each other. Every night when we returned from our meeting, we were supposed to hold our own discussion. The sessions were only intended to last ten or fifteen minutes, but ours repeatedly lasted over an hour. The only drawback there was that I started smoking cigarettes again.

We were given the option of having a counseling session with a family member over the weekend, and immediately I wanted to talk to Jimmy. As far as I was concerned he was the primary source of my depression. I was well aware that the numerous deaths I'd mourned through and concussions I'd sustained also played a role, but his temper, inconsistency, and constant attacks on my mother, her family, and Glenn were all at the core of my depression and needed to be addressed. Every day I walked by him and grunted a greeting on the way to my room, constantly stifling my hostilities.

He came in and we had a session with one of the therapists. I told him that I felt he was the reason for my depression and proceeded to tell him how and why. Years ago he'd declared that he would not attend any functions for his children to which Glenn was invited, including marriage and/or graduations. That turned out to be the reason he left my basketball banquet early. I tried to express to him my belief that no amount of hatred should ever overpower the love one had for their children, but he didn't see it that way. I specifically brought up the night he beat my mother up when we returned from the fair and, as was his nature, he denied any culpability saying that he'd never hit her. He had tried to grab her arm and inadvertently hit her in the face. I replied, "You gave her a black eye!" I called him an infantile, deluded sociopath and the conference was over.

That weekend Elaina and I got into numerous arguments with the night nurse who suspected we were sleeping together, but couldn't catch us. We became very defiant and decided we were going to do things our way. On Sunday I found out that Jon would be going home the next day. I wanted to do something special for him, so I stayed up all night writing him a poem. The night nurse tried to send me to bed when lights out came, but I told her I wasn't going until I finished writing and that ended up being after the sun rose. I have never acquired a taste for coffee, but I drank five cups that night. It had to be perfect. It had to flow and rhyme, but more importantly it had to express my profound appreciation for him and wishes for his future success.

On Monday morning everything fell to pieces. The two head counselors called me into a meeting and informed me that I would be leaving as well. Their explanation was that I was ready, but I didn't believe that to be the case. I had just been told the previous day that I would be there for a while, but all of a sudden I was ready. I suspected what the real reason was though. I figured the night nurse had told them of her suspicions of me and Elaina and they decided that one of us had to go. I guess they deemed heroin to be the more substantial risk so they decided to let me go although I was far from ready.

I recently found the notebook that I was given while I was there, and upon reviewing it I found the most useful exercise I ever did in any rehab. We were each to write a letter to what we felt our prevailing affliction was. I never believed that alcohol was my problem, only a symptom of the deeper issue which was depression, and I wrote:

Dear Depression,

I have known you for years but I didn't know your face, and now I realize that you don't have one. You are a phantom, like the antithesis of the Holy Ghost. You have been fighting a battle with Him inside of me for more than half of my life, and I have allowed you to reside there, but as of today you are evicted. This battle has raged for years because I allowed myself to be impartial to it. Just as the Holy Ghost brought love, understanding, unconditional trust of others, and empathy, you brought pain, fury, substance abuse, and denial, but no more. I will no longer stand by like a weakling without choosing a side while you ravage my life. I choose God, which is choosing love, hope, and redemption. You are hereby dismissed, by order of myself, and the Almighty, Everlasting, Creator and Father. Jesus Christ will be here shortly to assist you in removing your baggage from my heart, mind, and soul. GET THE HELL OUT! Better yet, go back to hell where you came from.

I found this exercise to be liberating and exhilarating, but I didn't expect the second part. Now we had to write a response, and my honesty frightened me. I wrote what I believed the devil (depression) would have, and realized that I was in for the battle of my life. My inability to realize the very real forces of evil working in my life ultimately doomed my recovery. Here is the response:

Dear Naima,

Catch me if you can. If you think I'm going to make this easy on you, then you really have no clue as to my power. Truth be told, this battle has taken longer than expected, but I'm not going to give up. I'm going to keep throwing s—t your way. If you and your God can beat me and eventually win this war, than I will move on. I cannot be destroyed. I don't need you either, but I fight one soul at a time, so although you may eventually get me out, it's going to be the biggest battle you ever conceived, let alone fought.

I didn't understand its significance back then, but when I finally got myself together, it was only upon acceptance of the constant presence of evil in the world and a steadfast decision to stand against it.

Back to Reality

When Sharon left my house she didn't want to go home so she moved in with her aunt and cousins in Newark. We were through but my commitment to Sha-Quaan remained. On my first night home I went to go pick him up. He was standing next to Sharon as she opened the door. He got so excited when he saw me that he tripped over the threshold of the doorway. He didn't fall though; he just got his feet together and ran to me. I'd missed him so much. I brought him home, gave him dinner, and got him ready for bed. From then on Sharon and I split custody of him. I wanted to be with him all the time and she usually obliged, and before long I was spending more time with him then she was.

Although I left rehab with the intentions of a champion, I fell within three weeks. As much as I wanted to change, I just wasn't ready. I hadn't done enough work yet. I was still living in my father's house, and I hadn't been given nearly enough tools in my week at Summit to deal with my depression. There was a lot more work to be done before I would have the strength and the information I needed to truly get myself together. I only drank in private though. I didn't want anyone to know that I had relapsed.

My return to the basketball team was triumphant. When I walked in the gym I was flooded with hugs. I had written them a poem from Summit and someone typed it up, printed it out, and posted it in the locker room. For as much as the Christmas tournament incident had torn the team apart, they rebounded from it. The day before I went to Summit they beat one of the best teams in the conference and dedicated it to me. They used my struggle and my poem as inspiration and it brought them together. We entered the county semi-finals against the two-time defending State Championship Shabazz Bulldogs with only two losses. We fought a valiant battle but came up five points short, so we refocused our efforts on the state tournament.

◆ ◆ ◆

Before the tournament began I experienced a personal tragedy on many levels. I was out eating with some friends when my phone rang. It was my brother and he was looking for my father. What he said next caught me completely off guard. His relationship with Jimmy was not in one of its finer periods, and in his angst for my father he dropped a ton of bricks on me. "Well, when you see Jimmy tell him Uncle Donald's dead." My jaw dropped. I hung up with Jay and called Nyerere to see how he was doing and find out what happened. I left the restaurant and went to find my father. I couldn't find him so I went home to wait.

My uncle was a political science professor at the University of Mississippi and Nyerere was there pursuing his Master's degree. He didn't live with his father but visited him often. He hadn't heard from him in a while and when he didn't answer the phone he went to check on him. When he entered the house he found his father lying on the floor. He called the paramedics but my uncle had been there for days. He was epileptic and everyone automatically assumed that he'd had a fatal seizure, but it turned out to be a heart attack that claimed his life at the age of fifty-seven.

I waited in my room for my father to come home, and when I heard the door I went down to the living room and sat across from him. I told him that

I needed to talk to him and he turned the television volume down. I didn't really know what to say, but I knew I had to tell him. "Dad, I got a phone call from Nyerere a little while ago." I could see concern come over his face as it was clear that this wasn't a social call. "He went to visit Uncle Donald today and he found him laying on the kitchen floor. It looks like he had a seizure, but he didn't make through this one. He passed away."

He covered his eyes with his hand and exclaimed, "Oh, no." He removed his hand from his face, his eyes welled with tears, and asked, "What happened?" I told him what I knew, which was only the limited amount that Nyerere knew. I sat there paralyzed for about five minutes as he processed what I'd just told him. I felt like I should go over to console him, but I couldn't. I just didn't like him. I stood up awkwardly, told him I'd be upstairs if he needed anything, and went back to my room.

My brother came over a little while later with his girlfriend and my mother. Although I was dealing with very strong emotions towards Jimmy, she had learned to ignore his stupidity in the interest of her own salvation and held no animosity towards him. My brother and his girlfriend came upstairs to get me, but I refused. My feelings for Jimmy were bordering on hatred and I could not bury them, even in a time of mourning.

The wake was not heavily attended and I was beginning to think my uncle should have been buried in New Jersey with his parents and where he had life-long friends, but his funeral was massive. He was honored by present and former students, co-workers, and various community leaders, and the church was packed. There were a number of moving speeches and bittersweet remembrances.

I mentioned that this was a tragedy on many levels for me. The first was obviously that my uncle died so young. The second was the awful state of affairs with my father and me. I count the third tragedy just as considerable. Reverend Doctor Mfanya Donald Tryman was truly a great man but I'd only known him as my Uncle Donald, and didn't realize his greatness until after his death. I spent two weeks in Mississippi in 1996, but besides that I had only seen him sparingly over the years.

From the time I was a child my father made a mockery of him saying that the more degrees a person had, the less common sense they possessed. His younger brother had earned his doctorate at the age of twenty-six, and Jimmy's competitive nature created deep resentments within him, so he tried to make us think he was a moron; but my uncle was far from a moron. He wrote hundreds of articles and papers and was invited to speak on many different panels. In 2002 *The Malcolm X Encyclopedia* was published. He co-authored the 664-page book with a colleague. He was a champion for equal rights and was president of the local NAACP at the time of his death.

Championship Run

Our run through the state tournament was truly momentous. When Jerry Citro took over the team in 1996, it was in shambles. He created a top-flight program and built it from the ground up. For as proud as we were to break the losing streak back then, finishing with a record of fifteen and nine would have been a severe case of underachievement for the 2005 squad. When Coach and I sat on the bus that day five years ago and discussed starting an AAU team, this was our goal. This was our dream and we had devoted thousands of hours of coaching, scouting, mentoring, summer leagues, camps, fundraisers, and sacrifice to realize it. Before our loss to Shabazz we'd rattled off fifteen straight victories. We were clicking on all cylinders and believed that we could win everything.

We beat Hackensack handily in the first round sixty-four to forty-four, and then disposed of North Bergen fifty-nine to forty-four. There was no major celebration as the game ended that day. We were headed to the sectional finals, against our nemesis Paterson Eastside. They'd won the sectional championships the previous three years, but we spanked them earlier in the season sixty-three to forty five. In our 2004 state match-up with them they defeated us on our court in a close game that Monica played less than ten minutes of due to a stomach virus, and it'd left a horrible taste in our mouths. Over the years we had made some remarkable tournament appearances but we could never secure a state title, and now we were playing for the championship.

The game was held in Secaucus as all of the championship games were at neutral sites. There was heavy support there for both teams and the gym was packed. In the first quarter our nerves showed terribly and we allowed Eastside to jump out to an eight-zero lead, forcing Coach to call a timeout. Although we only answered with two points, they didn't score for the rest of the quarter. In the second quarter we regained our footing and outscored them fifteen to twelve, but they headed into the locker room with a twenty to seventeen lead.

In the third quarter we dominated them, at one point leading by as many as ten points, but they managed to cut our lead to three with one minute remaining. We had been in this position so many times in prior years and walked away empty handed, but on this trip we would finally fulfill our destiny. In the final minute we were able to keep them from scoring again, and a basket and two free throws on our end sealed their fate. With seconds remaining and a seven point lead, Coach Citro pulled all the starters out so that they could be recognized by the fans, and we watched as the seconds ticked off the clock.

Three, two, one… "Bzzzzz." The game ended and our fans erupted, flooding the court. There were hugs and smiles all around, and Coach's wife sat in the bleachers crying. She'd been with him since his real estate days, and had watched and supported him for over ten years as he buried himself in his education and coaching, agonizing over each and every loss and determined to reach his goal. I sat on the bench for a while in shock. Aside from Coach Citro, no one had committed the amount of time and energy to the program that I had and the feeling was surreal.

The next day it was back to business as usual. We did not have time to enjoy our success. In the state tournament one loss ends your season, so our next test would be Bayonne in a game that would determine a finalist for the group championship game in Toms River. We traveled to Union for that game and although they gave us a fight, we emerged victorious and were matched up with Absegami for the biggest game any of us had ever been involved with.

For the next two days practice was extremely focused as we prepared for the game. There was no laughing or joking, and you could hear a pin drop as the girls hung on Coach's every word. On the morning of Sunday, March 13th we met at the school at eight to take the two hour trip to south Jersey. Coach chartered a luxury bus and the parents cooked a pancake breakfast for the team. We boarded the bus and settled in for the trip. I was awestruck when we arrived, and I can only imagine how the girls felt. The gym had jumbo-trons at both ends of the court and a huge marquee that hung above center court. It was like a miniature Madison Square Garden, and there were 2,300 people there to see the game. Jimmy even showed up.

Going into the game we were ranked thirteenth in the state, but Absegami was ranked third. The rankings meant nothing to us but made us heavy underdogs. The girls battled with everything they had, and in the end I still believe that game was taken from us by an overzealous referee. Coach taught me years ago to never blame a loss on officials, but in my opinion the game boiled down to two crucial calls. The first came in the second quarter. Denise was called for a foul right in front of our bench and she clearly hadn't touched the girl. It constituted her third foul and she had to spend the rest of the first half on the bench.

The second call involved Denise as well, and created just the swing in momentum that Absegami needed. Midway through the third quarter they were running down the court trailing by nine points. Erin stepped in to take a charge and it seemed like she was standing there for an eternity before being bulldozed by the girl dribbling. Upon the contact she threw up a wild shot that somehow went in. When the whistle blew we jumped off the bench in anticipation of an offensive foul call, and were dismayed to see the referee call the foul on us and declare that the basket counted.

Denise was by far the most emotional player I've ever coached, and her emotions erupted over the call. She didn't say anything, but fell on the floor and smacked it in frustration. The same lazy, incompetent referee that had blown the call in the second quarter blew her whistle again, this time signaling a technical foul on Denise which crippled us. They got the foul shot, two more free throws for the technical foul, and the ball back. To make matters worse it put Denise one foul away from disqualification, so she had to be taken out again. Absegami went on to take the lead and we fell sixty-two to fifty-seven, ending the most successful campaign in the history of our program.

I had been drinking every night in secrecy since I relapsed, but that night I didn't care. I figured I had an excuse and went to a local bar for a few shots. Afterwards I went to the liquor store for more, and then made an awful decision. I felt that Denise had carried our team all year, and I wanted to tell her how proud I was of her. All the girls had assembled at one of the player's house so I stopped by. I asked her to come out and she did with another girl with whom I'd grown extremely close. I don't know how I thought they'd react, but when they realized I'd been drinking they turned their backs and walked back into the house. Their season had been dedicated to my recovery, and I had essentially spit in their faces by coming to see them drunk the day they lost. My time in rehab had been a waste.

Chapter 13
Help Me

Down the Hill

When the season ended I started hanging out in Irvington. It's a city full of ghettos that sits right next to Newark, and is just as dangerous. Over the past six months Shea and I had been in contact via email. I'd never really gotten closure over our relationship and I missed her terribly. She had been honorably discharged from the military and was sharing an apartment with her mother. We resumed our romance and within weeks I was consumed with it.

Sharon and Sha-Quaan had also moved to Irvington and only lived a two-minute drive away. Within a few weeks of the season ending Shea and I were back together and for the next four months my life was there. Montclair was merely for sleeping, showering, and working. I was in Irvington every day I was off of work. Sharon always seemed more than happy to send Sha-Quaan with me and I was always eager to take him. Eventually he began to cry every time I brought him home and I'd have to bribe him with potato chips to keep him from crying. More times than not, I drove away crying myself. I hated leaving him. He and Shea's four-year old daughter became like brother and sister and I had delusions of becoming a family.

We began hanging out with her teenage cousins, Tony and his younger brother Buddah, who lived a few blocks away and were popular in the area. I started to live a double life. When I was at work I was a public servant and upstanding citizen, but when I was off I was in love with the "hood". I was hanging out daily with drug dealers that were selling a lot more than marijuana. We spent our days in the park with the kids playing and us drinking, smoking, and playing cards, and our evenings on someone's porch or at her sister Dee-Dee's house. Shea and I were an unstoppable spades team. We must have played a thousand games together and only lost once.

The previous summer I'd bought a navy blue '91 Camry from a co-worker. When he sold it to me it was a nice, reliable little car that would get me from point a to point b, but I trashed it in Irvington. I did more damage to that car than any other I've had. There were worse accidents, but it seemed like I was bumping into something every week because I was always drunk. One night I was driving with Tony and we went past the house we were looking for. Instead of pulling over I decided to back up at forty miles an hour down a busy street. The car behind me tried to swerve but I hit it anyway. I didn't want the cops called because I was obviously drunk, so I showed them my identification and told them I'd pay out of my own pocket, although I didn't know how.

On another night I jumped a curb, took out a "Do not enter" sign, and kept driving. In doing so I shredded one of the tires and when I realized it a block later we had to park the car. Luckily we weren't far from Shea's house and in my drunken thinking we decided to walk back to get her car and go about our business. I paid no mind to the fact that I had to work in the morning and my car was disabled. The next morning I called a firefighter named Kevin that worked the same shift as me, treated me like a little sister, and didn't live very far. He brought me to work and on the way expressed his concern for me, as I was visibly disintegrating.

I actually began taking personal days at work just so I could go to Irvington. Whenever I left work my first stop was to pick up Quanny. Sharon didn't have a phone so I would drive to where they were staying to get him, and she never denied me. I would like to think that she just recognized the bond we had, but unfortunately it turned out to be a situation where she was ready to get rid of him. She was unemployed, uneducated, and sleeping on the couch of family members. She rarely left the front stoop and I imagine was easily irritated by his presence. It always seemed like she couldn't get him dressed fast enough.

Although the area where Shea lived wasn't great, where Sharon lived was downright dangerous. The corner of Nineteenth and Ellis Avenues was a hotbed of drug and gang activity, and there was a steady State police presence in the area. I must have gotten pulled over ten times in transit to or from her house, because I look white and was automatically assumed to be in search of drugs. I only made my trips in the day time, because it was too dangerous of an area for me to be waiting in after dark.

One day when I went to pick Quanny up Sharon said she had to talk to me. She told me that she was taking Sha-Quaan to Georgia to get a fresh start. I had already been drinking that day and didn't handle the news well.

I pleaded with her not to take him from me and even grabbed her arms. I wasn't trying to hurt her, just emphasize my point, but her mind was made up. She went inside to get him ready and her cousin came out. Sharon had taken offense to my grabbing her and sent her cousin out to address it. Although she came to me peacefully, I took it the wrong way because I was inebriated and I took a swing at her. She was considerably bigger than me, and proceeded to pick me up and slam me on the hood of my car. I jumped in the car and sped off, but I was coming back.

I picked up Shea and we went to meet Dee-Dee. Dee-Dee and I had known each other for years through the martial arts, and I consider her to be one of the best fighters I've ever seen. While we were going to meet her Shea was busy making calls and preparing to fight, tying her hair up and removing her jewelry. By the time we returned there must have been fifty people outside of Sharon's house. Buddah was not far away and came with a number of people who were ready to fight. Sharon came out and we walked around the corner to talk. We were able to resolve the matter which boiled down to a drunken over-reaction on my part and a misunderstanding. From that day on Shea and Sharon despised each other.

I continued to see Sha-Quaan and we only grew closer. Sharon began referring to him as my son with comments like, "When are you coming to get your son?" and, "Your son needs Pampers." I bought him a Spiderman sofa made of cushions that folded out into a little bed, and took it with us everywhere so that he could nap if needed to, like when I had to work at the pool all day. He also had his own wardrobe at my house so that she didn't need to send a bag with him.

More Job Problems

My favor at work was rapidly deteriorating. I was back to coming in hung-over and I was beginning to lose weight and strength. My ability to perform was dwindling and so was my attendance. I took every opportunity I got to call out sick or take a personal day, and by the end of my relationship with Shea I had no time left at work. Every time I turned around one of my co-workers was pulling me aside to talk to me about my drinking. Although the only people that were supposed to know about Summit were my battalion chief, the chief, Mike, and the director of human resources, there had obviously been a leak and everyone knew my situation.

I was also becoming very lazy. There are a lot of old fashioned traditions in the fire department that I found to be archaic and mindless. As a new person on the job, I was supposed to jump up and offer to help every time anyone was doing any type of work, and while I understood the concept of teamwork well, I didn't understand why taking two garbage bags out required five firefighters. I hope that by now I have established that I am a great fan of logic, and fail to thrive in an environment where I find it to be lacking.

So on top of my waning physical capabilities, I was earning a reputation of being lazy. I began to dread work more and more, and I didn't hide it particularly well. I was well aware that people were talking about me and I was beginning to get the same sinking feeling I had in college when I couldn't get in shape. I had never been comfortable with inadequacy and I was turning into a model of it. I began reverting to the introverted ways I thought I had left in middle school. I didn't talk very much and just tried to stay out of the way.

I don't mean to imply that everyone was mean to me. In fact there were a number of guys that went out of their way to try and make me comfortable, but I just wasn't. I was caught in the grips of a disease I couldn't control, and for the time being I did not have the strength to ask for more help. My ego told me that I should have gotten it right the first time and prevented me from reaching out. It was obvious that there were guys that resented my being there and had little or no confidence in me. I didn't have any confidence in myself.

My depression was intensifying. On top of my struggles at work and my drinking, my relationship with Shea had become very unfulfilling. It really wasn't anything more than a glorified friendship. We had great fun together and never argued, but that was due largely to the fact that I didn't stand up for myself. Although I loved having the kids together and hanging out in the hood, we never had any time alone. We never went out to eat or on any dates. In the four months we were together we weren't intimate once, and rarely was she even affectionate towards me. I began believing that she was using me and because I didn't feel worthy of love, I allowed things to continue on in misery. After all, she was prettier and smarter than most of the girls I'd been dating.

Shellz

My life could not remain like this. I was in a downward spiral and headed for disaster, and all it would take for me to break was one more straw on my back. Tony was preparing to graduate from high school, but his senior prom was cancelled due to low ticket sales. I had come to love him like a brother and wanted him to have a prom, so I set out to find him a date to Montclair's prom. Ultimately I found that one of my players did not have a date, so we introduced them and she decided to take him. They exchanged phone numbers and we decided to go on a double date so that they could get to know each other a little better.

She picked him up and brought him to a movie theater in Montclair. We were going to meet them there after getting Shea's daughter settled in with her mother. Buddah was hanging out with his best friend "Shellz", and we told him we'd meet up with them after the movie and dinner. We drove to the movie theater and bought two tickets to see *Crash*, but we never saw one minute of it. As we were walking in Tony was rushing out to us. He had just talked to Buddah on his Boost walkie-talkie and something was wrong. Buddah was crying and we couldn't make out what he was saying, so we told Tony we'd go find out what was going on and call him. Shea gave Tony her cell phone and he gave us the Boost so we could talk to Buddah.

What was usually a fifteen minute drive back to the hood took me seven minutes. While we were looking for Buddah we rode past a number of people we knew who were just standing around in obvious shock. We didn't waste time asking questions, we needed to find Buddah and they pointed us in his direction. When we found him he was waiting for us on the corner. He climbed in and told us we needed to go to University Hospital in Newark. Shellz had been shot.

I raced down to the hospital where people were beginning to gather in the waiting room. Tony got dropped off and we all waited in terror while we pieced the story together. Buddah and Shellz and been sitting in an apartment stairwell minding their business when two men came in, pulled out guns, and demanded all of their money and jewelry. Buddah's phone was concealed and he was able to keep it, but they lost everything else. As the men were exiting one of them turned and said, "I should pop one of you little nigga's right now," and without saying another word he shot Shellz in the abdomen and fled.

There were a second group of people in the waiting room that night, and they were also waiting on news of a loved one that had been shot. After hours of waiting the doctors came out and told them that the victim had survived surgery and was given a good prognosis. He had been shot in the neck, so we instantly felt a wave of hope. If this guy made it, surely Shellz would pull through. Not even ten minutes later Shellz' doctor came out and we saw his mother collapse. Within seconds we learned that the doctors could not stop his internal bleeding and he had succumbed to his injuries. Sheldon "Shellz" Kelly was holding a job and enrolled at Montclair State, determined to get out of the hood and make a better life for himself, and his life was snuffed out in a flash by a worthless thug.

I slept in Irvington that night and basically remained there for the next three days. I had experienced the eerie feeling that death creates in numerous houses before, but it seemed that the feeling was over the entire neighborhood. We all drank and smoked even heavier than usual as we tried to cope with our grief. Everyone mourned non-stop for the next nine days as is Jamaican custom. I felt very distant from Shea during that period as she clung to Tony and Buddah. I began having panic attacks for the first time in my life. My heart raced and my hands shook uncontrollably. The day after burying Shellz I checked myself into the detox and mental health unit at St. Michael's Hospital in Newark.

In Search of Help

I only stayed at St. Michael's for three days. I signed a forty-eight hour release because aside from being removed from alcohol, I wasn't getting any benefit. There were no counseling sessions or activities and I was going stir crazy. While I was there I did run into a guy I had known years earlier through my father. He was the same age as me and worked the night shift in the ward. When everyone went to sleep he would sneak me up to the roof and give me a cigarette.

I left St. Michael's highly disappointed and still in search of help. I went to the emergency room at Mountainside and upon evaluation was enrolled in the intensive outpatient program. Three days a week I was to go there from nine to one for group therapy. I was able to schedule the days around my work days, and for a while it worked. When I was at Summit they suggested that I start on anti-depressants, but after seeing what they did to Amina in her battle with depression I declined. When the doctor's at Mountainside made the same suggestion, I accepted because I was getting desperate. I was assigned a psychiatrist and started on twenty milligrams of Paxil.

I finished the program the last week of June. I had been promoted to manager at the pool which would be opening up full time soon and basketball camp was beginning. I was assigned a therapist whom I saw once a week and I saw the psychiatrist once a month for prescription refills. The therapist was very nice and began helping me straighten out my life. We began setting goals and making plans to achieve them. My visits with the psychiatrist were always brief. They were just long enough for me to tell him I was doing well and get a refill.

My relationship with Shea had become extremely distant and I was battling with it in my head. I was in love with her and the potential we had, but I knew she wasn't in love with me. I loved her cousins and hanging out with them, and I longed for her to reciprocate my feelings. We barely even had private conversations and I was beginning to feel like a tag-along. I was convinced that she didn't want to be in a relationship with me but I was going to have to work up the courage to end things, because she seemed comfortable with the arrangement.

A Girl for Me

Since relapsing after summit I hadn't been able to string five sober days together. When I started at Mountainside I was able to get a hold of myself and didn't drink for three weeks, but it didn't last. Somehow I got back to drinking and was thoroughly inebriated when I arrived at the gym to coach a summer league game. We were playing Orange that day and I was feeling very bold. Monica and Denise had become friends with a lot of the girls that played there and we'd developed a friendly rivalry.

For years there had been a girl named Shonte that hung out with Monica a lot. I had seen her on a number of occasions but never paid her much mind because she always looked angry. She was at Denise's graduation that year and I saw her smile for the first time ever. She had a gorgeous smile and I was instantly attracted. I asked Monica to tell her I was interested but she never did, and Shonte had just walked into the gym with some friends. I yelled her name across the gym while the game was going on and invited her to sit on the bench. I had no idea that she had been the manager for Orange in years past and was unaware of the awkward situation I had put her in. The whole time the game was going on she was getting nasty looks from the opposing coach and players.

After the game we exchanged numbers and I promised to call her soon. The very next day I was in yet another car accident. I had been drinking all day and everyone wanted to go to Dee-Dee's house to play spades. I was too drunk to drive so I offered to let Tony drive. I sat in the back holding Sha-Quaan and we headed over. I had just bought the car from the same guy that sold me the Camry, and he gave me a great price. It was a '95 Cadillac and was a huge upgrade from the car I'd just trashed. Tony and I had been joking about the difference in power all day and he got a little out of hand when I gave him the chance to drive. After all, he had been drinking as well and I don't know what I was thinking about when I decided to let him drive. I was already making despicable decisions in that I was drinking and driving with Sha-Quaan in my care. We were less than fifty yards from her house when he lost control of the car and slammed into a telephone pole.

Neither of the driver's side doors would open and the glass in the back window shattered. Sha-Quaan began to cry and I immediately began checking him over, but he didn't have a scratch on him. Sharon had been itching for a reason to take him from me since the fight with her cousin but didn't want to look like the bad guy, so I decided not to tell her. We walked to Dee-Dee's and waited for her to bring us home. The next day Shea disappeared without a word. The voicemail on her cell phone said that she'd had a death in the family and would be away for a while. I couldn't believe it. She hadn't even called to tell me. That was the last straw. I couldn't remain in this relationship any longer and when she came back I would end it.

I began dating Shonte right away. We started talking on the phone and I got her a ride to Monique's house to hang out for a while. I asked her to step outside with me while I smoked a cigarette, and when we got out there I began telling her that I found her attractive and got the feeling that she was attracted to me. Gone were my days of sheepishly crushing on people. I figured that the worst she could say was that she wasn't interested, but she was. I asked her for a kiss, and she smiled and said yes. When she kissed me I felt a sensation I hadn't felt since Kim. I didn't like kissing Sharon and the rare times that Shea kissed me usually only amounted in a peck, but this was a kiss. I was hooked from that moment on. I have never been a cheater so the next day I called Shea and I left her a message ending things.

The next day Kelli and her boyfriend came to help me try and get the car together. We swept all the glass out and had to jump start the car. When I brought Sha-Quaan home I faced the car so that the damage could not be seen from the house and brought him to the porch. The next time I came to get him I would tell Sharon that I'd had an accident since dropping him off. She found a shard of glass in his diaper though, and was furious when I told her the truth. A couple of weeks later she moved to Pennsylvania with her ex and took my baby with her.

I began going to see Shonte every night. I would go to her house around ten with a pint of brandy and we would sit on the porch talking for hours. Even when I knew I had to be to work in the morning I would stay there well after twelve, just to talk to her. Although I never wanted to leave, I was always anxious for my kiss at the end of the night. This might be the one. She was entering her fourth year in college and was an elementary education major with a minor in psychology. She was a total sweetheart but she had a "streetish" edge to her as well.

Shonte and I entered into a whirlwind romance. We went to the village in New York fifteen days into our relationship and got matching tattoos. We got each other's zodiac signs on our forearms with our anniversary date underneath. Everyone thought we were crazy but we didn't care. We had fallen in love. For the next month and a half we spent the majority of our time together. She would come to the pool when I was working, and I would take her to and from her job whenever I could. She started sleeping over often and we couldn't stand to be apart.

When my birthday rolled around I was feeling particularly depressed and wanted to get away, so the two of us drove to the shore. By the time we got a hotel room I was so drunk I could barely function. We tried going out to eat, but I kept spilling drinks so we got the food to go. When we got back to the room I passed out and Shonte spent the night alone watching television, and therein lied the death of innocence in our relationship.

Shonte's father had been a drug addict and an alcoholic. She had endured numerous highs and lows with him and did not want to go down that road again, so I vowed not to drink after my birthday. I tried, but it was at the very least an imperfect effort. I would string nine or ten days of sobriety together and then relapse, and as much as she did not want to enter into that cycle with me, she couldn't help it. In my periods of sobriety I was everything she'd ever dreamed of, but every time I drank I let her down all over again.

I really wanted to get myself together, but I just didn't know how. My mother made a suggestion that would prove to be monumental in my recovery. I mentioned to her that I'd noticed having a particularly difficult time staying sober a week or so before my period. She told me that Amina suffered from something called Premenstrual Dysphoric Disorder (PMDD) that made the symptoms of PMS much more severe than usual. I had never gone to the gynecologist before but I would have to in order to be treated for this particular disorder. It was uncomfortable but I got through it and the doctor upped my Paxil to thirty milligrams.

Losing a Friend

At the end of August I got hit with two major events, the combination of which I could not handle. I was working on engine two which I wasn't necessarily thrilled about. Promotions and transfers had depleted the truck crew that I found so amusing and station two was now an incredible bore, but on this night it would prove to be an incredible blessing. Around three in the morning we received an alarm, but it was at the other end of town so we didn't have to go. There was a report of a car accident with a victim trapped.

Engine three arrived first and made a report of a one car accident into a tree with one victim. When the battalion chief arrived I heard him yell to engine one to drop their "jaws" and come to the car. My battalion chief was a cool customer. I very rarely heard him raise his voice or sound agitated, even at actual fires, so when I heard his frantic tone over the air I knew it was a bad scene. The radio was silent for a while and I went back to sleep.

When I came downstairs the next day everyone had a very somber look. They had received word that a twenty-three year-old young man, whose address was near the high school, had not survived. Instantly my mind went to a guy that had played basketball in high school and graduated a year after me. I was worried but didn't know who I could call at eight o'clock on a Sunday morning to find out. I sat racking my brain, hoping it wasn't him. Moments later the phone rang and surprisingly it was for me. It was Kevin calling from headquarters.

He was at the accident scene the night before, but I couldn't imagine why he was calling me as our shift was ending. "Hey Kev, what's up? I heard that kid didn't make it last night. I'm sure glad I wasn't there." Fires did not worry me nearly as much as my fear of finding dead or bloody victims. That was something I was hoping to avoid as much as possible in my career.

His response caught me way off guard. "Yeah, man it's tough. It's even harder when you know the person."

Instantly feeling sorrow for him I said, "Aw man Kev, you knew him?"

"No, but you did." My stomach dropped into my shoes. I had been standing for the conversation, but decided to take a seat at this point. "It was Justin Ashe, sweetie."

I couldn't believe my ears. It was Gus. My mind started racing as I tried to process the information. Still in shock, I thanked Kevin for the call, hung up, and stoically took my gear off of the rig. I had to find Kelli. I didn't want her to hear it in the streets. They hadn't been together in years but they spent five years together and this was not going to be easy for her. I drove to her mother's house but she wasn't home. After breaking the news to her family I headed for her boyfriend's house. By the time I got there she had already found out, but she didn't seem to be processing it at all. She was just wandering around in shock.

For the next five days or so the entire township was shocked. Between his storied football career and numerous antics off the field, everyone knew who he was. Whether they liked him or not, everyone in Montclair knew Justin Ashe's name. Gus always had an omnipotent air about himself. Not only was he the king of the gridiron, he was the king of Montclair. Gus was the kind of guy that transcended definition. His sweet nature endeared him to everyone he met, but he was known far and wide as someone not to be crossed. If he was in your corner than you were set, but if he didn't like you then it felt like the whole world was against you.

To this point in my life I had seen many funerals, but none like this. There had to be a thousand people at his wake. There were mourners there from every facet of his life, some who'd even made the trip from Hampton University where he'd attended the previous year. The wake went more than an hour past schedule. The wait to get inside was near an hour right from the beginning, and no one dared to try sending all of these people home without paying their respects. I can say unequivocally that it was the most heavily attended wake I'd ever seen.

The day of his funeral was heart wrenching, especially when they opened the floor for comments. One by one people came to the microphone to praise him as an outstanding friend, teammate, player, relative and father (he had a baby girl). The procession of testaments to him was very emotional, but none more than when his mother read the poem she had written for him.

The funeral procession went past his house which was in a section of Montclair known as "The Hollow", of which he was the self-proclaimed king, and it was undisputed. Everyone honked their horns as we passed through the neighborhood en route to the cemetery. That night many of us gathered in The Hollow to drink and pay final homage to Gus. The next morning there was so much garbage in the street it looked like there had been a ticker tape parade.

On the heels of burying Gus came Hurricane Katrina. As the storm swelled in size and intensity, all my family and I could do was watch in horror. The news reports were devastating and we were having a great deal of trouble contacting our relatives in Mississippi. It was days before we found that they had all survived, but our family property was destroyed. The house that my mother grew up in and that hosted so many of our family reunions was in shambles, and the entire area looked like a war zone. My cousins were spread all over the region and some ended up in trailers.

The Break

Over the course of the next six weeks I became increasingly self-destructive. It was becoming harder and harder to just stay sober for a day. Although I went to some AA meetings when I first left Summit, I never liked them and didn't think they could help me. Sharon had moved back to New Jersey and I was back to seeing my son regularly. Since I wasn't coaching basketball at the time, I was only truly able to stay sober when I had Sha-Quaan, and sometimes even then I failed. Shonte could tell whether or not I'd been drinking just by my tone on the phone, and was beginning to get frustrated. It was during one of these times that I finally broke.

I had been in a funk all day. I was miserable and even though I had Quanny back I couldn't shake it, so when he took his nap I went to the liquor store, wiping away tears as I walked in. I bought a pint of brandy and returned home where I commenced to try to drown my sorrows. When I spoke to Shonte she knew I was drinking and broke up with me, and my overall misery drove me to a point of absolute desperation. I had been trying to fight this disease for the better part of a year and hadn't gained any ground.

As a matter of fact, I'd only gotten worse. After I put Sha-Quaan to bed I swallowed every pill in my room. I took anti-depressants, muscle relaxers, pain killers, antibiotics, sinus medication, and whatever else I could find. I then began leaving messages for my girls on their cell phones stating that I loved them and always would, in essence announcing my suicide attempt.

I guess I hadn't thought things out very far to that point, because one of them called the police from college. When the police and ambulance units arrived they could not get in, so they called the fire department. I was supposed to be at work that day, but had called out sick. It was bad enough that the fire department had to come, but it was even worse that it was my shift. One of them picked Sha-Quaan up and he started crying. Immediately I tried to get to him but the police were holding me down.

I began frantically yelling his name, and eventually I had to be restrained with handcuffs. The firemen helped the ambulance unit carry me downstairs and put me in the ambulance. By this time Shonte, Coach, and Monique had arrived. From what I understand Coach almost went to jail that night himself because he thought the police were being too rough with me.

I was taken to the hospital and Shonte, her friends, and Monique went to the police station to find out what was going to happen with Sha-Quaan. Sharon had to be tracked down and Quanny would only be released to her custody. I probably should have been facing child endangerment charges but I'm told that things were smoothed over by a police officer I knew, who assured the family services unit that I was an upstanding person and just seemed to be crying out for help.

Meanwhile I was in the emergency room being tortured. The staff was trying to force me to drink liquefied charcoal to absorb the pills, but it was thick and tasted horrible. I fought everything they tried to do, cursing out a number of people along the way. I was screaming for Shonte and becoming belligerent. Eventually they gave me a shot that put me to sleep for hours. When my father arrived he was more concerned with the fact that Glenn was there with my mother than my condition, which was pretty much par for the course, and he had to be restrained.

Chapter 14
Hardship

The work of rehabilitation is grueling. That fact stands true for emotional and spiritual rehabilitation just as much as it does for the physical kind. My road to recovery seemed to be a particularly long and tedious one. My efforts in the past ten months had served little purpose other than to raise awareness of my problem. My therapist was helping me to get organized, but he wasn't helping me deal with the past and I was downright opposed to AA meetings. In order to recover I would have to make a solemn commitment to myself, and I felt I had reached the necessary point of surrender.

I slept the majority of my first day in the hospital away. I didn't eat anything and remained in bed until my father showed up around six thirty that evening. Even then I was feeling groggy from the medication, and only said a few words to him. My disdain for him had reached a simmering point and keeping my mouth shut was all I could do to keep from exploding. About ten minutes after he arrived, my mother arrived with Shonte. After the previous night's incident I wasn't even sure if I still had a girlfriend. At that point I sat up and began talking, and after ignoring Jimmy for about twenty minutes he left. I didn't see him again until I returned from rehab.

I spent a week at Mountainside. The days were loaded with group therapy sessions and even though they weren't mandatory, I attended them all. I became a leader in the ward and my attitude was positive. I made friends with everyone, even two guys that seemed to be suffering from severe psychosis. My mother and Shonte came to see me every single day I was there. Shonte took buses, cabs, and even walked in the rain to make sure that she was there when visiting time started, and she always stayed until they made her leave. She vowed to support me and help me to get better.

Two weeks prior to my break, Dutchess had puppies. I guess either her or my father's black lab had gotten loose and hooked up. She had ten puppies;

six black, two brindle, one white, and one tan. Shonte and I decided we were going to keep the white and tan ones. We would take them out of the cage often and play with them in my room. We named them Lady and Tramp, and I made the mistake of telling Jimmy that we were keeping them.

On my second day in the hospital my mother took Shonte and two of her cousins to my house to pack a bag of clothes for rehab. Dutchess and the puppies were in a cage on the first floor, and Shonte's cousins waited downstairs while she retrieved my clothes. When she came back down they both looked extremely apprehensive, and for good reason. While she was upstairs, my father had come in with two boys and given away two of the puppies. But not just any two; he gave away Lady and Tramp.

When I found out I was furious for two reasons. The first was obviously that he had given away the puppies that Shonte and I had planned on keeping. I couldn't believe he'd gone behind my back and done that two days after my suicide attempt. The other was that they were only two weeks old and far too young to be separated from their mother. The next day I arranged for Shonte and my mother to go get the rest of the dogs while Jimmy was at the barber shop, and Glenn kept them in his basement while I was to be away.

White Deer Run

After a week in the psych ward I was sent out to Pennsylvania to begin rehab at White Deer Run. A van arrived for me at the hospital and my mother and Shonte walked down with me. I kissed them both goodbye and left on the three-hour ride to the facility. It was almost eleven when we arrived. I was taken to the detox unit where I was evaluated and my vitals were taken. After a few hours there I was given a bed and I went to sleep. I was allowed to sleep later than everyone else because I had come in so late, and I joined my group later in the day.

While I was there I made friends fairly easily. My days were filled with various group therapy sessions and as I did at Summit, I learned a great deal about the disease of addiction, the process of recovery, and the symptoms of relapse. Many people actually looked forward to my sharing and felt that I gave them incredible insight. I was particularly close to two girls named Monica and Sasha, and spent most of my time with them. I liked being there a lot and was looking forward to getting better there, but it was not to be.

Due to my hospital visits earlier in the year, my insurance company informed me that I only had five days of inpatient care remaining, and I would have to leave. Fortunately, the company that ran the rehab also ran an outpatient facility about a half-an-hour away that included housing, so just as suddenly as I'd come, I left the rehab. I was terribly disheartened and felt that even after I had so desperately called out for help, my plea would be denied. My mother had to come out of her pocket for close to a thousand dollars to pay for what the insurance wouldn't cover, but she wouldn't even consider letting me come back without treatment, and thankfully my sister Juno helped her out.

There was a bright side though. Actually there were a few, but in this instance I am merely referring to my access to a phone. While at the inpatient facility phone time was limited, and the pay phone took a third of my calling card minutes as a connection fee, but the house that I was staying at had a landline so I loaded up on minutes. Although I was itching to talk to Shonte, my first order of business was to call Sharon.

I had not spoken with her since before my suicide attempt and didn't know what she'd say, but I had to try. She didn't answer and I left her a lengthy message apologizing for my actions. When I checked my cell phone messages the next day, I heard a nasty reply. She said that I had messed up for the last time and I would never see Sha-Quaan again. My second call was to Shonte. It was so good to hear her voice. Just as Monique had steered me through the fire academy on the phone, Shonte helped me to bide my time in rehab.

We were picked up early every morning and taken for the thirty-minute drive to the outpatient clinic. Once there we spent about six hours a day in different group sessions, and we also saw a personal therapist a couple of days a week. The main counselor was a guy named Frank that was in recovery himself, but had years of sobriety under his belt. Afterwards we would go to the local Y to play volleyball (which I enjoyed terribly) and then the men walked to their house around the corner and we piled up in the van to return to our house.

We usually got home around four and the rest of the day was ours, save for an AA or NA meeting at eight. A woman named Carolyn came to check on us every day and took us to the meeting, but she didn't stay there. We cooked our own dinner, and had a television and a phone. We were supposed to be off the phone at eleven, but I stayed on the phone with Shonte every night until she began to fall asleep. I didn't know much of anything at that point in my life, but I knew I loved Shonte. She had been incredible with all I'd put her through and I loved her for it. I wrote her a number of letters and poems while I was away because I couldn't get her off of my mind.

I was only at the outpatient facility for ten days when my insurance ran up there as well. My mother offered to pay for more days, but at what she was paying I couldn't allow it. I knew she didn't have that kind of money and I was anxious to get back to Shonte, so after a total of fifteen days away, I came home. I still hadn't had a full twenty-eight day inpatient stay but I felt strong in the work I had done and was ready to return home. Between Mountainside and the two rehab facilities, I'd been sober and in treatment for twenty-two days.

Moving Out

When I arrived at my house Shonte was waiting for me on the porch. I thanked my ride and we went inside. While I had probed a number of possible reasons for my depression, the prevalent factor still seemed to be Jimmy. As far as I was concerned his inconsistency prior to, and apathy for us following, the divorce had created a number of volatile and stressful circumstances that had crippled my growth process, and I had to get out. When I found out about the puppies I vowed never to sleep in that house again, and I didn't. I had been living there for years because I could do what I wanted, but in the meantime I'd developed a very powerful and frustrating disdain for him that was tearing me apart internally. Although we barely ever spoke aside from quick greetings, merely seeing his face made my stomach turn.

For the next few days Shonte helped me to gather all my belongings and move them to my mother's house. She didn't have much room but she knew as well as I did that I couldn't live with Jimmy anymore. I didn't even want to speak to him, so I didn't move the television and pictures until I'd already removed all of my clothes and other belongings that weren't in plain sight. Every night I slept on my mother's sofa and Shonte slept in the spare room. She could have stayed at home but after being apart for such a stretch, we wanted to be under the same roof.

It just so happened that there was a vacant apartment in the basement of the house my mother was renting, but I didn't have a security deposit together yet. I spoke with her landlord, whom both of my parents had known for years, and we made arrangements for Shonte and I to move in on November 15th. Although we weren't supposed to have pets, we kept one of the brindle puppies and named him Tiger. The rent would be six hundred and seventy dollars and I figured I could handle that, but things didn't work out as planned.

I went to see my psychiatrist and after evaluating me he determined that I was ready to return to work. He typed a letter saying so and I took it to human resources, but I was told that I needed to be seen by the township's forensic psychiatrist first, and I was given an appointment. When the time came I spent three hours with the doctor. I filled out questionnaires, drew pictures, talked with him, and evaluated inkblots. I left feeling that things had gone well, but it was weeks before I heard anything.

A week before Christmas I was called back to the human resources office and informed that I had been deemed unfit for duty. The psychiatrist suggested a six month leave of absence, over which time I was supposed to make at least three AA meetings a week, see my therapist weekly, and my psychiatrist monthly. I also had to submit to random drug and alcohol screenings. I wasn't happy about the news but I didn't mind so much. My disability checks were almost as much as my paychecks and that was six months I didn't have to see my battalion chief. Two weeks later my disability claim was denied by Cigna and I had no idea how I would make ends meet until June.

The doctor was right about my not being ready. By the time I got the news I had already relapsed once, although it was only for a day. I found out that my disability claim had been denied and my depression worsened. How was I going to survive the next six months with no money? For seven years I had only known one way of dealing with adversity, which was to ignore it and drink. For everything I'd learned in the rehabs about relapse prevention, I went right back to old faithful.

Huge Mistakes

When I was away at rehab I decided to write my father a letter. By the time I came home I had nine pages written in my notebook, and I was nowhere near finished. I had been working on it using my mother's computer, and when it was finished I had written Jimmy a twenty-one page letter. Having fully relapsed following the doctor's report, I was enraged with him. I blamed my father for what my life had become and I wanted him to know exactly how I felt. I delivered the letter to him a few days before Christmas, tacking it on his bedroom door.

When I came back the next day I found a brief handwritten reply and a copy of his will tacked to the wall. I ripped the will apart page by page and tossed it up in the air without reading a word; I wanted nothing from him. He'd also left a Christmas gift which I took and gave away. In his reply he again denied ever making any mistakes, and said to come and talk to him when I had an education. He further stated that he was sorry I felt the way I did but he made no apologies for his past actions, and that if he had it to do all over again he wouldn't change a thing. I was furious and had been drinking non-stop for days.

A few nights later I couldn't find my bank card anywhere and I went ballistic. I had already drunk a pint of brandy and I wanted more, but Shonte had taken my card and my keys so that I couldn't. I demanded for her to give me my belongings, but she denied having them. I tore the room apart trying to find the card, and when my search was fruitless I turned my attention back to her. Finally, in a state of blackout and utter belligerence, I cocked back and punched her in the face, demanding the card. When she continued to deny me, I grabbed a knife from the kitchen and chased her as she ran up the stairs to my mother's apartment.

I couldn't catch her, but I locked the door so that she could not come back down. My mother began calling but I ignored the phone. Since Shonte did not have any shoes on, she spent the night upstairs in my mother's spare room. I went back to Jimmy's madder than ever with a metal baseball bat, intent on caving his skull in. This was his fault. I was becoming just like him and he was going to pay for my misery. My drinking was causing problems with Shonte and me, my depression was causing the drinking, and he was the source of my depression. Feeling my life would never improve, I came to settle the score. Most fortunately for us both, he wasn't home.

When I woke up the next morning I felt awful. I was so embarrassed I thought I was going to vomit. After experiencing a violent relationship first hand as a child, I had resolved years ago that I would never be in a physical relationship. I would never hit someone I was with, and if they hit me I'd walk away. In one drunken swing, I had become my father. I made my way upstairs in total humiliation, and curled up on the floor next to Shonte's bed. I stayed there until she woke up, and apologized profusely. I hugged her and cried and said I would never do it again, but a few days later I was drunk once again.

For the next four weeks I went on an all-out binge. I was like a zombie, making my way to and from the liquor store. I was absolutely miserable. All I cared about, besides Sha-Quaan, was drinking. Sharon had reneged as usual and we were sharing custody again. I would sober up enough to go and get him, and tried not to get drunk in the day time, but when he went to sleep I drank. I had reached the pit of my depression, and he was the only person that could bring me any joy. In the following week I made another huge mistake while I was drunk.

I ran into someone in Monique's life that I had not liked for years, but since we'd recently buried the hatchet, I invited him to come back to my apartment and relax. I had already drunk a pint of brandy before running into him in the liquor store, and began working on my second. We got into a deep discussion and I told him some things about Monique's life that were very personal, things that she should have been allowed to tell him in her own time. I believed that I was helping everyone involved, because I cared deeply for Monique and wanted to see her happy. I was wrong though, and the result was one of pain, anger, and disappointment for everyone involved.

The next morning I remembered that he'd been there, but nothing about what I said. Monique called me and started questioning me about what I said, because he had come to her in tears over my words. She was incredibly hurt and didn't even want to hear my story. She told me that we were no longer friends and I was no longer her son's godmother. I couldn't believe it. Within two weeks I had crossed very serious boundaries with two of the most important people in my life, both times because of liquor. I was destroying everything in my life. Something had to give.

50 Days

I called Jade who was now in her home state of Virginia, and asked her if I could come and visit for a while. If I didn't get away soon I was going to have a nervous breakdown, so she told me to come down. When I got to Penn Station in Newark I was almost through my pint of brandy, so I bought another one. While I was waiting for the bus I threw up in front of the bus terminal. I was no different than the winos I'd always avoided on trips to New York with my father.

Once I was on the bus I got comfortable for the ride. I tried talking to Monique but she didn't want to hear anything I had to say. I continued to drink until I passed out. When the bus driver woke me up we were in Norfolk. I gathered my things and stumbled off the bus. I staggered out of the bus terminal to Jade who was waiting in her car. She looked horrified when she saw the state I was in. She took me to her house and I passed out on the couch.

Before leaving for work the next morning she told me to call her if I needed anything. This became another point in my life where God had obviously aligned things favorably for me. Jade had just moved and didn't have her television or computer hooked up yet. Ordinarily I would have laid on the couch watching television, or wasted my time on the computer, but in this case I couldn't. Although I was on a drunken romp when I was packing to leave, something moved me to grab the big book of Alcoholics Anonymous. Given my lack of options and dire circumstances, I took it out and began to read. I was enthralled with the book and barely put it down, except when I was on the phone with Shonte. By the time I got back to Newark I'd read the first seven chapters.

All of a sudden something clicked in my brain. That book had been given to me when I was at Summit nearly a year ago and I'd hardly touched it, but feeling that I had nothing to lose I picked it up and for the first time truly opened myself to the concepts of AA. It all made sense and doing it my way had gotten me three hospitals and a rehab, a suicide attempt, and suspended from work, so I dove in head first.

I began making at least one meeting a day. No matter the circumstance, I made sure I got to one every day. I began reading the second part of the book which was personal stories. I also began buying puzzle books. I'd always liked puzzles, and I needed something to keep my mind busy, so I made sure I never ran out of puzzles. Sha-Quaan started spending a great deal of time with me again. In fact there were frequently stretches of two or three weeks where he would be with me and Shonte.

Although I'd always loved Sha-Quaan deeply, our relationship grew tremendously close during that period. He was with me everywhere I went and his personality was really starting to develop. My license was suspended and expired so I would take two buses each way to bring him back and forth. We took cabs to basketball practice and games, and he had so much fun. In practice he'd play on the sidelines, and at games he'd run around in the bleachers with two other boys. The three of them were all right around two and a half and loved being together. I bought him toys whenever I could and loved to play with and tickle him.

Usually my mother or Shonte watched him while I went to my meetings, but sometimes Shonte had class and my mother was busy, so I'd bundle him up, grab a book or toy for him, and walk him to the meeting with me, carrying him when he was tired. When we got there I'd sit him in a chair and get him a hot chocolate and a donut, and he would sit quietly while the meeting went on. If he needed to say something he'd whisper, not wanting to interrupt. I was always astounded by his intelligence and desire to be good. He was truly my angel.

Some things happened over the next few months that made me wish I could keep Sha-Quaan forever, but I couldn't say anything because I didn't think I could prove abuse. I'd like to believe that my bond with Quanny was because I was so good and not because she was so bad, but unfortunately I believe it was a combination of both. One day he woke up with a considerable amount of mucus in his eyes, so I called Sharon and asked her to make a doctor's appointment for him because I thought he had conjunctivitis. "Naima, it's a cold. If you can't take care of him then bring him home." I told her to forget it and took him to the doctor myself; it was a very enlightening trip. For starters, I saw that he hadn't been there since I'd brought him a year ago. He was diagnosed with conjunctivitis and she wrote a prescription.

When I brought the idea of vitamins up with Sharon she'd told me that he could only have special vitamins prescribed by a doctor, so I asked the doctor for that as well but she stared at me puzzled. "He can have any multi-vitamin available in the store. Just make sure it's for two year-olds." *Hmm, a little Munchausen's by proxy here? Why would she deny him something that could only aid his health?* I also asked her to prescribe him another inhaler since I hadn't seen his in a year.

I went to Rite-Aid and got his prescriptions, as well as two bottles of gummy vitamins, two toothbrushes, and two tubes of toddler toothpaste. As much as I wanted to keep him with me I couldn't. Shonte could not afford to get sick at that point in the semester, so I brought him home. Although I wanted to say, "I told you so," I just gave Sharon the things from the pharmacy and arranged to come get him in a few days.

A few weeks later he was back with me and he woke up coughing in the middle of the night. As usual Sharon had neglected to send his inhaler with him, and he began to get worked up. He was wheezing terribly and bringing up massive of amounts of mucus. He was having an asthma attack. I tried to calm him down but I couldn't. I left him with Shonte and ran upstairs to wake my mother up. I wanted to use her car but she was apprehensive because my license was invalid.

Although I knew Monique wasn't speaking to me, I called her because her daughter had asthma and I was desperate. She wasn't home but told me to go to her house and use her brother's inhaler. My mother drove me there but without the chamber attachment the inhaler was useless. I didn't know what else to do, so I called Sharon's aunt so that Sharon could meet us in the emergency room. She lived right across the street from a hospital so we were going to take him there, but she told us to bring him home.

Although he was still wheezing I managed to get him to calm down on the ride to her house, but when he realized where he was he started getting upset all over again. She was waiting when we got there and I brought him upstairs. He was so agitated that she could not get him to take the inhaler so I asked her to give him to me so I could, but she refused. Her pride was obviously hurt because he wanted me instead of her, so in order to calm him down she held her hand above his face and said, "That's enough boy! If you don't stop that crying right now I'm going to smack you in the mouth!" When he eventually calmed down, she told me that he was staying with her so she could monitor him. I told her if she hadn't neglected to send his inhaler it wouldn't have happened in the first place, but she stood firm and I had no say in the matter. He got upset all over again when he realized I was leaving without him.

I've always been good with children, but I couldn't afford to do anything special for Sha-Quaan. At the time I was trying to stretch what little money I had as far as I could, so his preference of me over Sharon had nothing to do with money or gifts. I merely placed him first in my life and paid attention to him. Sometimes Shonte and I had to eat ramen noodles for dinner, but I made sure that Sha-Quaan got a nutritious dinner every night. With all of the free time my job afforded me, I had developed a very rigid daily television schedule, and was obsessed with *NYPD Blue*, *Judging Amy*, and *Law and Order*, but I surrendered them all to *Dora*, *Diego* and *Jimmy Neutron*. The only time I watched what I wanted was at twelve and seven when *Jeopardy!* came on.

After the noon edition went off I'd bundle him up and take him to the park to play for a couple of hours. He always cried when it was time to leave and I'd have to bribe him with *Shrek* or *Shark Tale* to get him to stop crying. I'd give him a sandwich or a Lunchable and begin a movie for him, and when he finished eating I'd tuck him into his bed and he'd take a nap. Every night when I returned from my meeting I would take his clothes off, put on the bathrobe and Elmo slippers I'd gotten for him, and take him up to my mother's bathroom. I only had a shower, so I would give him bubble baths in my mother's bath tub. I'd dry him off and take him back downstairs. On the way down we'd stop so he could wish my mother and Glenn good night. I would lotion him up adoringly and then put his pajamas on him. He would brush his teeth and take his vitamin, and then climb into his Spiderman bed after kissing Shonte good night. Then I would tuck him in, kiss him, and tell him I loved him.

I wish I could say that I did all kinds of spectacular things with and for him but the reality of the situation is that I couldn't afford to. He loved me because I loved him. Sharon was inconsistent with him and always seemed to be yelling at him. She claimed that she never spanked him, yet I did, and he still preferred to be with me because I even disciplined him with love. I only spanked him when he did or said things that he knew were wrong, and afterwards I always made sure he understood why he got a spanking, and then told him that I loved him and gave him a hug.

When the time came for him to start potty training I began making the transition from spankings to "time-outs." He actually preferred the spankings! He would cry and when I asked him if he wanted a spanking he'd say yes so that he could get off of timeout. He didn't take to potty training right away and Sharon's aunt said something to me that made me want to throw-up. She told me that if he had an "accident" without telling anyone he had to go, I had to make him stand with his arms at ninety degree angles. That's what they were doing and it had to be consistent. Although I was horrified at the idea I said I would to avoid an argument, but I never followed through.

This boy was being abused and neglected, and there was nothing I could do about it. Would he be better off in the state's care? But then I wouldn't be able to see him either. Sharon was no longer the sweet girl she seemed to be when we were dating. Whenever I suggested that she was doing something wrong she threatened to keep him from me, so I typically kept my mouth shut. Shonte and I had many arguments because of the way I allowed Sharon to talk to me, but I was terrified of losing my son.

Relapse

My recovery was going well. I was following all of the doctor's suggestions. I still felt quite depressed, but that could have been just from having no money and no car. I found seven meetings that I really liked and was going everyday no matter what. Shonte and I were happy and I spent a lot of time helping her with her schoolwork. Her college was about a twenty minute walk from our apartment, and when the weather was nice I'd walk her to school and hang out in the computer lab while she was in class.

Little by little I was making positive strides in my recovery. I had done the fourth step of the twelve-step process, which is to make a "searching and fearless moral inventory" of yourself, and was waiting to do the fifth step, which is to share it, with Coach. I had used the numerous worksheets and resources I brought home from rehab as a guide for my inventory, and felt satisfied with what I'd done. Something still wasn't right though. I should have been happy, but I still felt very depressed. I could feel a relapse coming on, and I let it happen instead of fighting it.

Shonte was going out with her friends and cousins for her birthday. I was never a big fan of clubs, so I was going to stay home and we were going to spend the next day in Central Park. That day I was itching to drink. I don't know why. Nothing out of the ordinary had happened, but I did get my period the following week. Monica came to pick her up, and moments after I thought she'd left for the night, I put Tiger on the leash and took him to the liquor store with me. I had to hurry because it was almost ten o'clock, but I brought him so that if she'd forgotten something I could say I was out walking the dog.

When I got back I saw Monica's car in front of the house so I hid the bottle before I went inside. When they left again I got the bottle and climbed in bed. That's the last thing I remember, but that wasn't the end of the night. They came back a little while later and Shonte found me drunk. Suddenly I didn't want her to leave and I tried to persuade her to stay. Her mind was already made up and all her friends were ready to go. Upon her denial I lost my temper and began swinging. Denise and Monica tried to hold me, but I didn't calm down right away. They got her and left for the night.

Shonte didn't come home that night or the next day. She was staying with her cousin and two friends in Newark. Her family cooked her a big birthday dinner but she was so disheartened and sad that she just kissed her mother and took a plate to go. Her lip was swollen and she tried to conceal it for the time she was home. After a few days of my pleading with her, she finally came home. I told her that I didn't know what had come over me and I was really going to get myself together. When she came home I resumed my work at recovery and we agreed to keep trying. I never put my hands on her again.

For the next month I was able to get back on track. I figured that I would need to do something more to defend against the PMDD next time. I hadn't been very successful trying to work out on my own, so I went to see Asatida. Over the years we had buried the hatchet and spoke in passing. I explained the nature of my situation and that I couldn't afford to pay him, but I desperately needed him to train me. In a supreme show of humility and kindness he allowed me to begin training twice a week, free of charge. He also bought me a new uniform and a brown belt. He said that I could not come back as a black belt because I hadn't earned it there, but I didn't care. I had a much bigger agenda than that.

It took a multitude of things to keep me sober, but I was doing it. Sha-Quaan was with me all the time and his very presence helped to deplete my depression. When I was in karate class he would be out in the office trying to imitate what we were doing, but he was never a distraction. I was making meetings and making my appointments. When I started training again I switched from cigarettes to Black and Mild cigars and I was beginning to get my wind back. Everything seemed to be going well when the bomb dropped. I was ready to face anything in sobriety-- anything except losing my son.

My Heart Shatters

Sha-Quaan had been with me for about two weeks. It wasn't supposed to be that long of a visit but I kept procrastinating because he didn't want to go home. He never wanted to go back to Sharon. He never thought much of jumping on a bus with me and would walk happily along with me down Central Avenue talking incessantly. When he saw the neon sign on top of the Chinese food store on the corner though, he'd stop dead in his tracks every time and start crying.

I would kneel down to him in the middle of a busy sidewalk and force a smile as I told him that his mommy was missing him, but he never took reassurance in my words. He'd shake his head vigorously and would say through his tears, "No, Na-Na. Can't see mommy. Can't see mommy, Na-Na." It tore my heart apart every time I had to bring him home.

I started trying to prepare him the night before. "Listen Fat Boy, tomorrow I'm going to take you to see mommy. She really wants to see you. Don't you miss mommy?"

No matter how I tried to sugarcoat it he would respond by shaking his head and with the same phrase, "No. Can't see mommy, Na-Na."

This is where I made the egregious mistake of using his fear to my advantage. If he was misbehaving I would say, "That's it Sha-Quaan. Put your shoes on, I'm taking you home." I would use different approaches with it. Sometimes I'd pick up the phone and pretend I was talking to Sharon, telling her that I was bringing him home. Other times I'd look at Shonte and ask her if she wanted to go with me to drop him off. It was a gross abuse of my knowledge of his desire to stay with me. I am embarrassed to admit it and I cringe as I recall it, but if this is to be an honest, introspective account, I must bear the weight of my sins.

So, having stretched his visit as long as I could, Sharon told me that I had to bring him home on Good Friday. Her mother, who had moved to Pennsylvania, was coming to get him for the weekend. She had no idea that Sharon was still letting me see him and Sharon didn't want her to know. I'd said a number of things about her in the past when I was drunk, and when she heard about the night I took the pills and that DYFS became involved, she didn't want me to see him ever again.

The date was April 14th, 2006 and I will never forget it for as long as I live, because it was the last time I ever got to touch my son. I brought him home and as usual when he realized what was going on, he began to cry. I thought I had him calmed down but when we got to the front stoop he began to cry again. I knelt down to console him, but before I could reassure him, Sharon threw the front door open and began screaming at him. "Stop that screaming boy! You don't cry when you come home! I'm your mother!" She grabbed him by the arm and he fell out, which I'd never seen him do before. She dragged him up the stairs kicking and screaming, as she yelled at him to shut-up.

I sat on the stoop and waited for her to come back down the stairs. I was horrified but I was helpless. When she came out she told me that I couldn't see him for a while, "until he learns how to act when he comes home." I came back two weeks later which seemed more like a month to me, and she told me I still couldn't see him. Apparently he'd acted the same way when her mother brought him back, so this was going to be for a while. I pleaded with her. I told her that he was the most important person in my life and played a major role in my sobriety, but she didn't care. Her feelings were hurt, and instead of considering that his actions were the result of poor parenting, she snatched him away from everyone he loved more than her.

I must have said the serenity prayer about a hundred times on the bus ride home, and was able to stave off relapse for that day, but it wasn't long before I collapsed again. Within a day or two I was on a binge as bad as any I've ever been on. It started with a half-pint. I had been sipping on it all day and I hadn't eaten. I was sitting on my mother's front steps smoking a cigarette when my friend Mary pulled up. Suddenly I got the idea to get her to take me to see Quanny. Surely Sharon would let me see him by now. I didn't do anything wrong.

She opened the door with an agitated look on her face and asked me what I wanted. I asked her if I could just take him to the park or McDonald's for a little while, but she said no. I tried to push my way past her and yelled his name. She started screaming for her cousin, who came running downstairs. I denied touching her, and her cousin and I went to talk in private. I pleaded with her to talk to Sharon. Everyone in that house knew how much Sha-Quaan and I loved each other, and she said she'd talk to her.

After another week passed I came back but Sharon wasn't home, and neither was Quanny, but I had a long talk with her cousin. She was the same cousin that threw me on the hood of my car in Irvington, but we'd since talked it out. She had a great deal of respect for the obvious amount of love I had for Sha-Quaan, and the way I'd treated him like my own son for so long. I didn't want to be on the outs with Sharon. She was expecting her second child and I knew that she'd need more help with Quanny than ever. Her cousin told me she'd talk to her and to give it a few more days. She gave me her phone number and told me to call so I could arrange to come and get him, but she never answered or returned any of my numerous calls.

I went back to drinking and that's all I remember. One morning the following week I woke up with a black eye, a hangover, and vague visions of climbing the fence atop a freeway overpass. I also had a sickening feeling that I'd seen Sharon the night before, and I was right. Apparently I'd talked Kelli, who was six months pregnant herself, into taking me to see him. She didn't know what was going on and I didn't tell her. When Sharon opened the door I once again began pleading with her to let me see him. When she said no I got on my knees. She said no again, and that after how'd I'd behaved the previous week I would never see him again. I snapped. I got up and punched her square in the face. She yelled for her cousins and they came down running. Once I got hit I went running off into the night.

When Kelli told me what happened I knew I'd really done it this time. I dodged any phone calls from numbers I didn't recognize because I knew I'd be getting some nasty ones. I knew Sharon needed some time to cool off. I'd made some drunken mistakes before, but this one took the cake. She'd kept him from me before, and then she'd cool off or need me and she'd give in. But this time I got the sinking feeling that I'd never see my son again.

I couldn't handle it. Once again I went on a binge. I drank liquor by the fifth. I even umpired softball games drunk. I had to do something for money so I could continue to drink. I'd lost my baby. *This God-damned liquor!!!* I was in such turmoil. I was ashamed, furious, depressed, miserable, and hopeless all at once. What did I have to live for? Sha-Quaan was my inspiration, and he was gone. I was an embarrassment at work, and I was destroying my relationship with a girl I loved. Sometime during that binge I ran a butcher knife across the inside of my left wrist. When I woke up I was mortified at the depth of the cut. I'd really almost done it. I'd really almost ended my life in a blackout. I had to get this right and soon. If I was ever going to see my son again I'd have to get sober. In order to do that, I'd have to stay alive.

Chapter 15

Recovery

In writing this book I realized a great number of coincidences throughout the course of my life. A major one was the way children always seemed to be born at a time when I needed an escape. April 18th, 2006 was the eight year anniversary of my car accident, and was also the day Khalea gave birth to her first child, Kenneth Jr., or KJ as we came to call him. Khalea went on maternity leave and came home for the duration. I spent a lot of time with him when I wasn't drunk and, although nothing could fill the void left by Sha-Quaan's absence, he helped to ease my pain

On May 21st, 2006 I began a new recovery, but this one would be for real. I had a new inspiration. Maybe I couldn't beat my disease for myself, but I could do anything for Sha-Quaan. I knew that I was going to have to toe the line if I had any chance of getting back into his life. Furthermore, my re-evaluation for work was two weeks away and I had to get it together. I had hit some considerable detours on my road to recovery, but I was learning and now I was prepared to conquer my disease.

I went back to making meetings every single day. I made all of my appointments and kept myself busy with puzzle books. Although I had disappeared at the end of the previous summer following Gus' death, I managed to talk the pool supervisor into letting me be the manager again. My mother had been helping me out financially by continuing to work a second job that was draining the life out of her. Khalea would also be a manager until she returned to Atlanta in July. I adored KJ and his presence helped me to get back on the wagon. Things began to improve with Shonte and I and my outlook began to change. I convinced myself that if I was going to drink liquor than I might as well drink bleach because the outcome would be the same, and that worked for me.

My re-evaluation for work was on Friday, June 2nd and I was nervous. This would determine my future. If he still found me unfit for duty I would be facing losing my job altogether. I may not have been crazy about the job but I needed it sorely at that point. I gathered documentations from my therapist and psychiatrist stating that I had followed his recommendations as they pertained to them. The first time I went to see the forensic psychiatrist I was dressed in sweats with my hair in a messy ponytail and stuffed under a hat, but I wouldn't make the same mistake twice. I took a shower and pressed a purple and white button down shirt and black slacks. I put on cologne and brushed my hair into a neat ponytail, detailed with gel. I walked into the office a few minutes early and full of confidence.

The doctor administered the same set of tests and asked most of the same questions he had the first time. The first time I tried to give him the "proper" answers, and obviously failed miserably. This time I gave everything to him straight. I felt like Morgan Freeman's character going up for parole in *The Shawshank Redemption*. I told him that I'd relapsed early on and had not resolved things with my father, but I was learning to understand that he is mentally ill himself. I told him I'd lost Sha-Quaan but was coping with it in meetings. I didn't tell him I was only two weeks sober, but I was honest about everything else.

The first time I waited weeks to hear the results, but this time I got a call from the chief on the ride home. I'd passed and was to report for duty the following morning at eight o'clock. I called my mother and Shonte ecstatic and told them the news. Things were coming together and I had to maintain them this time. You only get a number of chances before the fatal relapse and I'd already had more than my share. I returned to work the next day, and in a most triumphant fashion I got to ride in the African-American Heritage Day Parade by order of the chief.

My return to work was awkward for a while. Most of the guys were nice to me upon my return, but on this job people talked about you as soon as you left the room and I was very uncomfortable around some of them. Once again I got lectures from the chief down about redeeming myself and regaining my credibility. I felt the weight of the world on my shoulders, but in my quest for Sha-Quaan I was determined to succeed. I'd lost a good twenty pounds since coming on the job and with that weight went some of my strength, so I was struggling to perform the physical tasks of the job.

Getting It Together

For years Khalea had driven a silver '99 Mitsubishi Eclipse but now that she had a baby she needed a larger car, so we made a deal. I took out a pension loan to pay the remaining balance of the car and I got the title. I wanted a bigger car in a year or so and I would give it back to her when she could afford the insurance on two cars. It was a car that fit her personality perfectly and I know it was hard for her to give it up, but she didn't have much choice.

Shonte and I celebrated our anniversary at the shore with her cousin Tash, my cousin Subira, and Monique. It was already by far the longest and most serious relationship I'd ever been in. That weekend we went on rides, went swimming, and even had a little cookout. I won Shonte a bunch of stuffed animals on the boardwalk. We laughed and enjoyed ourselves, and more importantly I didn't touch a drop of alcohol.

I was catching up on the rent after a number of eviction threats and started catching up on my other bills as well. My relationship with Shonte seemed to be growing and life was slowly getting better. I enjoyed going to AA meetings now and usually learned something about myself every time I spoke. Often times my words would flow as if I was being spoken through, and when the words stopped I'd usually said something powerful. I realized a gift for talking to people in a way that they could relate to. Jimmy had retired and was in the process of moving to Georgia. My life was getting better in every aspect except the one that mattered most to me.

It was now the middle of August and I still hadn't heard from Sharon. I'd never gone this long without seeing Sha-Quaan. I wrote her a long letter of apology and mailed it to her aunt's house but after a few weeks I hadn't heard anything, so I stirred up my courage and went to the house. The second floor looked vacant and my heart fell into my shoes; they were gone. My legs went numb and I sat down on the stoop for about ten minutes trying to process what was going on, as the tears poured from my eyes. He was really gone this time.

I couldn't give up. Another week passed and I decided to call her mother's number in Pennsylvania. Sharon answered the phone and told me to leave her alone. I pleaded with her and cried my heart out, but she was unmoved. She said that they'd moved away and I would never see him again. I was devastated. I told her that I finally got ninety days sober because of him but she didn't care. She told me to forget about him and move on with my life.

Although I thought I had it together, I cracked. I went to the liquor store and got a pint of rum. I picked Monique up from school and cried to her about Quanny. I needed her to come with me to pick up Shonte and explain to her that I'd been drinking and needed my space for a day. She let her know that yelling at me was not going to make the situation any better. While they were both out of the car I removed my diamond cross necklace and threw it out the window. I turned my back on God because he hadn't rewarded me for my sobriety. I stopped praying before my meals and in general. For a few months my grief led me to completely lose my faith.

I Get A Break

Following that slip I got back on the wagon once again and focused on getting my life all the way together. When basketball season began, I was back full force. I began guiding the freshman point guard and I was having fun coaching. Shonte came to all the games and did our scorebook when she got out of class. My three main issues were missing Sha-Quaan, my unsettled issues with Kim, and my troubles at work. My unresolved issues with Jimmy still bothered me, but I tried to act like they didn't.

As I said, my battalion chief seemed generally fair the first year and we didn't really have any problems, but ever since I came back from Summit and more so since returning from my leave of absence, he seemed to be going out of his way to make my life miserable. I'd heard rumors and stories of his racist nature, but he seemed to have a special disdain for me. Whether or not he is a racist is a matter of opinion, but it was obvious that he had no tolerance for my disease. At a time in my life when I was desperate for some compassion and understanding, he nearly drove me to quit.

He was constantly moving me unnecessarily, even when it disrupted people that he liked. Other people could have laptops and conduct their side businesses as they pleased, but over the summer he got mad that I was doing the pool schedule in his presence. He wasn't talking about anything in particular, but it was a problem just the same. He knew how uncomfortable I was around him and took every opportunity he got to exploit my insecurity. I was becoming miserable at work and was thinking about quitting, when I finally got a break.

It was a Sunday evening and the acting officer had instructed me to wash the engine. I figured that he was just being a little arrogant because he was in charge, but he said that it was by order of the battalion chief. Like an idiot I called the battalion chief and asked him if he'd really said it and he said yes, then berated me for questioning my acting officer. Later that day I was returning from a call and my air tank was not in the holster properly. It fell out and as I reached to catch it my finger got wedged between the tank and the edge of my seat and for a while I couldn't move it. I went to the hospital to get it checked out and ended up going out on a line of duty injury.

When my battalion chief came to get me from the hospital he told me that I was to report to the chief's office the following morning at eight thirty. He'd spoken to the chief about my behavior and the chief decided that I should transfer to another group. I'd gotten into a pretty bad rut and needed a fresh start. When I came back from my injury I would begin in group four. I was ecstatic to get away from my old battalion chief, but I had no idea of the asset my new one would be.

My new assignment was like starting a new job. Each fire house held a different personality and the guys all got along. The battalion chief, Donnie, had grown up with my Uncle Donald and had reached out to me a number of times before I was even in his group. He understood that I was in the grips of a disease and honestly wanted to help me. I have always had a hard time accepting help, but once I opened myself to him he truly became my friend. The guys in his group were all nice to me and eager to help me learn new things.

Forever My Son

I called Sharon again to ask her about Sha-Quaan's clothing sizes and she gave them to me. I ordered him about a hundred dollars worth of clothes and four hundred dollars worth of toys, including a V-Smile learning system. I ordered everything online and shipped them to her mother's house. I was holding it together, but inside I was as miserable as ever. I couldn't take it anymore and I decided to get his face tattooed on my left shoulder. She could take him physically, but he would always be a part of me.

Somehow Sharon's best friend, Tanya, and Monique had become associates and although Tanya and I were on bad terms, Monique convinced me to show it to her. Tanya took a picture with her cell phone and sent it to Sharon's brother's phone. When she saw it she had a conniption. She told me it looked nothing like him and called me psychotic. She said she hoped I enjoyed it because it was the only way I'd ever be able to see him. Even after receiving the gifts she wouldn't let me speak to him on the phone.

I didn't relapse though. I had gotten stronger in each failed attempt at sobriety, and I was really starting to get the hang of it. I kept my head up and tried to keep a positive attitude. I began praying again and apologized to God for going astray. I knew that I needed Him more than ever at this point. I was getting stronger and pulling my weight at work. The basketball season was a lot of fun and Shonte and I were happy overall. My next relapse wasn't like the others.

Pain

All in all, things were going well. Shonte was in her final semester at school and was student-teaching. Things at work were getting better and I was finally getting my finances together. Every day I would pick Shonte up from school with a blunt and we'd drive around smoking. We'd cook dinner together every night and then put Tiger in the car and take him to the local dog park. It seemed like I had a grip on everything, but I still felt a great deal of discomfort inside. I wasn't masking it with alcohol, but I still wasn't dealing with my issues because Shonte and I were smoking over fifty dollars worth of weed a day.

On January 16th I lost another friend that I'd grown up with. Mike C. is a prominent businessman in Montclair. He owns a pizzeria and a jewelry store and is well connected. His son, Mike Jr., and Khalea became close friends in high school and we'd had our fair share of times together as well. I got a phone call that day and was told that he'd died of a cocaine overdose at the age of twenty-five. That wasn't really his scene and there was a lot of suspicion surrounding the death. He was a friend and it hurt to hear, but it hurt even more to tell Khalea.

I called her down in Atlanta and broke the news to her. She couldn't believe her ears, and I didn't really know what to say to her. Thankfully Mike Sr. called to break the news to her while we were on the phone and she hung up with me to talk to him. She came up for the funeral and we went to see big Mike at his house. He was obviously very hurt, and it was hard for me to see someone I respected so much in that much pain. Somehow I was able to stay out of the liquor store through that ordeal as well.

On May 5th tragedy struck yet again. My brother had taken a guy named Al under his wing years ago. He was the cousin of one of Jay's best friends and was a year older than me. He always had a hot temper and that night he paid for it with his life. He'd gone into a bar in Newark to get a beer to go, and while he was there he got into an argument with another man. I don't know what it was about, but the argument didn't last long before the man pulled out a gun and shot him in the head.

I had become numb to death after all I'd been through, but this one struck me for a different reason. When I heard the news my mind went back a few years to a night at Jimmy's. He was out of town and I had people over to drink and play cards. Al came in with Jay and Thud was also there. Somehow they got into an argument and went into the backyard to fight. My brother and another guy went out back to watch them fight, and I watched through the back window with a few friends. I don't remember what the fight was about, and it truly is irrelevant. What is relevant is that only a few years later they were both dead as a result of street violence.

It had been five years since Kim and I still carried a torch for her. Not one day had passed in all that time that I didn't think about her. The way things ended had been gnawing at me for years and I needed some closure. I needed to know why she had so harshly banished me from her life. The matter haunted me and I felt like I'd never be happy unless I was able to deal with it. I loved Shonte, but I'd been in love with Kim from day one. Since her many girls had come and gone, but none like her. I wrote her a long letter and used the internet to come up with an address for her. After umpiring a number of softball games one Sunday I decided to go see her. I got the directions from the navigation program on my phone and headed out on the thirty-minute drive to her house, sipping on a half-pint of brandy to ease my nerves.

When I pulled up to the house I summoned my courage and walked up to the door. Her mother answered and I asked to see her. When Kim came to the door she was none too happy to see me. "What are you doing here, Naima?"

"I don't mean to bother you, Kim. I just wanted to give you this letter."

As I handed her the letter she snatched it and said, "It was college, Naima. It was just an experiment." She almost spit the words out of her mouth as if saying them tasted nasty. She muttered something under her breath about me stalking her and went back into the house. That's the last thing I remember.

When I woke up I was on a bed in the trauma unit at Hackensack Medical Center with my head throbbing. My bottom lip was grotesquely swollen and had a ton of stitches in it, as my teeth had gone clean through it. Little by little I began to piece the night together. Somehow I'd run off the road on route forty-six in Lodi and right into the divider. I'd smashed my face on the steering wheel and been knocked unconscious. My mother, Shonte, and Monique were worried sick because I'd been missing for hours and it was after two in the morning when I finally called. I'd done it again. I didn't even remember drinking that much. Shonte, Monique, and Audrey came to pick me up. I started crying when they walked in and vowed never to drink again as Shonte hugged me. I apologized profusely and said this was really it.

We went to get the police report, and then to see the car. It was totaled. I had destroyed Khalea's pride and joy. I almost had a year of sobriety and in the tilt of a bottle I'd thrown everything away. I was lucky to be alive, and lucky that I hadn't killed anyone else. After years of driving home from the city in blackouts I guess I needed a serious warning. Instead of returning to meetings I continued to wallow in my misery, and this relapse would cost me any remaining chance I had of ever getting my son back.

Summer of Hell

Sha-Quaan's birthday was coming up and I sent him about four hundred dollars worth of gifts. I've never been one to try and buy the affection of children, but I wanted Sharon to see that I had my money together. I couldn't afford to buy those things if I was still drinking. Part of his gift was three tickets to the circus. The last I'd heard Sharon didn't have a license, so the third ticket was for the driver. Since she never bothered to call me when I sent things, I decided to go out there. I wanted to know if she would take him to the circus.

I rented a car and Shonte and I drove out the night before his birthday and stayed in a hotel, because I didn't want to take any chances with traffic. We relaxed for the night and checked out in the morning. The circus was supposed to start at one, so we sat in the parking lot of a building across the street from them and pulled out the binoculars I'd bought for this very occasion. I just wanted to see his face on his birthday and to know if Sharon was going to use the tickets.

Around twelve-thirty Sharon came out with Quanny, her mother, and a little girl. I began to get excited as I started the car. I followed them at a good distance, being sure not to get too close. They went into Sam's Club and I lost them, but it was right down the street from the arena. I figured that they were getting some snacks or a camera. Although I didn't see them go into the arena, I left feeling happy. He had a nice yard and what seemed to be nice neighbors. He looked well groomed and happy, and that was what I wanted more than anything.

A few days later I was just finishing my laundry and I saw Sharon's best friend, Tanya. She told me that Sharon wanted me to stop sending him things. *How could she say that? Had she not taken him to the circus? Didn't she give me his clothing sizes and her address?* I was confused. I told her that I knew for a fact that she had used the tickets, and when I told her how she freaked out. She called me a stalker and told me to stay away from her "nephew", but I had loved him more and better than any of them. This was so unfair.

I went to the liquor store and went on another binge. Sha-Quaan was my inspiration, and I could not be sober without him. Over the course of the next few days Sharon and I exchanged nasty e-mails and text messages. Her brothers eventually got involved and things got incredibly ugly. They called me suicidal among other names, and I made a comment about the fatal illness of a close family member.

This time it was all over. For the next few weeks I had trouble stringing more than three days of sobriety together, but this would be the summer that God would gun the engine. I'd wasted enough time and potential and it was time for me to get it right. That summer he lined up all types of signs and signals that it was time to get it together. It was time for me to start fulfilling my destiny.

Alignment

The first change had actually occurred at the end of the previous year. When I switched groups I began to truly get acquainted with Donnie. He gave me every possible way to contact him and told me to call him if I needed him, no matter what time it was. I'd been told that on numerous occasions by different people but he really meant it. He'd known many people that were diseased with depression and/or alcoholism and he had a great deal of empathy for me.

When the time came for me to reach out for help at an inopportune time, he didn't hesitate to step up. The worse I got, the better he was. I called him drunk and in tears on more occasions than I can count, and usually in the middle of the night. He never sounded agitated and never made me feel guilty. He'd get out of bed, pick me up from my house, and take me to a diner to talk. He went above and beyond the call of duty when I needed support the most and was happy to do it.

The next thing that happened was that the bond with my girls was broken. It was agonizing and depressing when it happened, but they'd all lost respect for me through my diseased actions and it was no longer a healthy relationship. They looked at me as a failure that did not want to stop drinking. My drinking created the situation that ultimately separated us, but I believe it was for the best. My past efforts had become meaningless to them and they were ashamed of who I'd become. I can't say I blame them.

Many of them came to my house to confront me about my drinking. They came out of concern, but they began attacking me. They called me a joke and said that Shonte deserved better. They told me I needed to grow up and act like an adult. They had no tolerance or understanding for what I was going through and were tired of watching me fall apart. I was initially hurt and began to cry, but eventually my pain became anger and I kicked them out of my house. We wouldn't speak again for months.

The next sign came on my two year anniversary with Shonte. The previous week I'd been on another binge and once again we argued. I decided to go to the city one night and on the way back I ran into a street vendor selling DVD's. I bought three of them, but the only clear one was Tyler Perry's play *Why Did I Get Married?* I watched it the next day and was blown away by the entire story, but particularly the lead actress. She had a spirit about her that was amazing and her voice was unbelievable. After making up with Shonte we watched it together. She was almost as impressed with the woman's talent as I was. Her name was Cheryl "Pepsii" Riley and I'd never heard of her before. She played a woman who was being mistreated and cheated on by her husband, and was searching for happiness.

Since it was our anniversary I wanted to do something special for Shonte, but I didn't have a whole lot of money. Kisha and I used to go to a lounge called The Village Underground in Greenwich Village that had open mic on Monday nights with no cover charge. I hadn't been there in years and I thought it would be nice. We went into the city and hung out for a while, and then we went to the lounge. As it turned out, Cheryl Pepsii Riley was performing that night, and as if that weren't enough, she was wearing a John Coltrane t-shirt.

I don't believe in coincidences, especially the big ones. Too many different things had to happen for that sequence of events to happen, so I refuse to believe that it was happenstance. First I had to relapse and go to New York. Then I took the train back instead of the bus. I had to run into the vendor at that time, and I happened to pick that movie because I liked Tyler Perry. Then Shonte and I had to make up and I had to decide to take her somewhere I hadn't been in at least four years. I don't know what sequence of events lead Ms. Riley to be performing at that particular lounge, but I think you get the picture. God was talking to me. I took a picture with her that night, but a few days later I found her on MySpace and sent her a message explaining the effect she had on me. I told her about my struggles with depression and alcohol and how I believed God put her in my life that night to show me that he was still paying attention to me.

I didn't know whether or not she would respond, but she did and I was blown away. She replied:

Wow. Well, first let me say, congrats on your 4th day. It IS a big deal for we can backslide, or relapse, but if given just ONE more day to turn our lives around for the benefit of us and those we love, then we are BLESSED! So, yes, keep goin', I believe you can do this. It was something that I had that shirt on, that you just saw the dvd, all of that. Forgiveness, aaahhh, a big thing, and in order to stay in sobriety, I believe you must forgive YOURSELF and then move from there. So, I am praying strength into your life for your quest to change things for the better. Thank you for sharing and know that you are in my prayers. Blessings, Cheryl.......Nothing is by accident... Nothing!

On the strength of that encouragement I stayed sober for the next eleven days, but then I fell again. No matter what I just could not get a grip on my recovery. I needed something tangible to turn to when I felt I couldn't do it alone. I decided to get a tattoo on my right forearm of Jesus and in the banner below I had *Phil 4:13* written. That scripture says, "I can do all things through Christ who strengthens me," and I thought that was exactly what I needed. When I wanted to drink I could look at the tattoo and draw strength, but that didn't work either. What the hell was I going to do?

A few days later I was thumbing through the newspaper when I was struck by an interesting advertisement. In big bold letters were the words ALCOHOLISM SUCKS, and underneath that it said, "And it will suck the life out of you." It was an ad for a website called *Live Outside The Bottle*. I went to the website and found it very informative. It was advertising a drug named Camprate that helped to diminish the cravings of alcoholics, and it had a doctor locator. I entered my zip code and found a doctor named Marc Watson in a neighboring town and there was a bus stop right in front of his office.

I made an appointment with his secretary and got a referral from my primary care facility. He was a tall black man around the age of fifty. He greeted me with a firm handshake and a huge smile and I felt comfortable with him right away. I spent the next two hours with him and he patiently listened as I outlined my problem. He started me on Camprate and gave me an appointment for the following week. I filled the prescription and remained sober for the next week.

I am arrogantly aware of my natural intelligence and I don't readily admit that people are smarter than me, but that was the first thing I told my mother about Dr. Watson. He was smarter than me and was really making me think. Although I managed to relapse again he never made me feel guilty and we began to attack the root of my problems. My two main problems were missing Quanny and my feelings for my father. My first therapist was nice but he wasn't helping me deal with my past issues. Dr. Watson began the work of digging through my past to find the source of my deep-seated depression.

One more thing happened that summer to set up my final break. Khalea was in between jobs and came back to New Jersey for the summer. She got a job at a summer camp and I watched KJ everyday that I wasn't at work. He and I bonded immensely over that time. He was now a little more than a year old and all over the place. He was right about the same age as Sha-Quaan was when I met him, and the similarities were hard to cope with.

They were both very smart, sweet, and active, and to top it all off KJ took his first steps to me just as Quanny had. Khalea went back to Atlanta and left him with my mother and I while she got settled in, but two weeks later she came to get him. When they left I felt like I'd lost Sha-Quaan all over again, and I didn't handle it well at all. I binged for the next three weeks and was barely able to crawl into work. Something definitely had to give.

September 17th was Shonte's first day at her new job. She had been searching for work since graduating in May and finally landed a job at a day care center. I had been sober for a week, but I was itching to drink that day. I had no idea why, because nothing had gone wrong. In fact, things were slowly getting better, but I wished I could crawl out of my skin and sure enough I got my period the following week. I went to the liquor store and bought a half-pint of brandy.

By the time Shonte got home I had downed two of them and passed out drunk. She came home excited to tell me about her first day and I had let her down. She couldn't take it anymore. I was taking her on the same roller coaster ride of happiness and disappointment her father had, and she couldn't stand it. As much as it pained her to say the words, when I woke up she looked at me and said, "It's over Naima. I can't do this anymore."

I got up and got dressed to leave. I decided to go into the city to get lost for a few hours. I bought another half-pint and started bar-hopping. I went to see Cheryl and she was standing at the door when I came in. She asked me if I was still doing well and I said yes, even though it was obvious that I wasn't. That night I passed out waiting for the bus home and when I woke up my money and cell phone were gone. I had to use a police officer's phone to call Donnie to come and get me from Port Authority at two o'clock in the morning.

I continued to drink around the clock for the rest of the week. I called out sick that Wednesday and once again I had used up all of my sick days, so taking that day cost me about four hundred dollars. I was drinking more than a pint a day, and eating nothing. All week I was caught in a cycle of drinking, vomiting, and sleeping. I was down to one hundred and eight pounds and my stomach felt like I'd developed gastritis from purging myself so much. That Friday night I had the dream and conversation with God that I outlined in the beginning of the book. When I woke up Saturday morning I knew that was it. I knew that I was really going to die soon if I didn't stop. I had all of the tools and support I needed to make it. I just had to put the pieces together.

Chapter 16
Diagnosis…

My life had been a series of addictions that I developed to defend against pain, hence the term defense mechanisms. Although alcoholism was the addiction that brought me to my knees, all of my addictions were truly unhealthy because they were merely emotional crutches, and when they gave way I was devastated. My addiction to athletics left me severely lost and disheartened when I lost many of my abilities following the accident. My addiction to children left me inconsolable when they were taken from me for one reason or another. My addiction to mentoring my girls left me feeling hollow when they went to college. It was no mistake that my first major breakdown came in the year that Monica and Jennifer went to college and my other girls were seniors. Each addiction served me well to avoid my problems temporarily, but when the circumstances changed each one ultimately drove me deeper into depression.

With each relapse I gained experience, and with each recovery I gained strength and hope for the future. Every time I began a new recovery, I tried to make adjustments in my life. When I got sober after the fight with Sharon, I changed my mind set. My focus was on getting Sha-Quaan back and the bleach reference helped to keep my thinking from getting clouded, but eventually that was not enough. What could I change about my approach to get it right this time? Depression had caused me to become terribly lazy in every aspect of my life. I was living in filth and was out of shape because I had absolutely no motivation. I needed to institute a plan of action to bring change into my life.

My plan of action consisted of a combination of a number of very simple measures. The next day I was back to work so I walked to the store in the morning and bought a notebook and two pens. Dr. Watson had suggested weeks ago that I begin keeping a journal and I decided to give it a shot.

Keeping it served two main purposes for me. The first was that it would help me keep an inventory of my thoughts, feelings, emotions, actions and experiences. Maybe if I was a little more aware of those things I wouldn't feel so sad all the time. The second reason was of equal importance.

Laziness and apathy were symptoms of my depression, and affected everything in my life. My apartment was atrocious and my hygiene was non-existent. I only showered for basketball games or work, and sometimes not even then. In some stretches I went weeks without taking a shower or even brushing my teeth. I wore the same sweats for weeks at a time, even when they were dirty or stained. I just didn't care about myself and that had to change. In the back of my journal I used a ruler to create a grid of daily tasks. I listed things like showering, brushing my teeth, eating three meals, taking my medication, and making meetings. These would seem to be simple, everyday things to many people, but the depression had stripped me of any desire to care for myself at all and I had to get out of this rut.

At the end of every entry I would make a list of goals for the next day, and when I wrote the following night I would go back and check off the goals I had accomplished. They were just as simple as the tasks in the back, but they helped me to get myself organized. I also made a list of different specialists I needed to see to begin getting healthy again, and assigned myself deadlines to make appointments with each one based on referrals and co-pays. My teeth were disintegrating from years of neglect and passing out with liquor on them, my neck sounded like bubble-wrap popping every time I turned my head, and I hadn't been back to the GYN since my visit two years ago. I also needed to find a new psychiatrist because the first one wasn't serving my needs.

This organized approach was a desperate attempt at jumpstarting my sobriety but, although it was a good idea, the journal alone would not be the solution to my problems. It did however, motivate me to go to the Y when I got off that Friday morning, and that was when the miracle happened. On the walk home I was compelled to stop in the used book store. As I walked past the spirituality section a title jumped out at me, but I'm not sure why. The name of the book was *The Road Less Traveled*, written by Dr. M. Scott Peck. I stopped to read the back of it and decided to buy a used copy for five dollars and fifty cents. It turned out to be the best investment I ever made.

The Road Less Traveled

When I began reading the book I was blown away. It's about spiritual growth, the meaning of life, and enduring pain as a mode of personal development. I hadn't even come close to reading an entire book since the seventh grade, but all of a sudden I felt like my love for reading resurfaced out of thin air. The book was written before I was born, but as I read it I felt like it was recently written especially for me. As I said, I believe that God had been lining this particular awakening and recovery up for a long time, and all of a sudden I started getting motivation from everywhere I looked, and in many different forms.

Kisha had graduated from the police academy in Maryland in August after eight months of tough training. By the end of September she realized that the Sheriff's department was not where she wanted to be. The first time she had to pull her gun out she knew that she had to make a career change. She quit her job and moved back home. I invited her over for breakfast and, feeling we both needed some inspiration, suggested that we watch my mother's copy of *The Secret*. I had watched it months ago with Monique and Shonte but I was distracted and I turned it off when they fell asleep. This time I watched it intently, and we were both inspired by the law of attraction. I won't try and explain what it is or how it works, but we immediately started applying the concepts we'd learned from the DVD and before long we began seeing results.

That very weekend I got motivation from another source. Two years after the hurricane, my family's property in Mississippi still stood gutted and my cousins were still living in a trailer. My mother organized the family and together we decided to raise money for the house. She started a non-profit organization in the name of the family and with the help of my cousin Andre, created a website to raise awareness and collect donations. We also began holding fundraisers, the first of which was this weekend. All of my mother's siblings and my cousins collected anything they could that was suitable for selling and we had a sidewalk sale.

We had the sale on a local corner and across the street from a tire shop. One of my first little league baseball coaches was getting a tire fixed and came over to say hi. As we began talking he told me that he was a teacher and had used me as an example of perseverance and determination on numerous occasions. He went on to tell me that his daughter had always looked up to me and if she turned out to be anything like me he would be overjoyed. *Boy, if he only knew.* Nevertheless, his recollection of our past together reminded me of the days when I was special. I knew that the person he spoke of still existed, although she'd been battered by life's experiences.

After reading more about self-discipline as a function of love I finally decided to attack my apartment. I had been lazy and undisciplined for far too long and one of the ugliest results was the state of my living space. I rifled through thousands of papers to make sure that I tore up any vital personal information, picked up handfuls of garbage, vacuumed the rug, mopped the kitchen, did laundry, rearranged the bed and one of the dressers to create more space, and threw away clothes I didn't wear. It was far too big a job to be done in one day, so I broke it up into parts. Over the course of that second week Shonte and I got our home together. The apartment was still overcrowded, but it wasn't nearly as cluttered and nasty as it had been.

I began to intently study Dr. Peck's teachings. As I read his book I tried to apply the principles I learned to my life, and it worked. I had developed a terrible misconception that life was supposed to be fun and easy, but he put that notion to bed with his famous first sentence, "Life is difficult." He went on to explain that once you come to accept that fact it becomes a non-issue, because in knowing that it cannot be changed, it ceases to matter.

One of the reasons I kept falling apart was because I could not handle disappointment. I felt like my life was unfairly tough and I couldn't help but pity myself. I had a million reasons why my life was too hard and I felt I should be able to just drink it away. I didn't really enjoy those drunken stupors, but they numbed me to the pressures of the outside world. When I realized that I was no exception to the necessary struggle of growth, a light bulb went off in my head. I was going to have to change the way I looked at life altogether, because I'd had so many poor models of some very important life values. As a result I had no idea who I was or how to love myself.

In my reading I learned that love began with self-discipline, and there were four tools that needed to be applied in order to maintain it: delaying gratification, acceptance of responsibility, dedication to truth, and balancing. Delaying gratification simply meant getting unpleasant things done first, allowing for a deeper enjoyment of the more pleasant things. Acceptance of responsibility meant one hundred percent, without excuses. Dedication to truth meant honesty in the face of scrutiny and discomfort. Balancing had to do with prioritizing, or bracketing as Dr. Peck put it. I used these tools in assessing my daily actions in my newly developed commitment to change.

I won't outline the entire book, but I'd just like to mention that in reading the third and fourth sections entitled "Growth and Religion" and "Grace," I finally developed a comprehensive understanding of spirituality that I could manage. I still believe in Jesus Christ, but now I have a deeper knowledge of how to communicate with Him and how to decipher His Will. I have a great deal to learn on the subjects of both Christianity and spirituality, but at least I became aware of how much I didn't understand. I began on my spiritual journey. I came to realize that there was a much happier, healthier life in store for me and I needed to renew my perception of life. This could only be achieved by examining the areas of my life that had caused me the deepest pain and figuring out how to cope with them constructively.

Love

The model of love that Jimmy set was poor and ambiguous at best. Growing up I learned from him that love was conditional. He was joyful and fun when things were going his way, but when we made mistakes it was as if he hated us. He had chased or kicked my brother out on more occasions than I care to count, which sent us all the message that our residence there was not automatic, and that it wasn't our house, it was his. The way he disciplined and terrorized us taught us that he loved us as long as we behaved. To make matters worse, I don't ever remember him saying the words "I love you" to any of us.

Since I could not process that version of love as a young child, I adopted my idea of love from the movies and television. I knew that my family was dysfunctional but I didn't really have anything else to go on, so I believed that love happened the way it did on screen. I thought you met that certain someone and you knew it right away and then bang, you were in love and lived happily ever after. I developed a crush on almost every close friend I ever had, both boys and girls. I could not differentiate between plutonic love and romantic love.

My experience with Kim was the closest thing to the dream I had of love, and it took me years to shake it. The moonlit walks, the notes, and long conversations were all it took for me to flip. It was just like a movie and I'd found my soul mate. I didn't understand that no matter how much time you spend with someone, you just can't know who they truly are after a few months. I convinced myself that I knew her because I wanted to be in love. I wanted her to be the one, and I believed that she was battling some internal demons, but she would ultimately follow her heart and come back around. This wasn't a movie though, and she wasn't coming back.

I convinced myself I was in love with other people over and over again, but it was always an effort to hide my feelings for Kim, and my flame for her didn't go out until that disparaging night in May. What did I think she was going to do, jump into my arms? Or maybe she'd apologize for shattering my heart and lying about it, and want to be friends. I was so far off of any path of conceivable reality. I was still consumed with a fairytale, and for five years I had been obsessed with this girl that didn't really exist. I was infatuated with who I thought she was, but that was only a facade. She had dismissed and avoided me completely and I was left holding the fragments of my heart in a cloud of confusion and denial. I dated all different types of girls with no real standards to speak of, but before long I was comparing them to her and they all came up short. I tried to convert them into something that resembled her, but it always resulted in disappointment.

I still didn't trust my judgment when it came to affairs of the heart. I knew that Shonte loved me and was by my side through thick and thin, but things changed with my newfound awareness and we'd reached an impasse. Shonte loved me beyond all of my shortcomings, but that was no longer enough to sustain our relationship. When I had my spiritual awakening, everything on my end changed. I had ignored our many differences and problems for years because I needed a companion, and I suspect that's the same reason she put up with all of my baggage, but I couldn't do it any longer. I had never loved anyone the way I loved her because no one had ever stuck it out with me through my struggles, but I had to come to terms with the fact that we were burning out.

After my awakening I realized that we just didn't seem to be compatible. I think I always knew it, but we always had plenty of distractions. Between my drinking, Sha-Quaan, her education, and my recovery we never really had time to stop and examine the merits of our relationship. Many aspects of my recovery were very painful, and this was no exception. Myrna, Monique, Shea, and Jade had become four of my very best friends over the years. It takes much more than love to sustain a happy relationship. I don't exactly know what that is, but in its absence I learned that the love can sustain beautiful friendships.

Shonte had become nervous around me because of my temper and our differences, and that wasn't fair to her. She tried to edit her words and walked on eggshells in her attempts to make me happy. I held her to a standard that she was incapable of maintaining, and the future of our relationship became doubtful. I wasn't sure what the end result would be, but I could no longer cling to relationships that did not serve my deepest needs in order to pamper my desire for acceptance. Whether she and I got married or became the best of friends it would have to be a conscious decision that we reached together after careful examination, and it would be based on truth, however painful.

The only people I really knew how to love were my family and children. They were the people that saw me for who I was inside. They didn't care about my sexuality, they obviously didn't care about my skin tone, and they'd forgiven my past mistakes. I'd put my mother through hell in the past few years, specifically the last two I'd lived beneath her. I'd caused her numerous sleepless nights and tearful prayers, but she stood by my side and tried to help me while I struggled. She suffered with me, and that was one of the greatest examples I'd ever seen of what love is really about.

The capacity in which I demonstrated my love for children morphed tremendously over the years, and was typically erroneous in some fashion until I learned that it would require much more work on my behalf. Guiding children is a harrowing task, and one that must be undertaken with great deference. I had many methods of dealing with children including strict discipline, childlike playfulness, and a serious effort at patience, but I always thought I knew it all. I thought that because I was able to communicate so well with them I always knew what was best, and that thinking was what lead me to lose my son.

I lost sight of the fact that I wasn't biologically his parent and because our bond was so strong, I could not deal with Sharon's decision to keep him home for any unspecified amount of time. I walked around in turmoil for over a year because I viewed myself as the victim. I deluded myself into believing that I hadn't done anything to lose him, when the truth of the matter was that I'd made a number of awful decisions when I had Sha-Quaan in my custody. Although I loved him more than I loved myself, I didn't love anything more than the bottle and as a result I had done just as much damage to him as his mother had. I could not come to terms with this fact until I took a hard look at myself, evaluating my actions honestly. The truth of the matter was that although she took him from me without reason, my response to her actions was the determining factor. I chose to pick up the bottle that day, and there is no one to blame for the result but myself.

Self-Worth

While the concept of love I developed was outright dysfunctional, the way I understood my worth was heavily confused. I had experienced life from a broad spectrum of positions. I was the child prodigy, the terrified daughter, the outcast tomboy, the star athlete, the last player off the bench, the instructor, the coach and mentor, the mini-celebrity, the alcoholic, and a token at my job to name a few. I felt like I wouldn't fit neatly into any category of people. The way I felt about myself hinged on my environment and how people responded to me. As a child I never knew how my father felt about me because he only seemed to express himself in fits of anger. Rarely did I feel that he was proud of me, although when I got older I learned that he bragged about me constantly. Yet and still, he almost never took the time to fortify our self-esteem with professions or expressions of his love.

Jimmy was quick to tell me that I could do anything I set my mind to, but when he set the bar too high I failed miserably, and the resulting damage was considerable. Since my athletic achievements seemed to get my father's approval the most, I worked twice as hard for them, but I was also twice as disappointed when I came up short. My eventual exhaustion from the task of trying to fortify my self-worth with my father's approval lead me to seek acceptance elsewhere. I carried myself with a mock arrogance that I developed as a defense against my feelings of inadequacy, because deep inside I felt worthless.

My desperate need to fit in somewhere put me in a number of unnecessarily dangerous situations. I gravitated to the nearby ghettos because I was accepted there. I was often referred to as "the cool White girl," and that was okay with me. They could call me whatever they wanted because they showed me loyalty. It was only by grace that I was not around on the nights that Thud and Shellz were killed, and I began to feel like I was invincible. I also had unprotected sex with girls I hardly knew on so many drunken nights, I can't fathom how I came out of that phase with a clean bill of health.

It wasn't just about acceptance though. I knew that I could find friends in less dangerous areas but I liked the danger and, because I didn't value myself, I enjoyed testing fate. Some morbid part of me felt like I earned a stripe every time I attended another funeral that was the result of a senseless tragedy. People had been dying all around me my whole life, and I was daring the devil to come and get me. I was incredibly depressed and hanging in the hood was actually an indirect suicide attempt. My self-worth was non-existent.

My inability to love myself was another problem that bred my addictions. I was uncomfortable with the prospect of who I was at my core so I used sports, kids, and eventually alcohol to avoid self-evaluation. I put so much effort into other activities and people that there was no time to feel the pain of my emptiness. I valued myself based largely on how other people treated me. When I was treated with respect and dignity I was proud, but when I was shunned and chastised I felt inferior.

I clung to children and my girls because they needed me in some sense. They all depended on me in one way or another and I needed that to feel important. I showered the girls with gifts and attention because they reciprocated the attention. I adored Cindy and our friendship, and since the age difference was the same I thought they would grow to adore me in the same way. My self-esteem hinged on my perception of what people thought of me, and I was desperate for admiration.

When I lost my son I was devastated. No matter how atrocious my actions, Sharon would always forgive me after a short period of time because she needed me. She needed my financial support and she enjoyed having an on-call babysitter, but when she realized her son loved me more than her, everything changed and she took him for good. When she didn't need me anymore I was again deserted, and I felt like I didn't deserve anything positive in my life.

When the children moved and the players graduated I had no purpose. I couldn't handle my girls doubting me. It tore me apart inside that I'd lost their respect in struggling with my disease. I deserved to wallow in this misery. This was how I used to think whenever things went wrong, and that thinking made it nearly impossible for me to hold myself together in my previous attempts.

I had a very powerful revelation during this period, and it hit me like a ton of bricks. While there were a number of events and people that contributed to my self-esteem issues and ensuing depression, I played a bigger role in my near-demise then anyone, and I was able to pinpoint the exact moment it happened. In the five months that followed my accident in high school, three people died in motor vehicle accidents. Eric was an All-American track star, Meikel was on her way to the University of Virginia on a full scholarship, and Joelle was one of the most popular people I knew.

The night of Joelle's wake, the night of my first real breakdown, I began giving myself an extremely detrimental message. These people were all better than me. I was a nobody. I barely made it through high school, and for as much potential as I was born with, I had become mediocre in everything in my life. Surely God made a mistake. Or maybe my survival was some freak accident. How could those three die, yet I lived on? That night I told myself that I wasn't supposed to be here, and I spent the next ten years trying to prove it to everyone around me. I don't think I was sober for one night of those next four years, and I only slowed down because I couldn't drink when I was in the firehouse. That night began a self-inflicted, self-destructive rampage that almost claimed my life on a number of occasions.

Patience

My understanding of the virtue of patience was just as confused as my self-worth. In this regard my mother's approach was paramount. My mother was always a model of extreme patience. She wasn't a saint, and she occasionally erupted as do we all, but she was aware of its importance when it came to us. She had the self-discipline to explain things to us out of love. We constantly nagged her and I'm sure she had enough on her mind just trying to keep her marriage civil, but she repeatedly extended herself in order to nurture our emotional health.

The confusion came when I tried to reconcile that ideal with my father's explosive temper and iron fist. He was a poster child for impatience and narcissism. He wanted his way all of the time, and there was hell to pay when he didn't get it. His favorite responses to our questions were "because I said so" and "we'll see." They were both conditioned responses designed to cut short our inquiries and minimize his obligation to explain himself. His comfort was always more important than our curiosity and even our emotional needs, and he was too selfish to change for our benefit. My last four months with Sha-Quaan taught me of the sacrifices you make when you love a child. They were simple sacrifices, but nevertheless they were sacrifices and Jimmy wasn't considering putting anyone before his own will.

I didn't have very much to offer Quanny in those last few months. I hardly had any money and my apartment was tiny. It was cold outside and there wasn't much to do but watch television and play with his toys. I never wanted to send him back to Sharon, but boy could he try my patience. He was now approaching three years of age and talking up a storm. He was rarely quiet and, although he'd learned to play well by himself, he usually wanted my participation.

One of the products of my depression was a substantial energy deficiency manifested in my laziness, but he didn't understand that. He wanted my attention, and who was I to deprive him? I put his emotional progress in front of my nagging desire to isolate myself. That was an act of patience and self-discipline. I didn't always feel like playing with him, but my love motivated me to put my selfish desires aside, which was something that Jimmy was never able to do.

I had to be very careful with my patience in general though. In my yearning for acceptance, I eventually became too patient. I became a door mat and most people didn't hesitate to use me. I overextended myself with an expectation of reciprocated concern and was hurt tremendously when I came up short. I thought that if I made life easier for other people it would get easier for me, but that was not the case. My excessive patience was really just a cover for my need to be needed, and had become an outlet for me to avoid the pain of denial.

Education

I viewed education as a burden, almost from the very beginning. I loved reading as a child, but as soon as I started with the gifted and talented programs I began to see it as a chore. As Jimmy constantly denigrated my efforts, achieving the goal no longer seemed worth the struggle. The bar was set far too high for me with no landings. My fall from grace was the result of numerous failures on my part that should have been seen as successes. My father made it an all or nothing situation. There was first place and there were the losers. There were A's and other grades. There were no moral victories.

There are many possible reasons for my years of apathy towards education. Obviously I became worn by expectation, but there was more to it than that. My early achievement left me bored by the time I was in middle school. I was discouraged by my father's phony attempts at incentive, and uninterested in the subject matter. The distractions started at home, but they didn't stop there. My inability to focus stemmed from many sources over the years. Initially it was daydreaming to block out my family life, but it also became a symptom of my concussions. I've been diagnosed with seven concussions and I've hit my head far too many times to even garner an estimate. After the accident my thinking became increasingly clouded and I began to doubt my ability to keep up in my classes. It put a damper on my already low self-esteem and caused me to recoil in the face of academic challenge.

I had given up on the idea of pursuing my education. I applied to Montclair State in the spring of 2007 and was denied. I don't think I was ready anyway because I was still very lazy and still viewed education as a burden. All I knew was that I was unhappy with my career choice and would do anything to hold on to sobriety. I applied as a last resort because it seemed like the only alternative, but I didn't even know what I wanted to do. I was too lazy to pursue my doctorate and I no longer had faith in my ability to understand Calculus.

The Road Less Traveled totally changed my view of education. In the book Dr. Peck explained that gaining knowledge is the whole essence of life. The more we know, the broader our awareness is. We can make more informed decisions by educating ourselves and then using that knowledge to constantly change the state of our environment. Education should not be seen as a burden, but as a privilege. Within the realm of knowledge lie the keys to the kingdom. Regardless of your particular field of study, preparation is almost always the best weapon. The more information and tactical understanding you gather, the more equipped you are to react accordingly when things go wrong, and in understanding this concept you can attack a primary source of depression.

Depression is a result of not being prepared to deal with controversy. In a knee-jerk impulse to avoid the discomfort of that controversy, we develop defense mechanisms that will only serve us for a limited amount of time, and when their usefulness runs out the final condition is depression. Such was the case with my addictions. As I wrote in the beginning of this chapter, even my seemingly healthy addictions eventually added to the worsening of my depression.

As I mentioned, I don't think I read an entire book since middle school, but in the next sixty days I read *The Road Less Traveled, Further Along the Road Less Traveled,* and *People of The Lie,* all written by Doctor Peck. Through my honest self-evaluation I was able to rediscover the passion for reading and learning I possessed as a child. I also purchased the seven hundred page study guide for my "Essentials" firefighting book. Maybe if I took a more proactive role in my development as a firefighter my circumstances at work would change.

Spirituality

In the entire scope of the factors contributing to my depression and difficulties in recovery, spirituality was at the top of the list. For a very long time I blamed Jimmy for my problems, and he was most definitely at the root because he didn't attempt to guide me spiritually at all, but I was my own biggest detractor. The second tool of discipline that Dr. Peck addressed in *The Road Less Traveled* was the acceptance of responsibility. My father was way beyond change, and for as long as my recovery hinged on his response to my pleas, my efforts would fail. I needed to examine my own participation, or lack thereof, in my spiritual growth, and then make the necessary adjustments that were within my power.

For the majority of my life I was spiritually disconnected from God. I believed in Jesus Christ but my understanding of Him was purely academic. My mother was far more devout than my father, but he crushed any ideas she had of us growing up with any type of connection to the Catholic Church. He detested it and wouldn't stand for us to be involved with anything at her family's church, with the exception of weddings. In his usual ignorant, threatening manner he browbeat her into stifling the faith she'd been raised in, and she made that sacrifice for the good of the family.

I was desperate for a spiritual connection to God and it manifested itself in many ways throughout my life. My father always denounced television evangelists like everything else he didn't like, and since I was so brainwashed by his negativity I didn't pay much attention to them either. Although I only went to church for choir rehearsal and on the third Sunday, I missed it when we stopped going. I wasn't crazy about the church itself, but it was the only spiritual outlet I had, which was why I became so heavily consumed with *Touched by an Angel*. It reassured me that there was a benevolent God that wanted my happiness. When that no longer sufficed I converted to Catholicism, where I started to understand fellowship with God and the forgiveness of sins.

From there it was Joel Osteen's Ministries, and he gave me incredible inspiration, but that soon faltered as well. When my addiction brought me to some of my lowest points, I would actually sip on liquor while I was watching him. I expected him to say something magical that was going to give me the will to put the bottle down for good right then and there, but it never happened. It had nothing to do with Pastor Osteen's abilities though. I was holding on to my will with all of my might because I still didn't feel my connection with God was strong enough, and I didn't trust myself to sort out what His will was. I'd surely mess it up, so I nestled in the comfort of my bottle.

I also made all sorts of tangible attempts to show my allegiance to God in the hopes of being enlightened. I had the praying hands tattooed on my shoulder and eventually added *John 3:16* underneath it, which says, "For God so loved the world that He gave His only begotten son, that whosoever believeth in Him shall not perish, but have everlasting life," and that summer I'd gotten the tattoo on my forearm. When I was sixteen my grandmother gave me a gold crucifix, and from that day on I always wore some type of cross, whether it was made of wood or diamonds. When I threw my cross out after speaking with Sharon I was ceremoniously abandoning God. I felt like He'd turned His back on me and I was pissed. I stopped praying altogether and no longer even referred to Him. Although I'd reconciled my anger early in 2007 I didn't buy another cross until September, finally reversing my renunciation of God, and that was when I started to gain steam.

When I got into the heart of *The Road Less Traveled*, Dr. Peck systematically proved the existence of God within our sub-conscious. He made the distinction between religion and spirituality and I needed that because I'd tried being religious, but I just wasn't. Religion was never able to teach me how to truly achieve fellowship with God. I knew to pray but I wasn't connected. Whether you refer to it as God, your conscience, or some other term, he makes it quite evident that there is a higher power that exists within us. This power reveals itself to us in a number of ways, including dreams, premonitions, and random thoughts. If we pay attention to these revelations we will come to know God's will for us, and therein lies the foundation of spiritual growth.

These revelations become more and more frequent as you learn to look for them. I'm not talking about cosmic signs and omens, but little voices and inklings. They arrive in different forms and at different times, but they can be very powerful and insightful if you take the time to evaluate them. I began to listen to my inner voice whenever it was possible, and things began to work themselves out. Dr. Watson and Coach Citro both helped me to take a very graphic and honest self-inventory and when I opened myself to the idea of spiritual change, and making changes in general, my life began to transform.

Managing My Disease

My recovery and emotional healing boiled down to choices and awareness. For more than two and a half years I stumbled through the process with a great deal of difficulty because I chose to blame the world, specifically my father, for my problems. I didn't understand that I held the key to my own future, because my impression of the world had tempered my aspirations. Long ago I had shut the door on my destiny because I had such a distorted understanding of the five life concepts I just outlined. I didn't realize that I had the capacity to redevelop those understandings into a working compilation of values. I knew that I had a ton of issues but I was overwhelmed by the prospect of dealing with them alone, so I tried to ignore or shirk responsibility for them just as I had witnessed my father do my whole life.

My healing only truly began when I committed myself to finding out how I could affect my own recovery. I had to examine my problems with stark honesty, figure out what was in my control to change, and then dedicate myself to applying the solution. For years I had done any and every thing to avoid this process because it seemed like too much work, but Dr. Watson drilled home a very encouraging point on my first visit with a sly little joke. "How do you eat an elephant?" I stared at him blankly for a second realizing it was a riddle, and then it came to me.

A slow grin came over my face and I replied, "One bite at a time." He smiled and nodded, and he didn't need to say anything more. I got it.

The week of September 23rd, 2007 spurred a spiritual awakening greater than anything I ever could have imagined. Over the course of the following two months I was able to readjust the scope of my entire life, but I had to make some very difficult decisions regarding my surroundings and relationships. As my addictions eventually failed to serve me, so did some of my relationships. I had heard in AA meetings that to maintain sobriety I would have to change people, places, and things, but for a long time I understood that to mean the people, places, and things that were directly contributing to my active addiction. I didn't realize that there were certain situations I had to rid myself of that were indirectly adding to my depression. I had to separate myself from people that had carried me through some very dark periods in my life, and that was extremely painful.

I took my life apart piece by piece and sifted through years of destruction to arrive at my rebirth. I matured exponentially in those two months, but my recovery took much longer than that. With all of my might I had struggled to be normal, but this battle would require more strength than I could possibly muster by myself. Once I was presented with a spiritual connection that I could understand, I became able to place my trust in grace and let God guide my life. I stopped trying to control the overwhelming factors in my life and focus on the solutions within my immediate grasp. Bit by bit I began to assimilate all the various tools I had been given for recovery in a grand effort, intent on building a solid foundation. I forced myself to take more showers, brush my teeth, and be vigilant with my medication. I switched psychiatrists and made an appointment with my dentist.

I made myself the most important person in my life. My recovery was still fueled by my desire to get another chance with my son, but it no longer hinged on the success or failure of my attempts because that was beyond my control. I came to realize that all I could control is whether or not I was a person that he would want to return to, be it in two months or twenty years. I needed to be a sober, healthy, thriving adult in case Sharon ever changed her mind or if I ever crossed paths with Sha-Quaan years down the road.

I stopped bemoaning my circumstances and focused my efforts on carrying out God's will so that he could fight my battle, and I did my part as well. I got up extra early on work days to go to a seven o'clock meeting by the firehouse. I took time off to go to meetings and this time I was extremely humble. In my years as a coach I'd developed a somewhat dramatic flair for monologues, and that spilled over into meetings. Often times when I spoke in meetings, people around the rooms were smiling and nodding in mutual understanding. I got a rise out of that and usually made a point of saying my piece at every meeting in order to feel good about myself.

This time around I rarely spoke, although it wasn't a rule. If I thought that I had something particularly beneficial to share or felt the need to get something off my chest than I did, but I tried to focus my efforts on listening and absorbing information. For years I needed to feel like I was the smartest person in the room, which was a major reason I hung out with teenagers and ran around in the ghetto. Now I'm trying to be the dumbest person in the room, because if I surround myself with people that are smarter and more knowledgeable than me, it can only improve me as a person.

I began leaning on every resource I had. I made all of my assorted appointments, I went to meetings, I got serious about writing my book, and I started calling my sponsor and Donnie more often, just to say hi and that I was okay. I went to see Coach at least once a week, and would talk to him in detail about my recovery and progress. They were all such simple actions, but their sum total began to change my life. I buried myself in reading and writing, and filled my down time with pencil puzzles. I didn't cut television out altogether, but I tried to choose programming that would provide me with knowledge or insight. All of a sudden I was no longer terribly interested in dramas and sitcoms. The only things that really mattered to me were my recovery, my spiritual growth, and the potential of seeing my son again. Everything else took a backseat. I couldn't control the major things, but I could begin to sway them by taking control of the little ones.

Jimmy

Dr. Peck makes a clear distinction between mental illness and evil possession in his book *People of the Lie*. People possessed by evil have no interest in self-evaluation. They are so incredibly uncomfortable with their own shortcomings that they will do anything to keep those flaws from coming to light. They are opposed to the truth and will take exhausting measures to place blame on everyone but themselves, which is what makes them people of the lie. My father is a person of the lie.

Having come to terms with this fact, my father is no longer a factor in my life. There is no need for me to continually try to bring him to a point of enlightenment, because he is strictly opposed to the practice of introspection. Most psychiatrists cannot get through to these people and to perpetuate our relationship in the hopes of improvement is pointless. I have finally cut the reigns of control he had over every aspect of my life, and the bottom line is that he is just not someone that will ever make a positive contribution to my life, which makes him expendable.

Even with all that we've been through there is a part of me that wishes I could have an adult relationship with my dad, but it is simply outside of the realm of possibility. I have however, been provided with four men that are better substitutes than I ever could have asked for. I have already expressed my opposition to the theory of coincidence, so having Leon as a Godfather was for a very distinct purpose. He grew up with Jimmy and was one of the few people that were able to provide me with insight as to his history of absolute dysfunction. He helped me to understand that my father was very sick in his own right, and that I had to find a way to shake his effect.

My first interaction with Coach Citro was one of an adversarial nature, as I had come to request an apology for what I'd deemed to be disrespect. The similarities in our stories are startling, from the athletic prowess, to the physical setbacks, to the addiction, to the passion for children. He has been a beacon of light as I have walked through times of dark solitude, and his guidance has been paramount to anything Jimmy ever could have attempted.

Leon is my Godfather, and Coach is my mentor, but Donnie has become my friend. Just the sight of him brings a smile to my face. When I am with him I am completely at ease and I feel safe. I know that he will always stand up for me and always has my best interest at heart, which is a lot more than I can say for Jimmy. If it wasn't for him I would have been fired from the department, and more than likely lying in a gutter somewhere.

Dr. Watson has been my spiritual surgeon. He spent twenty years as a vascular surgeon but felt he could do more to ease human suffering, so he took the strides to become a substance abuse counselor and therapist as well. One step at a time, he has given me the direction to straighten things out. If you look at my life as a disabled car, you could say that he didn't fix the car, but he provided the tool box and an instruction manual. He put me in a position to realize my destiny.

All four of these men have one thing in common: they are educated and aware. They constantly seek out ways to better themselves and the people around them. Having been extraordinarily blessed with them, Jimmy is now nothing but a shallow memory. His only purpose in my life is to serve as a constant reminder to be vigilant of my own behaviors. In my active addiction I came frighteningly close to turning into him, and the only way to prevent that is to remain dedicated to the truth. As he is a person of the lie, I must be a person of the truth.

My Future

I don't like being a firefighter. It's not a fact that can't be changed, but that is my current feeling after twenty percent of my career has gone by. It is an extremely noble profession, and I never intended to demean it with my physical frailty or complacency towards learning, but I have done just that because of my personal struggles. My co-workers as a whole have mixed feelings towards me.

Some of them like me well enough as a person but most of them see me as a liability, and deservedly so. There are some extremes. There are a few guys like Donnie that truly care about me and have broken their necks to help and guide me, and there are a few guys like my first battalion chief that wouldn't piss on me if I was on fire. There are also some guys that feel sorry for me, and a few guys that could care less about me as a person because I suck at the job. There were a few guys that had close personal experiences with alcoholism and depression and truly wanted to see me beat the disease with or without the job, so they made a point of pulling me aside and tried to guide me.

I guess that such a range of personalities and attitudes could be found in any workplace, but I have to spend twenty-four hour clips in close proximity with these guys. My comfort level during that time depends on what combination of men I'm working with on that particular tour of duty and I hate that. At the very least my role has to change, and that is why I bought the study guide. Hopefully as I learn more about the job and get back into shape I will be able to prove myself competent, but this isn't what I was put here for. Even as I get stronger I will be mediocre at best. As a 5'3" woman I'm never going to be one of the better firefighters and I can't accept that. Being a firefighter is a great job, but I'm not going to make any major contributions to society in my capacity there and that has become one of my life goals, so I must move on.

My being a firefighter has served its purpose in my life, but now it is time to look to a happier future. It kept me out of jail on a number of occasions, and who knows if I ever would've recovered from that? I now realize that God has special plans for me, and I did not suffer as I did for all this time so that I could get sober and become a good firefighter. I did need to come here though, because if it wasn't for this job I'd be dead. I would have gone to Florida and partied my life away. I would have killed myself or someone else in a blackout, and there's no doubt in my mind about that. Even if I realized I needed help I wouldn't have had health insurance, and that was the biggest blessing of the fire department.

I see the way these guys love the job and I know I am holding a position that someone else could be enjoying just as much. Conversely, I could be off doing something else that I'd enjoy the same way. It would be irrational for me to quit my job without any other significant career options in place, but that day will come soon enough. Many people, especially the ones that wish they could get into the fire department, will call me stupid. They will cite the generous pay, the schedule, and the benefits as major reasons to hang around for twenty-five years, but I won't be happy if I feel that I am squandering my existence. That season of my life has passed and now I am focused on progress and production.

I don't have any idea where I'll be in five years, but I seriously doubt it will be the fire department or New Jersey. Day by day I make strides to better myself and figure out what my true calling is. Whether it's coaching basketball, motivational speaking, teaching karate, or counseling, my days as a firefighter are numbered. I can no longer rest in the security of a career that does not fulfill me, knowing full well that there is so much more within my reach. My very existence after so many poor decisions is proof of my destiny, and I know that if I continue to follow my heart and stay disciplined in the work of spiritual growth, I will achieve spiritual and financial prosperity.

When I began writing I had no idea of the change my soul would undergo. I knew I had a remarkable story, but I really just hoped that somehow it would show Sharon how sorry I am about my actions. The driving force behind this book was Sha-Quaan, but it would've been selfish of me to focus on him when the message I carry is so crucial to so many people. If it weren't for him this book would never have been written, and for as much as I wanted to focus on children, I am simply in no position to do so. As I earn degrees and the accompanying knowledge, I hope to write a book about child psychology and loving child rearing, because that is my passion.

Chapter 17
The Revelation

* This book was written between September 23rd and November 21st of 2007. It pretty much ended with the previous chapter, but my work was not complete. The following was written in August of 2009.

A year after my awakening my life had improved exponentially. I gained twenty pounds and the dark circles that shadowed my eyes had disappeared. I got my driver's license back and got financing for a fairly new car. Shonte and I broke up early in the year but wanted to be friends, and we moved into a two-bedroom apartment in a quiet garden community ten minutes from Montclair. I quit smoking and I worked out three times a week. I was in the best shape I'd been in since I had the car accident in high school. I was showing up to work consistently and was getting better at my job. After contacting an advisor at Montclair State in February, I'd enrolled in county college in order gain re-admission to Montclair State.

Given the discovery and self-examination I expressed in the last chapter, you may think that I had it all figured out, but I wasn't quite there. When I sat down to write this chapter I began to detail the ups and downs of the last year but I changed my mind, because ultimately they don't really matter. What matters is how I chose to respond to them. I've read ten or so books in the past year, the majority of which were about psychology or self-help, and there is one theme that has been consistent in all of them, specifically *The Road Less Traveled* and *The Success Principles* by Jack Canfield. It is that of taking full responsibility for your actions. Canfield uses the equation E + R = O: an event plus your response equals the outcome. It is a concept that I came to understand quite clearly when I had my rebirth.

By the Grace of God, my life did an about face following that September. When my desire to survive and thrive exceeded my yearning for comfort, there was a windfall of opportunity in the way of inspirational literature and a resulting awareness of myself. But as life happened, my determination wavered and my awareness waned. Self-pity crept in and with it came more depression. I didn't fall off the cliff as I had in previous years, though. It was more of a gradual descent, frequently interrupted by weak attempts at resistance on my behalf, but nowhere near the depths to which I had previously sunk. As my life improved, I lost the sense of urgency that allowed me to make such a powerful and sudden turnaround in my life.

Three things happened that next summer that affected me tremendously and made serenity very difficult for me. The first was that I got into a nasty argument with Monique that carried on well into the winter. She was my best friend and her absence was excruciating. Two weeks later I got into a violent argument with my brother that almost turned physical, and we stopped speaking for months. In both instances I believed I was right and wrote them both off altogether. By the time August rolled around I was fighting depression over the loss of these relationships, not to mention an unending tension over my issues with Jimmy and considerable financial burdens resulting from all my previous poor decisions. I then got smacked in the face with a sobering reality.

In February I'd signed a six-month contract with a literary agent in San Diego. In August I received a letter stating that she was not able to find a publisher willing to put the book out. I knew that I had a story that needed to be told, and I believed that it would be published when the time was right, but I was deeply hurt because of what it meant with respect to my son. It had now been over two years since I'd seen Sha-Quaan and I knew that I was probably fading from his memory. My inspiration for finally writing the book after years of procrastination was getting him back. I hoped that Sharon would come across it, see the work I'd done, and give me one more chance.

When I got the letter from my agent, I was forced to come to terms with a devastating concept. Maybe God put him in my life solely for the purpose of getting it together. Maybe He knew that I didn't love myself, and needed to be presented with someone I loved so much that I would do anything to get to them. Maybe it was time to truly let him go. That was a terribly tough pill to swallow.

I'd made a vow to myself the previous year that I would never return to the train wreck I'd become. Never again would I disregard my life as unimportant and wallow in self-pity, but this was a lot. To make matters worse, my insurance changed and I could no longer see Dr. Watson for guidance. I was under great pressure to perform well in school and living with Shonte was not working out as planned. I'd begun dating other women and she was not prepared to handle that yet, which magnified my already elevated stress levels. I lost my way some, and I stopped working out and started smoking again. I hated being on anti-depressants because they made me so numb to all of my emotions, and I'd weaned myself off using a pill cutter the previous December.

The next six months were very dark for me. At the end of the year when Shonte realized that I had a new girlfriend, our relationship turned into one of contempt. Many of her feelings exploded and we argued daily. She couldn't live with me anymore and would move out at the end of the month, but meanwhile our only words to each other were said in anger. Somehow we'd reached a point just short of hatred for each other. She deeply resented the fact that in my awakening I realized we were incompatible, and felt that I didn't think she was good enough for me. I, in turn, resented her for not understanding that I was moving on out of love, because I didn't want to perpetuate a relationship that was not serving either one of us. She moved out right after Christmas, and I didn't think we would ever speak again.

In the days leading up to her leaving, I began to realize that my new relationship wasn't working either. Once again I'd rushed into something without taking the time to see where I was going. I was unhappy and knew I'd have to end it before the situation got any deeper, so a week later I broke up with my girlfriend. I was lost in a quandary of pain, loneliness, and confusion. Monique had been my best friend ever since our relationship ended and I needed her desperately. I reached out to her but reconciliation was a slow process after all the words that were said. All of my other friends were wrapped up in some combination of work, school, and raising children. I spent my days alone in this huge duplex with my thoughts echoing off of the walls like BB's, piercing my soul with every ricochet. The tears I cried that month could have flooded a desert.

As the saying goes, the darkest night is always right before the break of dawn, as was this case in this period. When you've viewed your entire life through tainted glasses, the period of adjustment that comes with removing them can be terribly painful, not unlike removing your sunglasses on a bright, sunny day. The difference here is that to put those glasses back on, in terms of spiritual growth, would clearly be regression. Using substance abuse, excuses, and denial to deal with my problems would only lead me to break that vow I'd made to myself, and the result would surely be a return to insufferable misery and chronic depression. When I read *The Road Less Traveled*, I became well aware of the fact that spiritual rehabilitation would be hard, and now I was seeing that concept manifest itself. For years I'd solved, or rather dealt with, my problems in one fashion. Instead of dealing with the problem I tried to kill the pain, while the problem festered. That was the "easy" way out though, and would only lead to more of the same circumstances as the past.

But this loneliness was suffocating. I'd hit a wall and my depression was back full force, threatening to wash away all the hard work I'd done. I was in between semesters and waiting to get word from Montclair State. I laid on my couch watching television all day, dying for three o'clock to come so I could go to basketball practice. I began to question my entire life philosophy. Was this worth the effort? Was this pain any different then what I'd just escaped from? Would I be better off passed out half of the time so that I wouldn't have to feel this way? No. Absolutely not. I had to continue to fight, even though I wasn't sure if I had the energy, because the alternative was terrifying.

I tried to return to the things that had worked for me the previous year. I started reading more and I began working out again, although giving up the cigarettes again took more effort than I anticipated. I had become terribly undisciplined in writing in my journal and reading The Bible nightly, so I got back to doing those things. After physically going to Montclair State and pleading my case I was re-admitted for the spring semester, and I started classes on January 20th. I could only afford to take two classes because I was paying out-of-pocket, and I still had a lot more free time than I wanted. I started looking for a new therapist but had a hard time finding one that could fill Dr. Watson's shoes.

I was reaching a breaking point. I could feel it. I wanted with all my might to get this right, but even with all the reading and growing I'd done in the last year, my understanding of how to handle loneliness and depression was still elementary. I wanted desperately to return to the euphoria of those first sixty days, but it seemed like no amount of reading, organizing, or reflecting could bring it back. I was terrified, because this time I had a lot more to lose. I prayed daily that some relief would come, but it seemed to be in vain. I invited my cousin to come and take Shonte's place, but I knew that wouldn't be enough. The solution to beating my depression could not be based on anything external. There was still something missing inside, and until I figured it out my battle with depression would be unceasing.

I had spent the last year and a half studying about and trying to foster mental health, but as hard as I tried I was fighting a losing battle. I never picked up The Road Less Traveled again and I began to get fuzzy on the details. I knew I had to delay gratification and listen to God's messages by way of dreams and idle thoughts but I got lazy and ceased practicing, which opened the door for my depression to return. The problem was that when I did those things life got harder, and I didn't have the faith to stay on course. It was at this point that my understanding of psychology merged with an unshakeable faith in God.

A friend gave me a book titled The Shack by William Paul Young and implored me to read it, but I tossed it aside. Within a week I found out that The Road Less Traveled was a required text for my psychology class, and began reading it a second time. I finally picked up *The Shack* a few weeks later at work and I was hooked. In two days I was finished and emerged a totally different person. It was the story of a man that was furious with God after suffering heart-wrenching tragedy. I could not possibly do the book justice in attempting to sum it up but I do want to share what it did for me, because it gave me the missing piece.

The missing piece was a true fellowship with God. I was trying intently to find it, but I was still riddled with fear. I knew that if I followed my heart it would ultimately mirror God's intentions for me, but I didn't quite trust that His path was better than my own. One thing *The Shack* did for me was to help me understand my difficulty in trusting God fully.

I spent the majority of my life with a severely dysfunctional relationship with my father, and at this point I hadn't spoken to him in over a year. Although I thought I'd resolved my issues with him, they were a clear road block in my quest to trust my Heavenly Father completely. I thought I'd forgiven my father, but I was simply choosing to ignore his very existence. Somewhere deep inside I wanted things to be different with us, but only on my terms. I wanted to see him humbled and broken and I still hoped for the day he would come to me in that condition. Holding on to my own stubborn will was destroying any chance we had to heal our relationship, and therefore stood between me and God.

The book also changed my perception of God once again. I still looked at God as a sort of genie that answered prayers like granting wishes. I felt like I had to work hard to gain His favor. In that last bout with depression I felt like my loneliness was either some type of penance for past transgressions or a rite of passage to happiness. Maybe if I could just hold on long enough I'd be granted a blessing. By the end of the book I saw Him as a friend that labored and suffered with me every step of the way. He couldn't control everything that happened to me by virtue of free will, but He was my biggest supporter and greatest protector. When bad things happened, I could still trust Him to see me through to a victorious ending. There was nothing to fear, because He was with me every step of the way.

Once I truly processed this I was healed almost instantly. My entire disposition changed. I went from reluctantly dragging myself out of bed in the morning to waking up before my alarm clock because I was so excited to start the day. I also made a conscious effort to thank God for another day as soon as I woke up, and it soon became a sub-conscious habit. When people asked me how I was doing I would reply with an enthusiastic "Great!" instead of the typical "Oh, I'm okay," and the best part was that I meant it.

My quality of life improved drastically, although nothing tangible changed. I was still $40,000 in debt and over a year away from my degree, but all of a sudden I didn't really care. The money and getting my degree were still concerns, but I knew that nothing I could plan could possibly compare to whatever God had in store for me. The daily hassles that used to aggravate me to no end became irrelevant. I took each day as an absolute blessing and joyfully looked forward to whatever it brought. Even if my day had disappointment, pain, or hardship coming I welcomed it, because I knew in my heart that whatever it was had the capacity to make me a better, stronger person.

This revelation was exhilarating, but I realized that there was still work to be done on my end in order to sustain this happiness. There were some things affecting me that were well beyond my control like not getting to see my son, and I was going to have to give those things to God. But there were other things that I was avoiding, and for as long as I ignored them they would continue to poison my spirit. Although I thought it was best that I never spoke to my brother or father again, the truth is that perpetuating the stiff silence that stood between us was eating me alive. In my reading I also learned about the power of forgiveness and unconditional love. If I wanted true fellowship with God I would have to do my absolute best to live in His image, and holding grudges was certainly a step in the wrong direction.

The decision to reconcile with my brother was an easy one. Neither one of us really wanted to re-hash what happened, and we decided to just move forward. It was really a combination of a number of small arguments that eventually came to a head, but I still adored him and wanted peace between us. Deciding to forgive my father came with a lot more thought. This would truly be a test of my faith, because our issues were deep-seated. On top of forgiving him, I had to accept the fact that he would probably tell people I came crawling back, which had always been a huge detractor for me. My pride never allowed me to get past that before, but I realized that my pride was going to be the death of me. It was going to be my way or God's way, and for the first time in my life I submitted to the belief that His way was better.

But how did I know that this was God's way? How could I be sure that forgiving and/or reconciling with *everyone* that had hurt me would be the key to my salvation? As I said, this was the point at which my psychology and spirituality became one. As I re-read the last section of *The Road Less Traveled* I gave new weight to the importance of hearing and heeding the internal messages that God sent. I'd been having recurring thoughts of reconciling with my father for years, but he always seemed to do something to push me further away before I could reach out. I would write him off all over again and place the blame for our dysfunctional relationship squarely on his shoulders, but it wasn't all his.

I was just as stubborn and hard headed as he was, and while I may not have caused the problem, I wasn't doing much to rectify it either. It wasn't my job to fix him. For all I knew, God may have made him like that so that I could become exactly who I am. I finally realized that as an adult he no longer had any power over me, my thoughts, or my emotions... unless I gave it to him. I could love him with his shortcomings and step back when I felt they would affect me.

He'd moved to Georgia upon his retirement in 2006, but he still made frequent trips up north. When I heard he'd be coming up, I called him and asked him to go to dinner with me. He sounded like he was in shock, but when he recovered he agreed and we made plans. We sat down and I told him that I wanted a clean slate. I was finished trying to punish him for his past mistakes, and I'd already forgiven him for any he made in the future. There were clearly some topics we needed to avoid like his thoughts on my mother, her family, Glenn, and my siblings, but there was a world of other things we could discuss and enjoy together.

We are building a relationship piece by piece now, and I've never been happier. After our reconciliation, I became weary of how I portrayed him throughout the book. When I wrote the initial manuscript I was still very resentful towards him, and I wanted to crucify him. Once we reached our new understanding I struggled with the idea of softening his image some, but eventually I realized that I just couldn't. What I wrote was exactly how I experienced things, and for my story to be complete, I had to be true to it.

Serenity

I've received a number of blessings over the course of the past year. My physical and financial rehabilitation was a miracle in itself, but the greatest gift I got in the entire process was the removal of my greatest fear. In the grand scheme of things, loneliness and emptiness terrified me more than death itself. Every compulsion I developed was a product of me trying to avoid those feelings. I was afraid to deal with myself. Once I'd put my faith fully in God, I was ready to face what I'd previously been terrified to do.

It was time for me to live alone. I really didn't want to, but I knew that it was time. I needed to embrace solitude in order to make my own well-being my first priority. I'd be a full-time student in the fall and substitute-teaching to boot, so I would have a full plate with regard to my time. Once I added in working out, my job, writing in my journal, and time for prayer and reflection, I wouldn't really have time to feel lonely. I told my cousin that when my lease was up in June, I was moving into a one-bedroom apartment.

Listening to God was working magnificently for me, but there was one more ideal that I was still clinging to, and I knew that it was time to let go. When I first attempted to get this book published, the title was *A Lesson*

Learned: Confessions of an Alcoholic. Eventually I came to believe that the alcohol wasn't my problem. It was just my poorly rationalized solution. I was my problem. Depression was my disease, and it manifested itself in excessive drinking. Make no mistake about it, I was severely alcohol dependent, but my inability to cope with my life and take full responsibility for it was at the core of it all. I had been suffering from stifling depression for years, and used alcohol to mask it. Upon that conclusion I began drinking socially and did so uneventfully for over a year, which is why I refer to September 23, 2007 as the date of my rebirth instead of my sobriety date.

In all my attempts at recovery I tried different approaches, all tailor-made to suit my will. I would smoke weed but not drink. I would drink but not smoke weed. I would do neither but smoke cigarettes and not work out at all. I would go completely dry and workout, but I couldn't trust God. In psychology, insight is defined as the sudden perception of relationships among various parts of a problem, allowing the solution to the problem to come quickly. Like a ton of bricks I got hit with tremendous insight all at once, and the solution was clear. In order to claim complete victory over my life, there was but one option: complete and total submission to God's will.

In childhood I'd developed a need for instant gratification. My father's inconsistent behavior and broken promises taught me to live in the moment and deal with the future when it came. I had no faith in tomorrow because I didn't know what would change by then, so I got as much as I could whenever I could. I needed to readjust my view of the world. My compulsive behavior served me well as a child because I needed it to make life with Jimmy bearable. When I grew up and began dealing with the real world, I wasn't ready to let that behavior go. It was my security blanket.

My drinking was never about the alcohol. It was about avoiding legitimate suffering. It was the strongest and most crippling tool I had to assuage the insecurity that my identity issues forged, and the pain those issues created. Ignoring reality and compulsively engaging in activities that distracted me were the only coping mechanisms I had. As my depression deepened my penchant for self-destruction grew, and alcohol served me well in both respects.

Whether or not I am an alcoholic is irrelevant, because I have chosen to stop drinking. I don't have to quit. I drank responsibly for a year and kept everything in order, earning five A's and a B+ in school, paying my bills on time, and staying out of trouble. My life was no longer anywhere near unmanageable, and no one was forcing me to stop. I chose to give it up because I could hear God telling me to. The message was coming consistently and I got it loud and clear. I didn't feel that drinking would affect me adversely with respect to my job or school, but I came to realize that I was blocking God's blessings.

I don't need mood altering substances to mask any pain or enjoy myself. The Holy Spirit has filled the void I was trying to fill for so long with chemicals and company. I never feel alone anymore and my depression has lifted completely. I am excited about my life and am amazed daily as I watch it unfold. I used to live in the past, reminiscing about my high school days and wishing I could return to them. I used to say that if I had a time machine I'd go back to ninth grade and do things differently. I would have done my schoolwork and talked to a counselor about my problems at home. I would have played four years of basketball and switched over to softball as a freshman. I never would have picked up a drink, a drug, or a cigarette. I would have put that balloon in the back seat.

I don't feel that way anymore though. If I had it to do all over again I wouldn't change a thing. Everything that happened to me, and every decision I made, resulted in the person I am today, and I couldn't be happier about that. I love myself for exactly who I am and am proud of the obstacles I've overcome. I am exactly where God wants me to be.

It's hard for me to believe that only two years ago I was a disaster. I have come so incredibly far in such a short time, and I'm chomping at the bit to see how far God has brought me in a few more years. Whatever it is, I am waiting anxiously. My only desire is for my will to match His, because His is so much better than mine. I pray the same prayer every day. It's simple and short, but it has been so powerful in my life. I used to pray daily that I'd reach a point of serenity. Now I pray daily that I'll stay here. God, grant me the serenity to accept the things I cannot change, courage to change the things I can, and wisdom to know the difference. Your will, not mine, be done.

"Therefore I take pleasure in infirmities, in reproaches, in necessities, in persecutions, in distresses for Christ's sake: for when I am weak, then I am strong."- II Corinthians 12:10.

A wise Cherokee grandfather once told his grandson, "On the inside of every person, a battle is raging between two wolves. One is evil-- it's jealous, angry, unforgiving, proud, and lazy. The other one is good-- it's filled with love, kindness, humility, and self-control. These wolves are constantly fighting." The grandson asks, "Well which one will win?" The grandfather replied, "Whichever one you feed."

Manufactured By: RR Donnelley
Breinigsville, PA USA
May, 2010